HISTORY
OF THE HOLIDAY

Our holidays lie near the heart of our emotional life, enjoyed for a fortnight, fed on in imagination for eleven months of the year. What we want from our holidays tells a lot about who we are and what we wish we were.

In this charming account, Fred Inglis traces the rise of the holiday from its early roots in the Grand Tour, through the coming of Thomas Cook and his Blackpool packages, to sex tourism and the hippie trail to Kathmandu. He celebrates the bodily pleasures of generations of tourists – from Edwardian banquets in Paris to fish and chips on the beach, from the Bright Young Things on the Riviera to the chosen hardships of the sea, the desert wastes and the mountain tops. He considers the ideals and the spiritual aspirations which are part of what we look for in a holiday, but he also warns of a darker current – how we have increasingly destroyed what we take most pleasure in and how the dealings between those who have much and those who have little can seldom, however good our intentions, avoid the taint of exploitation.

Fred Inglis is Professor of Cultural Studies at Sheffield University.

THE DELICIOUS HISTORY OF THE HOLIDAY

Fred Inglis

London and New York

First published 2000
by Routledge
11 New Fetter Lane, London EC4P 4EE

Simultaneously published in the USA and Canada
by Routledge
29 West 35th Street, New York, NY 10001

Routledge is an imprint of the Taylor & Francis Group

© 2000 Fred Inglis

Typeset in Times New Roman by Taylor & Francis Books Ltd
Printed and bound in Great Britain by TJ International Ltd, Padstow, Cornwall

British Library Cataloguing in Publication Data
A catalogue record for this book is available from the British Library

Library of Congress Cataloging in Publication Data
Inglis, Fred.
The delicious history of the holiday / Fred Inglis.
p. cm.
Includes bibliographical references and index.
1. Vacations–History. 2.Tourism–History. I. Title.
GV186 .I54 2000
306.4'8–dc21   00-032829

ISBN 0–415–13304–1 (hbk)
ISBN 0–415–13305–X (pbk)

FOR EILEEN: HOLIDAYMAKER

CONTENTS

ILLUSTRATIONS

PREFACE

This book stands well enough, I hope, on its own. But it is conceived as part of a larger venture intending to trace the rise of consumerism over the past two-and-a-half centuries and to describe and judge what sort of people, at least in Northwest Europe as well as, from time to time, North America, consumerism has made of us. The book is planned to have its successors, the first as identifying the extraordinary dynamics of celebrity as being somehow integral to that system of modern society which we identify as consumer capitalism, the second purporting to chart those deep drives of that system, codified in the handbooks of advertising, marketing, and management, which incline the world towards a quite new and, it seems, happily assented-to kind of totalitarianism.

In saying so, this book is earnest at all times to avoid merely uttering curses over the name of consumer society. It offers to speak self-consciously from that admirable tradition of English and American social criticism which, taking much from the great canon of socialist commentary which sees for what they are the evils of waste and cruelty inherent in capitalism, is also eager to live the only life we have as well as possible, and to encourage others in the same endeavour. The books I revere and the writers with whom I claim community in these pages – the work, for example of Richard Hoggart or Clifford Geertz, C.L.R. James or Charles Taylor – are uncompromising in their opposition to the much that is frightful in everyday life, but are also characterised by what Dickens so finely identified as a 'freshness and gentleness and capacity for being pleased' which he saw as a much-to-be-desired residue of childhood and which transpires in their writing as a keen pleasure in the customs of everyday life and in a celebration of life's dependable facts.

Consequently I have taken holidays to be one of the local triumphs of consumer capitalism, however much its fearsome engines drive towards destruction. Happiness and fulfilment are my themes and these necessarily emerge from the shadow of all the reservations one must have and feel about the uses of vacationing. Anthony Crosland once admonished the then Left for not seeing the great freedoms and satisfactions brought by the acquisitions, on the part of the working class, of such consumer prizes as washing machines and automobiles. So, in my view, too, with holidays.

My method, if you can call it that, is historical, my tone celebratory. The emancipation and fulfilment brought by the colossal extension of holidaymaking in the past fifty years take their shape and rhythm from the only place in which they could be found, the past, and in the past these were first formed by those wealthy enough to invent the vacation.

PREFACE

The fieldwork, as I hope is plain on every page, was done, first and heartily, on holiday. That apart, the University of Sheffield has provided handsome time and generous money to make the writing possible, particularly in its contribution towards an extended return as a Summer Fellow in 1998, to the Institute for Advanced Study in Princeton, doubtless the best place in the world in which to enjoy the unrivalled happiness of scholarly sojourn. The thing was then finished and revised under the burden of comparable privileges at The Netherlands Institute for Advanced Study, a young sibling of the great original, to which I owe my thanks.

I am grateful also to Susan Bassnett for her critical reading of the manuscript, and to Hilary Britland for the gift of many photographs which might otherwise have helped eke out her living with a camera; I am similarly indebted to Kathy Williams for the gift of her pictures of Manhattan. Amie Barker gave indispensable help in the selection of the illustrations. Finally, and as before, I owe more than it is the convention to record to my editor at Routledge, Mari Shullaw, for her patience, acute and stringent commentary, enormous good humour and unfaltering concern for her author's well-being.

ACKNOWLEDGEMENTS

The author and publishers would like to thank the following for granting permission to reproduce material in this work

Bamforth & Co. Ltd/Dennis Print for the reproduction of Brian Perry's Egg and Spoon race postcard; Hilary Britland for photographs of Venice, Clevedon Pier, Brighton Pavilion and Paris; John Cleare/Mountain Camera for the photograph of Snowdonia, North Wales; Derby Museums and Art Gallery for the reproduction of Joseph Wright of Derby's *Rydal Waterfall*, 1795; Faber and Faber, London/Noonday Press, New York, for permission to reprint Philip Larkin's poem 'To the Sea' and Faber Ltd for *The Collected Poems* of; respectively, T. S. Eliot and Wallace Stevens; Galleria Nazionale delle Marche, Urbino, Italy/Bridgeman Art Library for the reproduction of *View of an Ideal City, or The City of God*, probably painted by Piero della Francesca (panel) by Luciano Laurana (*c.* 1420–79) (attributed to); the Hutchinson Library, London/R. Ian Lloyd, for the photograph of a Thai massage parlour; the Mary Evans Picture Library, London, for the illustration of Claridge's restaurant, London; the Mary Evans Picture Library/The Barry Norman Collection, London, for the photograph of a 'Quad-ro-bike' at Butlin's holiday camp; the National Gallery, London/Bridgeman Art Library for the reproduction of Claude Lorraine (Claude Gellée), *Landscape with Cephalus and Procris reunited by Diana*; National Museums and Galleries of Wales for the reproduction of Thomas Jones' *Buildings in Naples with the north-east view of Il Castel Nuovo*; the Robert Opie Collection, London, for the reproduction of the Imperial Airways advertisement; Kathy Williams for photographs of Brooklyn Bridge and Manhattan Island; Worcester City Museum and Art Gallery for the reproduction of Forbes Stanhope's *Chadding at Mounts Bay*.

Every effort has been made to contact copyright holders for their permission to reprint material in this book. The publishers would be grateful to hear from any copyright holder who is not acknowledged here and will undertake to rectify any errors or omissions in future editions of this book.

1

THE PERFECT HOLIDAY

I

This is a book about the love of vacations and of their history. It is also a book about the rise of consumerism and how the two coincide. Whether as holidays or vacations, each has a meaning. They have many meanings; are, in the jargon, polysemic. Those meanings arise in the course of historical experience and out of the vanity of human wishes. They are woven, one upon another, into so thick and heavy a rope of usage that many become overlaid and forgotten but remain embedded in the dense coil of association and significance with which we pull along our lives.

In the pursuit, as we are, of meaning, better to refuse simplification. Vacation-taking and holiday-making turn up, as the *Oxford English Dictionary* informs us, at more or less the same moment as the consumer, that crucial partner to the manufacturer in the modern political economy. From some time early in the second half of the eighteenth century, consumers began to take vacations.

For two centuries since, vacation-taking has expanded and the consumer has figured more and more largely in our social consciousness. So much so that as the consumer came to supersede the producer as the dominant force in economic life, so at the same time the consumer replaced the citizen as the agent of political life. By that moment, the mighty juggernaut of capitalism became synonymous with consumerism, and a modern human being became defined by the new, insatiable capacity of humans to consume commodities.

That, at least, was how the algebra worked and the economy was planned. But it seems likely that the all-powerful term 'consumerism' has its limits. Its enemies name and curse it for so swelling up to absorb all historical energy and leaving no room for nobler ends or ideals. They say that the ethics of consumption are not only monstrously inegalitarian, they cut out all thought of human reciprocity, loving kindness, the gods of self-denial, thrift and modesty.

Put like that who wouldn't agree to join in the curse? But it will be the point of this book to present its protean subject as gathered within the force field of consumerism. No-one can doubt that, for a season in the wealthy countries of the world, the success of capitalism in making a sort of abundance very unequally available has released a modest orgy of self-indulgence across the globe and among the sufficiently well-off.

One manifestation of this is the multitude of tourists perpetually criss-crossing the skies above the heads of other peoples intent upon their civil wars, famines or merely the still desperate business of scraping a living and keeping out of the way of tyrants.

1

But the tourists in the skies are only rarely orgiasts. The jumbos come down on the ground and the visitors spill out into an unknown country. Unevenly, for sure, but as never before, the people of the world mingle with one another and the moral and political consequences of that mingling, whatever the profits shown by airlines and travel companies, cannot all be enclosed by the economic metaphor of consumption.

We may use these visits for our cognitive and emotional emancipation. Moreover, it hardly makes sense to speak of our being consumers of objects or experiences which are not consumed or used up. The paintings gazed at, the buildings sauntered through easily survive, a little erosion apart, millions of consumers. It seems likely that to characterise these economic and social exchanges as patterns of consumption fails to do justice to the love of happiness, the sense of beauty, the energy to experience new places and people, which are all apparent on the sunny piazza.

One would make many of the same points about that other unattractive agent of economic theory, Rational Economic Man, forever maximising his solid male gains. Insofar as this history offers one version of the rise of consumerism since the middle (or thereabouts) of the eighteenth century, then 'consumer' must remain the name of the main character of the action. Like all historical actors, however, he and she are irreducible to the single simple performance of consumption. What he and she are actually doing, let alone feeling and thinking, in the ceaseless busyness of consuming commodities can always be debited or credited to capitalism's vast account. This is no more than to say that in order to eat and stay warm we must all be monetary actors in a capitalist economy. But unless you take a very old-fashioned and flatfootedly Marxist line about all of us being driven willy-nilly by the forces of economic production, the consumer turns out to be a vividly modern mixture of decisiveness, anxiety, irresolution, childishness, and an earnestly reasonable, loving, sometimes generous-hearted, at other times mean-minded judge and advocate of what may be afforded of life's embarrassment of riches.

The present efflorescence of capitalism will last for a while yet, however subject to the usual slumps and revivals. Since that is where we all live, it cannot suffice to damn the whole culture as consumerist and stand aside, waiting for the end. The forces of emancipation and the quest for a self-aware self-fulfilment are still seeking and finding expression, even in our happily self-indulgent moment. That expression rises from our past, for it can only be from the past that we learn to live in the present.

Consequently, this turns into a study of how we learn to match aspiration to action in such a way as to hope to achieve certain fulfilments. It is a study of the way the social meanings of the vacation gradually accumulated and wove themselves thickly upon themselves. It offers to assemble the material bits and pieces – the geography and the history – together with the ideas and ideals which shape them – the values, the thoughts and passions – into the international and unprecedented practice of following the tour; going on holiday; taking a vacation.

This is, finally, an inquiry into the origins and forms of happiness and fulfilment. It is an essay on how we learn to feel. Forming our feelings is another way of naming how each of us assumes a place in the world. It is the contrivance of identity.

II

It all begins in the dark and cold of early January. Outside, the satisfying patter of heavy rain on the windows, the tyres of passing vehicles swishing over the drenched roads; inside, the tumbling images of summer on the screen, the endless nowhere of the blue sky, the flash of palm trees along a white promenade, brown bodies, white teeth and laughter, a glimpse of a scrubbed plank table piled with fruit and bread and green wine ...

It is time to dream about the summer holidays. The seasons turn; their ancient rhythm is now marked and timed by the unquenchable liveliness of the advertisers, clearing away the used-up glitter of Christmas and all its confectionery, promptly replacing it with the irresistible medley of July and August.

The great French historian, Fernand Braudel, opened his classic history of the geography in which our holidays were born with these words:

> I have loved the Mediterranean with passion, no doubt because I am a north-erner like so many others in whose footsteps I have followed. I have joyfully dedicated long years of study to it – much more than all my youth. In return, I hope that a little of this joy and a great deal of Mediterranean sunlight will shine from the pages of this book ... My feeling is that the sea itself, the one we see and love, is the greatest document of its past existence.[1]

Braudel came from north-west Europe, from that corner of the globe which goes dark in November and stays dark until April, where the flowers and plants withdraw their juices into the cold earth for a third of the year, and the trees go bare and black as iron. Up there, the stories people used to tell while the dark, bitter weather lasted were full of trolls and troglodytes and chthonic people, of waste lands frozen ringing hard and long, starving journeys to warmth and firelight. No grapes grew there, but men made themselves blind drunk on the harsh distillation of malt and birch, and saw winter out on a diet of salty meat and saltier cod.

These folk-memories stir in us when the time comes round, and they are called up by the mesmerising powers of our contemporary storytellers on television and the effortlessness with which they magic for us pictures of all we long for in the days of night. Braudel writes movingly and from the north of the southern sea he loves and the joy which writing its history has brought him. Vacationing has its roots in that love of a loving place, and in the joy we may all feel in anticipating our return. The folk-memories, of sunshine restored and stiff, cold limbs warmed and softened, are then bound in with other, more recent memories, in which holidays represented time won for our own freedoms from the killing round of heavy industrial labour and the grim, unyielding masters who only unclenched their grip on the days which made up other people's lives one hour at a time. One way of writing the history of the nineteenth century is as the slow process whereby labour won some time for itself from capital in order to call such time 'free': free from work and from producing things for the profit of others.

So a different picture of holidays is joined to the dream of sunshine. It is one in which we are freed from the unremitting demands of work and the dreary insistence of our superiors that we keep at it. It is a picture in which, as we say, we can do as we like

3

according to a timetable, the point of which is to overturn the usual working day. The time being our own, we fill it with the pointless productivity of building sandcastles or catching fish we could buy in the shops; or we fill it with a happy recklessness of waste, spending the money it took so many days of living and dying to earn in a giddy gesture of liberality.

Over the mere two hundred years or so in which 'taking a holiday' has been a natural and self-explanatory thing to do, the activity has also gathered to itself a little cluster of special values, so that to be on vacation is to become conscious of these values and to cherish them in a way often excluded from everyday life. If we have been lucky enough to enjoy them during our childhoods, vacations become, especially in anticipation, a short moment in which a childish kind of rapture and ardour, an utter abandonment to the feeling of happiness may be glimpsed from the hotel balcony above the bay or leaning on a stone wall beside a meadowful of lambs. I have in mind the story of the 10-year-old sister of a dear friend who, when she arrived at the family's country cottage on the Kimmeridge coast in Dorset, flung herself down crying out, 'I love it here so much I want to bite the ground!'

Holidays are dreamed of as restoring the abandon and bliss of childhood. They will repair the ravages of old time. Once away from work-discipline where time is spent and time is money, away also from the industrial city, its dirt and noise and fearful, nameless crowds of people, we shall restore time's losses, rediscover the magnificent freedoms of both familiarity and strangeness, natural beauty and civic ritual.

So the vacation cavalcades go back, back to the pretty little seaside villages in Cornwall, in Maine, in Provence, to recover the incomparable feeling of coming home

Figure 1.1   Forbes Stanhope, *Chadding at Mounts Bay*
Source: Worcester City Museum and Art Gallery

after a long absence, of finding at first the delicious taste of strangeness and then, gradually, recovering familiarity, as the loved and remembered details are rediscovered and gathered into the frame of the known. People revivify these small experiences every day: pieces of furniture or corners of the garden, even stretches of a much-travelled street or a view from the train, may all speak their friendly welcome.

You walk down a garden path to the bench, placed crosswise at the end of the path, overhung by a tree. You sit down and look back along the path, the climbing roses on a lattice to the left, the ranks of vegetables neatly regimented at right-angles to the path on the right. It's early evening, in July. The minutes you have to sit where you are match themselves to the homely, fragrant space and its fading colours. The fit is perfect.

Or the train stops at a station well known to you on a line you've travelled, off and on, for years. It's not large, and behind the neat slate shelter with its fretted bargeboarding, you can see pleasant hills, the road going downwards out of the station car park, two or three houses on the slope. The space is shapely but not quite enclosed. You crane your neck a little and watch the tall woman with the child walk out of the gate. Small events alter the little picture. A post office van sweeps round out of sight behind the station office. A stiff breeze moves through the trees.

> Suddenly an experience of disinterested observation opens in its centre and gives birth to a happiness which is instantly recognisable as your own. The [view you are looking at] appears to have the same proportions as your own life.[2]

This matching of space to time, of one's own life to the natural landscape in front of you is one of the promises held out by the dream of the vacations.

The dreams are powerful and beautiful. *Of course*, dedicated dreambusters in their big boots will, correctly, point out the horrors and the boredom of actually existing tightly packaged trips, the mutual exploitation of tourist and native, the drunks, the syringes, the dead babies. They will tell us, just as correctly, of that expanding third of the populations of the rich countries of the West which has absolutely no hope of affording any respite away from the dereliction and pointlessness of unemployed life on the estate.

But as Walter Benjamin once said, 'each generation imagines the epoch which is to succeed it',[3] and to be without a television is to be very poor indeed. Television is the source of the imagery with which we do our imagining of the future, and the holiday imagery now so omnipresent on the screen – in the soaps as well as the ads and in the travel programmes of all sorts – is one best place to find our fantasies of the free and fulfilled life.

It is the first contention of this book that those dreams be cherished and are cherishable. No doubt there are awful tattiness and worse kitsch in both the desire for and actuality of holidays. Certainly, there is extortion, fraud, mendacity, brutality and abominable wickedness in the very middle of tourist life and the industrialisation of our leisure. But luxury herself has always been the realm of the imagination. The origins of art lie in the dream of luxury, where body and soul will be freed from the frightful demands of subsistence, shelter, hungry children, dying dependants and where nature, restored to comity with humankind, will provide plenty and ease. This is the Garden of Eden, and the special effects of the Club Med holiday village, Swedish log cabin settlement or Caribbean beach paradise are alike the tribute paid to that ageless work of imagination.

Each generation, you could say, in imagining the next one, takes what it believes to be the best or happiest days of its present life and, shaping them into ideal forms, bestows them upon its children as a picture of how it hopes things will be. Naturally, this generation here and now hopes for prosperity for its children, hopes on their behalf for comfort, safety, happiness. It is part of that same naturalness that the icons and images in which those great values are pictured – comfort, safety, happiness; joy, laughter, open-handedness; troops of friends, courteous strangers – that many of these are drawn from the sacred realm of luxury, as it figures in the contemporary imagination. Even when personal taste comes out badly – and we can't ignore the fact – treat it tenderly; for this is the stuff which dreams are made of, before all these little lives are rounded out by the big sleep.

III

We shall therefore take it for the moment as read that the vast industrialisation of tours and travel may bring dire consequences in its train. This book contemplates a few. But for a value to *be* a value, it concentrates, in action and symbol, something of the best of life. Vacations mean what they mean because we look to them to bring out that best, in life and in us.

As any value does, this one gathers its meanings together over time and loses them also. The present English meaning of 'the holidays' began to accumulate sometime during the eighteenth century, taking its magical charge, as everybody knows, from the antique associations of the 'holy days' of the agricultural year on which heavy collective labour was replaced in brief respite by collective recreation – the dance, the race, the Christmas feast. The symbols of such moments – Maypole, Harvest Home, Yuletide – have been powerfully colonised by the inventors of tradition whatever their historical reality. Modern holidays, as we shall see, weave into their structure many such glimpses of these origins. In antique times, the palaeontologists tell us, the Lord of Misrule had his moment on the holy day, and the world was turned upside down. Excess, ecstasy, abandon, recklessness were given their usual lead in the pleasures of food and wine, sex and talking dirty, extravagant display and indecorous attire.

Plenty of all that on vacation. The discipline of work, the ethics of thrift and denial which, they say, set capitalism on its road, make welcome victims on the beach. These are the rites, customs and ceremonies at the genesis of the holiday.

It was the idle rich who took all the vacations in the eighteenth century, and what they did and had became obvious models for those who aspired to that condition of life to copy. So the practice of tourism became part of the decoration of the good life, stylishly mingling extensive and difficult journeys, exotic locations, special provender and a little educative self-improvement.

Sacred-pagan recreation and ruling-class tourism: the birth of the vacation lies *there*. The long history of the first inculcated the easy pleasures of transgression; the shorter provenance of the second illumined the satisfactions of going places.

This simple compound, however, hardly exhausts the manifold nature of the meaning and value lodged in the idea. The idea of the holiday occupies a corner, often a large corner, of the realm of *luxury*, and it was luxury, as Theodor Adorno suggests, which migrated into art and made art the place where we criticise this life and imagine a more abundant one. Adorno, a cultivated, wealthy and sort-of-Marxist Jew was exiled from Nazi Germany to Morningside Heights in Manhattan and embodying as he did the best, austere aestheticism of modernist Vienna found himself bowled over by the sheer vulgar plenty, the glittering showiness of American consumerism. Torn between human solidarity and his own caustic standards of judgement, he struggled to do justice to the dream of luxury. The ancient tales of opulence promise to hand over the secret spell which will bestow upon us the freedoms of wealth, the release from the necessities of labour and subsistence. There will be no call to screw a living out of the hard earth; the plenty of a loving Nature will surround us. So (he says):

> radiant things [jewels, stars, flowers, fruit, precious metal] become transformed into images of gentleness, promises of a happiness cured of domination over nature ... This is the primeval history of luxury that has migrated into the meaning of all art.[4]

Adorno began by thinking in this connection of precious jewels, the antique power of *treasure*, and those countless fairy stories in which diamonds, sapphires, silver, gold give power to those who find them and therefore bring freedom, fulfilment and delight, a life in which the natural world no longer has to be bullied and implored in order for us to win our shelter and food from it, but yields up the magic stuff which will do all the work for us. This victory won, we will then easily become our best selves, assured, loving, gentle. We shall live happily ever after.

'Once upon a time ...' all stories begin, and stories, whether told aloud, on the page, in the painting or by the music, were once stories about the imaginable world on the other side of this awful, short, contingent one. This is Adorno's 'primeval history of luxury' and after it 'migrated into the meaning of all art', the vast juggernaut of capitalism, whirling on its way a few centuries later, spotted what might be done with it and stepped smartly in to capture art for itself.

It couldn't, of course. Our ideal imaginings cannot merely be sold as commodities. The line from daydream to art is quite direct, and art does rather more for us than picture beautiful lives. But the resulting muddle in which our best hopes for the human future and our sentimental and indulgent longings for a good time now tussle with each other and set the terms of the new millennium as they do so, may nonetheless be sympathetically grasped and understood, I think, by way of interpreting our holidays. The best shot one can make at a perfect vacation partakes equally of being on our best behaviour, finding the nicest spot imaginable and fashioning a memory for the future to which one may return for restoration. I shall therefore rewrite Adorno by saying that luxury has migrated into that realm of the social imagination where our art, our politics and our ethics struggle together to replace the communality of a shared religion, and where, as a result, we do what we can to picture paradise. Butlins holiday camps and the Pure Crete villa, the Seychelles beaches and St. Tropez, the Brighton Pavilion and Coney Island, are all attempts to render that ideal home.

IV

Home, no doubt, is where you belong; vacations are somewhere to go away to. But one goes there for repair work, to put things right, to remember how to be better when one comes back. If home, as Philip Larkin said, is a glorious shot at getting things as they ought to be, that is why, as he also said, home is so sad. Homes get messed up by the everyday resistance of things and events. If we take out Adorno's licence and think of art as being our ideal imaginings, these ideals may be read in the piles of our keepsakes and souvenirs of the other places; in the way in which, when we have the money, we redecorate and refit our kitchens and bathrooms to come closer to the ideal. In our plans for the perfect back garden, the serene order of the prize allotment and, as I say, in the holiday places pictured on television and in the lifestyle magazines before being sold to us as our July and August, our Christmas and Easter, we find Adorno's 'promise of happiness' held out in the gorgeous colour photography of commercial art.

In all this busy dreaming at how things ought to be, one day in our future or our children's, the future is compounded (Walter Benjamin further suggests[5]) with the best bits of the past. Whenever men and women write books about utopias, even including Thomas More who invented the term, they go back to different aspects of different pasts and reassemble them as a different future. There is nowhere else to go for a bright idea. Since their picture of paradise is likely to be one in which people are happy and things go well, they are at pains to eradicate the causes, as they see them, of cruelty, waste, want and exploitation. So they go back, often a long way back either in history or in geography, to find images of life which escape those evils. They reinvent classlessness alongside independence; the irresponsibility of childhood as well as the ease of maturity; the rapture of spontaneous feeling together with the benign steadiness of self-control.

These are qualities of being rather than doing, and it is true that paradise has always had a problem with action. Even in the celestial city, all that hymning and harping looked as if it would get terribly boring, going on as it did for eternity. But purposeful action is a decidedly pressing matter in our more secular circumstances. It's damned hard to know what anybody can *do* which will make a difference, as we so frequently tell each other. All the same, action in the form of our duties to work (if you have work) and to families in any case keep people tied to what for most of them is drudgery: drudgery because unfree, because dutiful, repetitive, purposeless, deeply boring. Paradise will be free and it will be meaningful. It won't (obviously) be dreary; it won't bore us.

The dream of paradise begets, consequently, great expectations. I suppose boredom in its lethal form is simply an intolerable awareness of the disuse of one's gifts. That's why children hate it so violently. (Benign boredom – just 'sitting on your stalk like a mushroom' as D.H. Lawrence put it – is another matter altogether.) The human capacity to anticipate future fulfilment is one of the best things to come out of the evolution of mind. We can look forward. No economic system has yet bettered capitalism in its exploitation of this faculty. It sells the pleasure of infinite anticipation, smoothly replacing disappointment with the promise of another, future satisfaction.

The business has become unrelenting. The competition to keep up expectations must be kept up for the greater profit. In this little frenzy of the age, the difficulty is then to find time and space – both of them 'free' enough – in which to live where and when you are. If the consumer stops consuming, the whole mad rout of money stops as well, and nobody wants that. (They *really* don't.)

This puts the honest vacationer at the twistpoint of radical difficulties and contradictions for the industrial managers of the leisure industries. They are competing for the limited commodity of time itself. People only have a certain amount to allot to their holidays. The sales staff are also competing for limited quantities of capital: people can only afford a certain, generally fixed sum for their excursions. Finally, the industries are struggling to capture something grasped and won as one's own, *free* time, and such time is not to be spent at the behest of others lest one's possession of it as one's own be violated.

All this goes to make the commercial regularity of leisure infernally difficult. The industry must leave plenty of room for impulsiveness, last-minute decisions, sudden change, unexpected novelty and switches of interest and direction, all of which, by definition, are hard to accommodate in the Business Plan.

None of this need do anything other than exhilarate our holidaymakers with a keen sense of their own independence. But it all serves to remind us just how intense a concentration of meaning is to be found as we wait, all eagerness, in the airport terminal.

V

Holidays, I said, prefigure utopia, and 'utopia' translates from the Greek as 'the place of human flourishing'. 'Paradise', in turn, remains a powerful word, even when it has become the cliché of the brochures. In David Lodge's admirable little fable about a visit to Hawaii, *Paradise News*,[6] the appallingly zealous sociologist falls ardently on the Waikiki free paper of that name, while Lodge appends a dry anthology of all the grisly rendezvous on Main Street, the dire fastfoodery and the grim arcade of slot machines which ticket themselves as corners of paradise.

Paradise: word and concept remain gratifyingly indestructible. It lends its aura to all our holiday fantasies. The primary act of the human mind is to make sense of things by turning them into a narrative. We find meaning in form. The form of the holiday is given by certain feelingful maxims to be found in all the vacation-taking classes. There are, of course, ten such maxims. No one holiday includes all ten. Some contradict others. All, I claim, have a place in our common definition of the vacation.

First, vacations take place in bracketed time. That is to say, they are anticipated as 'time out', 'time off' (a well-known agency calls itself this), 'free' time, and so on. This is not time to be 'spent',[7] but time quite inflexibly marked as to its beginning and end, and also as to its recreational, deliberately non-productive content. Happy times, by and large, pass quickly and one sign of the good holiday is that its beginning is as eagerly looked out for as its end is held off as much as possible, its passage marked by little rituals, its finality given its own sad ceremony ('goodbye house, goodbye hills, goodbye river …').

There is much of our childhoods in this, and as I have twice suggested, holidays attach a permission to adults to regress to the terrific anticipatoriness of childhood and its passion to be free of all these encumbering, imperious, unignorable others.

The second maxim, therefore, is there must be no work while on vacation. Or if there is work, it cannot be the work for which one is normally paid. A banker may mend the plumbing in his Tuscan cottage but not phone the bank. A plumber may back horses or fill in his pools form but not dismantle the cistern. One meaning of the holiday is, as we saw, that it marks free time won from work. It therefore refuses the invasion of capital into all corners of life. On vacation, you do not make a profit and there should be no measures of productivity. (Capitalism being the monstrous force it is, I fear that people *do* nonetheless apply productivity criteria to their sight-seeing: they polish off the entire Piero trail, from Florence to Urbino, in two days; they pack the Louvre, the Quai D'Orsay, the Eiffel Tower and Notre Dame into one.)

Third, the places may be strange *or* familiar; they may be both. The one true holiday fills us brimful with the sweet anticipation of returning somewhere we know and, because we have been happy there in the past, somewhere we love. For a child this unbearable excitement of return, deepened by the escape from school work into perfect freedom, is ritualised by precious landmarks as she approaches the loved place. First, the signpost off the main road, then the far glimpse of the sea, then a house set well back from the road and behind the lush lawn, where she once bought a pot of honey; then the ugly but homely grey little town street with the harbour below and the gulls wheeling overhead; next, the coast road and the distant jumble of roofs, and finally the crunch of gravel under the wheels. She's *there*!

The return is from exile, where work rules and families become strangers to one another in the grip of their timetables; it is a return to what is known and trusted, because it restores the order of sweet and natural sounds and smells and sights. But the other true holiday is strange; it is *not-home*. Some vacations are pilgrimages, others voyages of exploration. The thrill of waking up unsure where you are is zestful and sparkling, the pleasure of finding out not only that things are as they were but also that you do not know how they are, that you have to search out the shop for the milk and the day the rubbish is collected, the pleasure of new picnic spots and hiding places, of unknown language and indecipherable passages, these are the delights of the strange, the foreign and exotic. Paradise, you see, will be a homecoming; but it will also be an amazing apotheosis. It will be the world as you never dreamed it could be.

Fourth, the place must be beautiful *and* luxurious. As we have seen, these notions are very close to each other. Like all cultural practices, the desire for luxury also lives in its negation. Some holidays – trekking in Mongolia or sledding in Alaska – derive their meaning by withdrawing comfort entirely and refusing the beauties of order, cultivation, settlement for the more taxing aesthetics of natural wildness and tempest, the ugliness of untechnological hygiene ('cat sanitation' as the Army used to call it), crude, badly cooked food (marioc, tortoise, snake), temporary shelter (tents, Land Rovers, brushwood shelter). These ideal opposites confirm the original. The hotel, the villa; the aircraft, the bus; the shops, the museums; these must all signify luxury, luxurious display, luxurious vegetation, implements and adornments. To say that these are the accoutrements and illusions of old power is to miss the point. The power lives in the luxury.

Luxury is ripest, no doubt, in the *city*. Pastiche being what it is these days, and the imitation of the iconography of luxury being so readily reproduced, as jewellery, gilded glass, blue marble and indoor fountains playing over mosaic peacocks, luxury is pretty well synonymous with kitsch.

Fifth, the vacation must be safe and it must be dangerous. Home is neither. The safety of home is taken for granted; when it *is* dangerous, it's a matter of routine. The holiday, however, encloses us in the safety of luxury (the amazing bathroom in the hotel, the little square below the balcony) and piques us with the scent of danger (don't go down to the edge of the town, take care of the waves on the sea front).

Sixth, contrariwise, the good holiday relieves us of the grubby city and restores us to the fresh bosom of nature. It will be *natural*. This is an echo of Adorno's belief that real happiness is only possible when human beings no longer need wring subsistence from an intractable earth. No work on holiday, obviously; but more than that, not only no need to drive to work but also one rediscovers the beatitude of being back on terms with one's natural and unpolluted surroundings. Nature-as-good-for-you has deep roots. In Shakespeare's magical comedies, the forests of *As You Like It* and *A Midsummer Night's Dream* are the places where, after comic trials and tribulations, things come right and all is well that ends well. Nature mothers us back into complicity with her. Holidays make time to recover that gentleness and complicity – it is surely this restoration which is covered by the catch-all 'relaxation'. From all of which it follows that ...

Seventh, the vacation must improve and enhance our minds, spirits and bodies. Western spiritual development theory is piled high with recent doctrines of earnestness and puritan self-improvement for everybody. But the Grand Tour, as we shall see, took out a licence on learning as well as licentiousness, and the tourist has always travelled with a heavy burden of improving literature and a clear duty to see the sights and take the walks. The world is full of its wonders, cultural and natural alike, and holidays mark the time to read the books and see the buildings and do the hikes which will do us good. A brown body, in the sexual aesthetics of today, is healthier than a white one (Billy Connolly: 'Who's that blue prick on the verandah?'); someone who took the trouble to gape at the Sphinx is better educated for it.

These last two qualities of every good holiday whether in city or country – the restoration of naturalness and the tribute paid to self-improvement – are also aspects of the utopian society. The good holiday will briefly place us in that society, by ...

Eighth, being both civic and solitary. It will be civic because we return to the familiar well-loved place and to people who are strangers but whom we restore to the familiar (though not to the intimate) by our greeting. At home there are only intimates and the anonymity of the crowds. On holiday there are traditional social roles occupied by cordial strangers: the shopkeeper, the postmistress, the fisherman, the farmer-landlord, the coastguard, the vicar. It is a bit like living in Trumpton or among the Amish: old appellations revive (Doctor, Officer, Monsieur, Signora, Effendi); lapsed and local ceremonies quicken again (the cricket match, the jazz cellar, the village fête, the church service). Appreciating these traditional roles probably involves an agreeable touch of histrionics: one acts up to their walk-on part in one's private play.

As with so many of these maxims, this last happily contains an opposition. The holiday is civic, but it is solitary as well. In other words, like all good societies it expresses an ideal balance and a clear but implicit boundary between public and private life. It not only marks the boundary, it facilitates the easy expression of both. I am public and civic when I go, as I never would at home, to the lecture on seabirds of the region; I am private and personal when I stand on the headland by the lighthouse to watch the sunset. (In both cases, let it be added, I am restoring my union with mother nature.)

Ninth, the holiday must be plentiful and it must be licentious. The end of every good holiday is a vast meal. Every holiday lives on the liminal, which is to say at the edge of things: duties, work, routine, financial responsibility. On the edge, those clouds lift. I shall eat what I like and drink more than I can. I will behave disgracefully, wearing weird clothes or no clothes. I will be invisible to my reputation and my respectability, because here such actions have their licence and misrule its day. I will buy food such as I would never buy at home and cook dishes never attempted there either. I will drink gin at midday and Chardonnay at three … And easy, edenic and guiltless sex will assail and delight me, in fact and fantasy, on any corner and at every hour.

Last and tenth of these notes towards a supreme fiction of vacations is that, as the great poet of the subject, Wallace Stevens, said: 'It must be abstract … it must change … it must give pleasure …' and he went on, magnificently:

Two things of opposite natures seem to depend
On one another, as a man depends
On a woman, day on night, the imagined

On the real. This is the origin of change.
Winter and spring, cold copulars, embrace
And forth the particulars of rapture come.

Music falls on the silence like a sense,
A passion that we feel, not understand.
Morning and afternoon are clasped together

And North and South are an intrinsic couple
And sun and rain a plural, like two lovers
That walk away as one in the greenest body.[8]

Stevens was a full-time, wealthy businessman as well as a poet. He lived in Hertford, Connecticut and endured its bitter beautiful winters, but he loved Florida and vacationed often in Key West, his favourite seaside spot. He is the twentieth-century poet of happiness and our grand romancer of travel, of art, indeed of seeing the sights.

We need such a poet for this book; Stevens is the heir of Keats and Wordsworth in England, the two poets who first really canonised the landscape for the people. He is also the heir of America's greatest nineteenth-century philosopher, Emerson, and Emerson's distinctively American cheerfulness and dreaminess, his certainty that he will get the best out of new experiences, all make him a member of the party, too.

Such poets and philosophers confirm by their trade the last of my maxims, which is a platitude. It is that all good holidays, abstract, changeful, pleasurable as they are, must leave a deep sediment of folklore, myths and family jokes in the collective memory and the culture which carries it. The immortality of the vacation lives in the recollection of a past which causes laughter and fond tears in the present. 'Do you remember when …?' is the potent trigger which fires the gone vacation back into your heart, and what you remember may have been catastrophic then but is a splendid joke now; it may simply have been loved companionship in a loved place, the memory of which presently renews the sweet regret of loss; best of all, the jollity and triumph brought up for recollection confirm all that has been built up since and holds us now.

These maxims and their contradictions give the form of the vacation as its idea moves in our imagination. Their contradictoriness is unsurprising; the mind has to hold together the bits and pieces of a world which is constantly flying apart. Holidaying is a time to pretend that they all come together. It is so designed that, on a good day, they do.

2

THE INVENTION OF TOURISM

I

The meaning of a social practice and the value it has for us are, as I said, made up of the many interweavings of its use. 'Holiday', 'vacation', mean the many things they do because of the many uses to which we put them in our lives. Things that mean a lot to us do so because they accumulate uses. Accumulation is by definition historical. To make useful understanding of our corner of cultural history easier, the origins of modern industrial society need be set no further back than the second half of the eighteenth century, when capitalism in one country – Britain, as it happened – started to roar unstoppably away. It would be quite adequate to date the beginning of the Grand Tour which gives us the word 'tourism' quite precisely from 1763 when the treaties were signed that ended intermittent hostilities in Europe lasting most of the preceding century. Thereafter, in spite of the interval of renewed warfare between Britain and France and assorted revolutions on either side of the Atlantic, travelling for fun grew and grew across the European continent and, later, up and down the eastern seaboard of the United States, until the working classes were allowed to join in, travel turned into tourism and on 5 July 1841 Thomas Cook, a Baptist teetotaller-preacher, chartered his momentous railway excursion from Leicester to Loughborough.

Tourism by then was rather less than eighty years old but its origins go back to the first pastorals. In John Fowles's admirable novel *Daniel Martin*,[1] the novelist lends his hero a favourite passage from Restif de la Bretonne's eighteenth-century quasi-autobiography, *Monsieur Nicolas*, set in the decades before the French Revolution. In it, while remembering his childhood in deepest Burgundy, the Frenchman describes shepherding his father's sheep into an unknown, rich and beautiful combe – 'la bonne vaux' – where he finds unparalleled fecundity, rare (but not legendary) birds and wildlife which he has never seen before and what he senses as a perfect congruence of man and nature, a harmony of free, mutual life which properly belongs to Paradise. Momentarily, the sacred valley, which he never found again, realises the dream of perfect peace which was to haunt the Romantics and remains for us as their potent legacy.

These sacred valleys and lost domains are scattered through the geography, the demography and the poetry and paintings of the next two centuries. In Britain their line is traced both northwards and westwards by a route whose landmarks are the ruined Cistercian abbeys left abandoned after the dissolution of the monasteries, pillaged a little for their stones by the locals, muffled and girded in outline by ivy and erosion. Then at a moment heralded by Thomas Gray's great poem 'Elegy in a Country Churchyard' in 1753, a bold new cadre of homegrown painters fell to imitating the grand ruins and sunny prospects of the mighty French classicists Claude and Poussin, turning ruins into lovely natural phenomena the point of which was to occasion sublime and beautiful feelings in the beholder.

Taking his cue, the young philosopher and politician from Ireland, Edmund Burke, published in 1759 his definitive essay[2] explaining the difference between the two. The beautiful was, as many commentators have pointed out, a feminine creature of soft-ness, delicacy, a hint of gratifying voluptuity and of humane congeniality. The sublime, on the other hand, was a fearsome patriarch, full of 'horrid power', bleak, massive, unyielding, enormous. The home of the first was the cultivated English garden with its soft curves and seductive boskiness. Its painter was Claude. The realm of the second was the Lake District, or better still, the Alps, where the mighty rocks and chasms, the torrents and peaks combined the authority of grandeur with the discipline of indifference. Its first painter was the seventeenth century Neapolitan, Salvator Rosa.

Either way, there was a moral lesson to the sentiments in all this. For it was more than a coincidence that the so-called Grand Tour inaugurated itself some time during the 1760s. There had been great political commotion in England and Scotland in the previous couple of generations. Monarchs were still to be found underneath their

Figure 2.1 Claude Lorraine (Claude Gellée), *Landscape with Cephalus and Procris Reunited by Diana*, 1645 (oil on canvas)

Source: National Gallery, London/Bridgeman Art Library

crowns to be sure, but they were much more domesticated creatures, kept in their place by the sedate Tory settlement,[3] itself the outcome of the deal between old aristocracy and new bourgeoisie which, among other things, gave such celebrated traveller-tourists as Lady Mary Wortley Montagu and James Boswell their money and their lives of leisure.

These two figures will act, in a moment, as the stars of our tour of the Grand Tour. A generation or so apart, the two of them may stand for the great affective change which came over all those with the money and the time in the second half of the century. The new class system which transpired in England and southern Scotland at the end of the seventeenth century was one in which the feelings in general, and family sentiment in particular found much more room to move[4] than had ever been possible in the large households and exigent economies of the previous century.

It all seems not to have been just a matter of that old historical standby, the rising bourgeoisie. Even in the absolutism of France, the petty princedoms of Germany, a new language of the sentiments broke out from literature and entered daily life. Leisure provided the time for the new freedoms, sexual, social, aesthetic as they were, and for a new kind of town, joined in its many variants by a new kind of travel and the spacious theatre which went with it.

It was a town for visiting rather than for the responsibilities of the estate or of exchange. Work, money-changing, adding value and moving freight happened there, or somewhere else, of course; but in this new kind of town, thrown up at headlong speed by eager speculators and shady jerry-builders, people took houses, which is to say rented homes, in order to meet and mingle and to be seen as members of fashionable society.

These towns, generally expansions of little places happily situated where the newly affirmed life-giving properties of salty waters, warm or cold, might be readily suffered, constituted one kind of new urban creation. The spa, the watering-place, and the resort entered the English language together. In such towns, the gleaming new assembly-rooms, the colonnades and little squares, the long crescents and terraces, took their lead, naturally enough, from the Palladian style books of old Italy but lacking the historical resonance of the original because they are (as Jane Austen shows us) a novel sort of theatre for the arrangement of marriages and the parleying of political settlement between old and new money.

On the other hand, however, when the same people set off across the Channel, for Paris, for the Rhine and Rhône and across the Alps, their reasons for going where they went were scholarly and historical: they went to Italy to see classical antiquity. Or they were aesthetic: they went to Rome and Florence to admire the great buildings and paintings. Or they were cultivatedly acquisitive: the collectors bought for their collections. Or they were healthful: if they went to Carlsbad or Aix, they took the horrible-tasting salty waters for the sake of their skin or their digestion and because Germany was more daring than Scarborough. Or they went for sex: they went, like Boswell so ardently did, to indulge what was, in his case, an unslakeable sexual appetite and they did so because, well, on the Grand Tour as a young blade, anything goes. It was hard to damage a reputation in foreign parts.

They did these things in Bath, Cheltenham, Leamington, Droitwich; in Carlsbad, Aix-les-Bains and Lausanne; wherever the waters could pass as salutary, John Nash, architect of the tourist boom, would design his splendid white stucco terraces and his imitators would do the same down the road. Meanwhile, the ancient capitals – Paris, Dresden, Grenoble; Venice, Florence, Naples – had only to adjust themselves slightly to the new ways: they had all the historical buildings and paintings in the first place, and the word 'hotel' meant at that time no more than a large town house. Old corruption in the capitals had no difficulty rearranging itself as headquarters to the new traffic. Each already had a name in the business; each had been an item in the education of young diplomats, poets, gentlemen of position since the Renaissance first lit up. Thomas Hobbes spent a decade of exile from the Puritan revolutionaries in Paris; Milton went to Avernus to sense the shade of Virgil; ever since the Levant company marked the route to Venice and beyond at the end of the sixteenth century, there had been a little group of expatriate English in each of the stages of the Tour. So they cleared a promenade for carriages – Naples first – found plenty of houses to let, views to contemplate, historic associations to vibrate, and dug antiquities out of the ground as fast as they could sell them.

More than an industry, a culture and a way of life arose from this ferment. The Peace of Paris concluded the Seven Years War in 1763. Between then and 1796 when Bonaparte invaded Italy, the Grand Tour was dominated by the British. Over those three decades, the ratio of passports issued in Rome to British visitors (a passport being at the time just that: paid permission to step from the boat to the quay) outnumbered all other nations by five to one. Already, by 1784 over three hundred elegant English wintered in Nice, another one hundred and thirty in Naples.[5]

They went for all the reasons I have given and they certainly went to keep warm. They were completely serious about their purposes. The maxim that a tourist should be improved and educated by the Tour was inscribed in the practice from the start. These were men (and a few of their women) who had undergone, whatever else, a full grounding in classical education. France had little more than Paris but Italy was not only Rome, it was Florence, Venice and Naples, a constellation of four cities which, in the words of Cesare de Seta:

> had assumed much of the splendour of the city of Pericles and Phidias, and now inspired the same passionate responses that Athens had once awakened in the Romans ... As Hadrian said when he took Athens, the conqueror had become the conquered.[6]

The tourists were schooled in the new classic painters of the Alps and the Roman Campagna, Claude, Poussin, Rosa. But they were up to date also with the latest theories of optics and the pictures which experimented with them; the panoramic paintings by Canaletto and Panini were made possible by the arrangement of a dish of mirrors placed below a high funnel in a dark room, the *camera obscura*.

In either genre – classical landscape or townscape – the painters taught their admirers what to *see* (and what not to), and they went to see the sights armed with one of the newly classic texts to which Grand Tourism gave rise, the guidebooks. In 1730 Edward Wright published an early bestseller in the form[7] and he was followed by a long line, the prominent titles in which included Thomas Taylor's *Gentleman's Pocket Companion for Travelling into Foreign Parts* (1722) (less a guidebook than a vademecum of tips to tourists flavoured with strong doses of chauvinism), Breval's *Remarks on Several Parts of Europe* (1738), Nugent's *Grand Tour containing an exact description of most of the cities, towns and remarkable places of Europe* (1749), Grosley's *Observations on Italy made in 1764*, Duclos' *Voyage en Italie* (1766), assorted volumes published as *His Guide through France Etc.* by *The Gentleman's Magazine*, Smollett's famous *Travels through France and Italy* (1766). Nor were such books by and for men only. The *Letters* and travel notes of the ladies Miller, Eliot-Drake, Radcliffe, as well as the fame of Wortley Montagu all attest to the presence of a comfortably-off, new, all-women reading public, travelling not alone but independently.

Taylor's *Companion* of 1722 marks the change. In effect, he stands at the end of the previous century. His readers were *travellers*, and if the distinction between those two concepts, so popular in the literature of travel and tourism is to mean anything useful, it must be that travellers go with a purpose other than seeing what there is to see. Then again, the purpose of travelling might be to travel. 'Fare forward, travellers', the poet says, and the implication is that travelling is its own satisfaction. Taylor is full of advice for the hardy and the provident, cautioning, for sure, against villainous innkeepers, mosquitoes and frostbite. His successors make nothing of footpads though they do warn against poor food, but their attention is given solemnly to the chronicles of antiquity and association: here, in Smollett, we are commended to the gentlefolk of Piedmont after the rough peasants on the wrong side of the Alps; there Nugent encourages us at Ulnbrae to breathe the same air as Horace breathed; Wright is particular about the masterpieces of the Italian peninsula which, naturally, he takes to be the Campagna (mentioning Claude) and Hadrian's villa. Each volume is almost casually pedagogic; to be on the Tour, whatever else you were there for, was to be acquiring an education.

The trouble is that to be described as a tourist, especially a self-improving one, has for many years been a term always of condescension and often of contempt. In that excellent study of travel literature *Abroad*,[8] Paul Fussell allows himself a frequent use of the downward inflexion. Travellers are free to go anywhere; they go pretty well alone; they overcome all obstacles in their way, an awkward official in Turkestan, a lame horse in Tartary. They live hard but romantically; they are brave (naturally), light-hearted, trenchant, well-off but never rich, mechanically resourceful, home-lovers *and* home-haters, cultivated … oh, the good traveller, mostly male but with a few tough women thrown in, is quite wonderful. But the tourist, hemmed in by 'passports and queues and guided tours and social security numbers and customs regulations and currency controls',[9] this creature is not only in a state of 'lamb-like subservience to red tape which is perhaps the most striking characteristic of modern man', he and she is a *bore*, and almost certainly lower middle class as well.

No-one could doubt that tourists, on some more cordial definition, are the people who mostly do the travelling these days. They are those who follow where the solitary traveller has been first (well, not *first*, you understand, people live there already, but first from your place). Even then, the travellers almost certainly had predecessors. In the end we may have to say that the distinction between tourist and traveller is either a historical one (early visitors in small numbers and having had a bit of a hard time count as travellers), or a snobbish one ('my dear, there were such crowds of tourists').

For our purposes, we shall say that travellers went there first and marked out the route for tourists. Every generation of tourists has a traveller predecessor; the travellers not only invented the route, in most cases they wrote the sacred texts which first recruited the tourists. They shaped the story whose charm drew people after them.

One can see this process at work in the celebrated, at times notorious life of Lady Mary Wortley Montagu. Although the tale of her travels was never published in print in her lifetime, those times and tales were pretty public; some of them found their way into news and gossipy journals like the *Weekly* or *Saturday Post*; she was much celebrated in poetic print by Alexander Pope as well as publishing pamphlets herself (one prominent one, for example, supporting the new and daring practice of inoculation against smallpox, a disease which had disfigured and nearly killed her[10]). Her personal and much admired correspondence passed from hand to hand and quickly constituted an early example of travel literature from the pen of a woman (it was published only seven years after her death in 1762), while her celebrity meant that her name and some version of her appearance were commonly known by virtue of the numerous full-length society portraits of her by, among others, Godfrey Kneller, Jonathan Richardson, Charles Jervas and Jean Baptiste Vaumour (the last in the National Portrait Gallery, London[11]).

In most of those portraits she appears in a version of the Turkish national dress for women of standing, Constantinople being the Embassy to which her husband, a not-very-bright career politician, was sent. But she and her husband, in spite of their romantic elopement, never got on well and his wife's disfigurement by smallpox destroyed the beauty which was to have helped his preferment. Lady Mary, a woman of remarkable and daring independence, as well as of taste, wit and intelligence, set an example to her sex and the Grand Tourists who queued up for the life she led so brilliantly and for half a century between 1716 and 1762. Her most resounding *coups* for future tourists were her frequent visits to the Seraglio of the Sultan and to the women's warm baths at Sophia.

> To tell you the truth, I had the wickedness enough to wish secretly that Mr. Gervase could have been there invisible. I fancy it would have very much improved his art to see so many fine Women naked in different postures, some in conversation, some working, others drinking Coffee or sherbet, and many negligently lying on their Cushions while their slaves (generally pretty girls of 17 or 18) were employ'd in braiding their hair in several pritty manners. In short, 'tis the Women's coffee house, where all the news of the town is told, scandal invented, etc.[12]

It is a fine piece of description though she rather turns the women from Muslim prisoners into gentlemanly Londoners – a very modern tourist trick. It is also deservedly well-known, not least because Ingres used Lady Mary as a sourcebook for his own, necessarily fantasied paintings of the harem. In so doing he marked another, tantalisingly inaccessible but of course erotic station on the tourist track.

Lady Mary was a formidable pioneer-anthropologist. She took the veil and wore a *djubbah* and passed unknown through the streets, praising in her letters the extraordinary freedom this bestowed upon her. She was an antiquarian also, paying her dues to the beauty of the city, dressing up as a man to visit the Mosque, taking her copy of Homer to visit the few stones left of Troy, before returning to England, squaring herself to the mutual disesteem she shared with her husband, and becoming a secular widow and hostess of high society across the great cities of the Grand Tour. She published fierce political pamphlets, she cultivated an ardent and poetical love affair with a handsome Italian half her age, Count Francesco Algarotti, and in 1739 took up residence, naturally, on the Grand Canal and became leader of the *haut ton* which gathered in Venice for its famous and indiscreet masquerades, the elaborate *levées* of a dozen princelings, the dalliance, and the gondola and barge trips, then as now, across the lagoon to the islands of Torcello and Murano. The cosmopolitan traveller Lady Mary sets the style for the later tourist.

She goes to Florence to join Lady Pomfret at the Palazzo Ridolfi, admires its Medici splendours, stays two months, drives out to the Cascine park to take the air beside the Arno, visits the Uffizi three times, holds her regular *conversazione* and proceeds to Rome. In her thank-you letter to Lady Pomfret, she writes of her tourist discipline that: 'I go to bed every night at ten, run about all morning among the antiquities, and walk every evening in a beautiful villa.'[13] The tour turns round in Naples, crowded but 'gayest of all', still warm in late November, with an excellent opera house and the newly excavated and fascinating remains of Herculaneum just down the road.

She was dazzling wherever she went, the star of the new tourist firmament, and drifted disjointedly north, meddling in the politics of Genoa, pausing in Chambéry and Geneva, settling at last in the far from fashionable but safe and comfortable city of Avignon. In every place she gave the stature of her name and good taste to all she approved, the which, she being a generous woman, was plentiful. She loved the *Palais des Papes* in Avignon and its prospect of the magnificent Provençal landscape, so she built her own belvedere at home. She ventured boldly on little tours never before undertaken by an Englishwoman and over territory much interrupted by brigands and hardly under any kind of control. She travelled to Nimes, Narbonne, Montpellier, carrying with her, as a French admirer wrote, '*la république des lettres*' before moving again for ten years to Brescia by the Garda Lake, restored a tumbledown mansion, grew tea and game, led a little scientific society, encouraged the locals to build a theatre in her stables, and added the Lake to the statutory list of Grand Tourism. It was a way of life almost precisely reconstructed by Lisa St. Aubyn de Téran in the Tuscan hills in the 1980s.[14] Every well-told traveller's tale is repeated as a tourist's biography which in turn became a new tale. This is how life imitates art and art, life.

Thus, in a strict sense, Lady Mary led an exemplary life, an example to tourists. James Boswell, being a man, and a foolish, passionate and observant one as well, admired her writing undoubtedly but had other fish, when he set off to France and Italy in 1765, to fry.

He was, after all, son of Alexander, Lord Auchinleck who, like all fathers of his class, saw the Tour as an essential part of his heir's education. Lord Chesterfield, in his classically pedagogic and minatory letters of advice to his son, assumes the young man to be with his tutor six hours a day in Rome, warns against the whores and gamblers who are simply everywhere in Paris, breathless to ease a gullible youngster of his money ('I must absolutely hear of no tavern scrapes and squabbles'[15]) and directs him to speak German, French and Italian to the native speakers of those tongues. Boswell who, whatever his failings, was very intelligent and very well educated, spoke and wrote all three languages fluently. But he had come not only with the paternal admonition to get educated but also with the licence of the gentlemanly tourist and he was going to enjoy himself. He was going to eat too much, drink too much and take as many women to bed as he could. He would also fall in love with quite different women, for sexual desire and the tender passion were firmly separated by social class and opportunity and, after zealous gaming and bouts of remorse, he would view the educative sights of antiquity which would restore a little sacred incense to his enthusiastically profane world.

> At Rome, I ran about among prostitutes till I was interrupted by that distemper which scourges vice in this world. When I got to Venice I had still some small remains of disease, but strange, gay ideas which I had framed of the Venetian courtesans turned my head, and away I went to an opera dancer and took Lord Mountstuart with me. We both had her and we both found ourselves taken in for the punishment I had met with, at Rome.[16]

The terrific zest with which Boswell participated in all the life he met was inseparable in the man from his ingenuousness, his egoism, his openness, his sheer likeability. It makes him an irresistible reporter of his vacations. This is how to enjoy yourself; it is to *feel* things so fully, partly because they are worth it, partly because he's like that. He lives it all, and mitigates nothing. This is feeling in the big Romantic sense, for he is on his Sentimental Education.

Boswell reminds us, for example, just how frightful crossing the Channel could be, just as Turner was to do a little later. Six or seven hours on a bad day, and then a violently buffeted trip in a rowing boat taking you off the packet and to the quayside,

Figure 2.2   Venice
Source: Hilary Britland

sick, bruised, exhausted. No wonder after four or five days on the road, travellers, pilgrims and tourists gave themselves a week or so in Dijon to thaw out and unstiffen.

Stopping only for nights, it was two more weeks to the foot of the Alps, the roads getting worse all the time from Nice, Boswell's wretched little dog Jachone iced up its paws so that his master carried him on horseback, until they came to the steeps of the pass of Mount Cenis where horses could not go, and the tourist was carried by four men on a rough litter, hardly more than two logs bound together, and so laboured on until Italy was visible. They would stop, perhaps (depending on the route) at the St. Bernard monastery, famous home of the famous giant tracker dogs, for a bitter night before a roaring fire.

Some travellers perforce ventured the crossing as early as April and had to brave crevasses in spiked snowshoes; mostly they crossed when the snows were thinner (still drifted up to six feet, Boswell says) and the porters cheerful, and so came down to the warmth of Piedmont, to Turin, where the Tour could properly begin, and education of the sentiments could divide itself easily between wine and song.

> I had an excellent apartment at Siena. I ate well. The wine of the district was very good, and on holidays I regaled myself with delicious Montepulciano … Every morning for two hours I read the divine Ariosto, and you can imagine the effect which that produced on my romantic soul … a professor of music who had very fine taste came to me every afternoon, and we sang and played fine airs on the flute … a city completely at peace where not a single soldier was to be seen … I was the only foreigner there.[17]

In Milan, Boswell 'drank chocolate and got into spirits', admired the *Duomo* to sincere distraction, imagined himself in contemplative old age at the convent, quoted well-loved Latin poetry on cue and for his own pleasure, and so to Rome to join his dear, unlikely friend, radical and atheist John Wilkes, found the 'campagna charming', but here he is at St. Peter's: 'Entered church; warm. Ah! noble, immense; quite rapt. Walked around. At last, kneeled and adored …' on to Naples ('a delicious spot; *praetor omnes ridet*'), admires the bay briskly and sincerely, Virgil in hand, suffers from some sort of eczema, back to Rome after a month for a six-day 'course in Antiquities and Arts', talking Latin to his friend Morison, and keeping a notebook in French (this is full-dress Grand Tourism, all right). He leaves nothing out, this consci-entious (but all-delighting) fellow:

> We saw the ceremony at the Minerva, where his Holiness was carried on a magnificent chair, decorated with a figure of the Holy Ghost … After this there was a procession of Roman girls … some to be married and others to become nuns … Only a few were pretty and most of the pretty ones were nuns … We viewed the celebrated Forum. I experienced sublime and melancholy emotions as I thought of all the great affairs which had taken place there … We entered the famous Colosseum, which certainly presents a vast and sublime idea of the grandeur of the ancient Romans … It was shocking to discover several portions of this theatre full of dung … climbed the Palatine hill in the afternoon … walked to where the house of Cicero stood. A statue there resembles him a great deal. Struck by these famous places, I began to

speak Latin. Mr. Morison replied. He laughed a bit at the beginning … saw the Baths of Diocletian … saw a strange fellow sitting in the sun reading Tasso to a group of others in rags like himself … saw 'Moses' by Michelangelo; horns, though sacred, yet ludicrous as like satyr; rest of the figure superb.[18]

On and on, tireless, energetic, sybaritic and egotistical for sure but also ingenuously attentive and alive to everything about him; our Grandest Tourist.

II

Boswell is a charmer, a hard man to leave. Erudition, enthusiasm, licence and extravagance mingle in him in such immediately recognisable ways. He is one of us, but one of us because he was like it first. Innocent as he is, he teaches succeeding generations what and how to feel, arranging himself and the landscape of Virgil's birthplace at Pietole under the spreading beech ('patulae fagi') sitting on the spot, no doubt, where the master beheld the gentle slope to the water's edge and penned the first lines of the *Eclogues* – 'qua se subducere colles / Inapiunt monique … usque ad aquam'. This was the pastoral image invented by the new pedagogues of sensibility in the eighteenth century, authorised by Virgil and turned into pictures everybody could find in the Campagna by Claude and Poussin.

These latter painters were more than imaginary presences in the luggage of the cultivated Grand Tourist. One indispensable item of kit was the Claude glass which, when held up to the prospect, would thereby frame it so that the spectator could adjust his or her vision correctly, ensuring a foreground, middleground and background; an overarching tree just *so*; a declivity ahead, a lake at its foot, the hills mounting beyond; the great orb of the sun (or, with an appropriate darkening of detail, the moon) not quite touching the horizon, slightly off-centre.

One can only tease the Claude glassholder affectionately, for these are the forms and composition of the landscape colour postcards of our own day, the most popular pictorial culture imaginable to the middle classes, as every kitchen or office noticeboard will testify. The Grand Tour was an education – a very expensive one as many parents complained, especially Boswell's father. Centrally, it was an education of the feelings and, as usual, those feelings were a jumble of desire – desire for the good, the true and the beautiful inextricably mixed with desire for the forbidden fruits of freedom, ecstasy, excess, all that stern fathers forbade. So Alexander Pope, his eloquence most fired, as always, by malice and hatred, caricatures the archetype:

> Led by my hand, he saunter'd Europe round,
> And gather'd ev'ry Vice on Christian ground;
> Saw ev'ry Court, heard ev'ry King declare
> His royal sense of Op'ras or the Fair;
> The Stews and Palace equally explor'd
> Intrigu'd with glory and with spirit whor'd;
> Try'd all hors d'oeuvres, all liqueurs defin'd,
> Judicious drank, and greatly daring din'd;
> Dropt the dull lumber of the Latin score,

Spoil'd his own language and acquir'd no more;
All Classic learning lost on Classic ground,
And last turn'd Air, the Echo of a Sound!
See now, half-cur'd and perfectly well-bred,
With nothing but a Solo in his head.[19]

Plenty of paternal letters and filial excuses to back that up; but the poetry wins over the moralising: Pope, in spite of himself, turns the tour into a riot. Spotting the Prince, sporting at the Opera, diving into dens of iniquity have always been measures of a good time, and if some of the younger students missed their Latin lessons, plenty of others, including Boswell, paid full tribute to antiquity.

The scholarly and *cognoscenti* aspect of so much tourist life was richly distributed in the eighteenth century and is its bequest to the nineteenth. Johann Zoffany painted an extraordinary *tour de force* during the 1770s, placing in the celebrated *Tribuna* room at the Uffizi gallery portraits of most of the leading British collectors genially admiring the greatest works in the gallery, each faithfully copied by Zoffany. Sir Horace Mann and the painter Thomas Patch consider Titian's 'Venus of Urbino'; Zoffany himself is showing Lord Cowper a Raphael for which his lordship intended to trade a more senior peerage with King George; over on the right, the Bright Young Men, ignored by their elders, vindicate Pope's strictures by gaping at the perfections of the Venus de Medici .

Latterday art historians are a bit apt to see such a picture as testimony to the acquisitiveness of the capitalist class as it picked up speed at that date. Pope, and plenty of people since, would have seen it as an occasion for animadverting upon the snobberies, rivalries, pretensions and worse which quite obviously Zoffany saw very well, and which both he and Thomas Patch[20] painted for us to judge. But there is much more besides. There is the unrivalled splendour of the Uffizi's paintings. There is, of course, the achievement of the Renaissance. And there is also the true and disinterested connoisseurship of that social class, its *love* of art and of conversation about art, which transpire from the countless paintings commissioned by and for the British Grand Tourists.[21]

These people had come to see and learn, as well as to take. They had to overcome considerable hardships to do so, as they were well aware. The hazards of the journey were serious, its disagreeableness often turned into revoltingness. The detestation felt by so many travellers and recorded so pungently of the sheer squalor of so much Italian and southern French wayside and tavern life cannot all be put down to that universal tourist recital about the grasping hotelier and his filthy rooms. In Venice, stinking water stood stagnant inside the Doge's Palace. Goethe pointed out [22] that intelligent use of the tides could really cleanse the city of the soft heaps of sewage which reeked along the inner canals. Urban myths about Italy as the cesspit of Europe gathered in the guidebooks and memoirs, Arthur Young noticing that passers-by simply glanced at and ignored a corpse in a ditch, one Dr Sharp finding an inn with no privy, Catherine Wilmot an inn with no windows, and everybody complaining of the food, 'hard, black, stinking buffalo', boiled giblets, 'a profusion of oil but a general taste of dirt'.[23]

The dangers of crossing the Alps, during which *banditti* and the *char-à-banc* were of equal menace, gave way to the severities of the food and dreadful roads which were regularly such as to tip out the occupants of lighter vehicles like the post-chaise, break the axles and clog the wheels immovably in mud to the rim.

The *cognoscenti* made light of all that. They had paintings and sculptures, broken stones and statues to see and, where possible, to bring home. The less knowledgeable hired themselves a courier-guide of more or less unscrupulousness and went to find classicism and the Renaissance. Since there were in many places only laws of great age, complexity and inapplicability with which to determine the ownership of long-buried marble, many were able to take classical treasures home as precious souvenirs.

They knew what they were doing. These broken statues and acanthus leaves in marble were extremely valuable on the collectors' market. But it should be added that they were not removed, as they very often would be today, as mere tokens of invest-ment, nor would it have occurred to anybody that their removal constituted in any way an act of piracy or a theft from the national heritage. They were bought, as bargains, from those who owned the land on which they were found, and if no-one laid claim to the land, which was the likelier the further south the collector went, the treasures were taken home anyway.

The heart of the matter was classical scholarship and the Italian landscape was the site of an open university, attended by an international posse of students and their teachers, the majority of them British, and all of them holding a copy of the *Geschichte der Kunst des Altertums*, Johann Winckelmann's celebrated history of the art of classical antiquity. Winckelmann was librarian to the Cardinal Albani and Prefect of the Papal Antiquities in Rome and his great pioneering work not only offered an eloquent account of its subject-matter, it also provided a new, confident way of seeing its ennobling beauty. The Cardinal was, in effect, the Pope's Foreign Secretary,[24] a genial peacemaker on good terms with the House of Hanover, thereby disappointing the exiled Stuarts in Rome and offering his distinguished librarian as tutor to the most prominent of the visiting British scholars as well as their Protestant royalty.

The Italians, of course, as Boswell has shown, had their museums and collections already at, for example, the Musei Clementino and Capatilino, as well as their sensa-tional fragments of classical townscape on the Appian Way, at Tivoli, and at the Coliseum. But this period also inaugurated the excavations of Pompeii and Herculaneum, followed by the discovery and restoration of the wonderful Doric temples a little way down the coast at Paestum. Thomas Jenkins, Gavin Hamilton, Colin Morrison and Robert Fagan were the British entrepreneur-archaeologists who dominated the excavations and their customers, especially Charles Townley and his remarkable collection housed at 7 Park Street in Westminster, alongside the haughty collector-landowners of Petworth, Lansdowne and the like.[25]

The new industry ran away with itself. The costs of excavation were high but the thrills stupendous. Think of it. You're the first person to walk the paved streets and enter the pillared gardens of Pompeii since the stifling clouds of dust blotted the sunlight and squeezed out all the air 1900 years before you. The excavators needed wealthy partners and found them. They needed restorers of the marble, and that became a thriving and very well-paid craft in a trice. Demand far exceeded supply, so first copiers of the classics and then forgers throve as well.[26] The business expanded as the tour stretched east, through Albania and Greece, to Turkey and Egypt, round the corner to Tunis.

Winckelmann taught his lessons painfully well: he was murdered for a few of his treasures in 1768. He taught that contemplation of the beauty of the ancient sculptures was a lesson in the best parts of humankind, moreover, that such study gave the student his best chance of self-ennoblement. The strong link between tourism and edification goes back at least to him. The souvenir, on the other hand, is the invention of Jenkins, Hamilton, Townley and company. One can say, I suppose, as people do, that souvenirs of this precious kind represent an effort to possess for oneself the art of antiquity, and if one feels like name calling, to say that this is a symptom of bourgeois acquisitiveness: 'Ancient Naples is hereby *mine.*' There must be a bit of such a feeling in the collector's heart. One can also say that the valuables brought home were merely objects of trade, intended for cash profit; that also must have been true at times.

But these men were serious and devoted archaeologists and classicists. They acquired their pieces of ancient Greece and Rome as tokens of those idealised civilisations. The busts were certainly beautiful; we can check that any time in the British Museum or the Museo Capitolino. More than that, however, they stood for the calm, the serenity and rationality, the wise beauty attributed to classical antiquity by this whole system of education, and every bit as much a part of it as the drunken evenings in tavern and bawdyhouse. The marble souvenir was (and remains) a talisman of those best parts of the Tour which recalled its owner to the classical virtues. It was also a testimony of his and her having *been there.* A souvenir carries a little magic charge which whisks its owner back from dark, north-west Europe to the sunny spot below the olive trees and beside the vines where it was purchased. It is a promise that one will go back and find the place again.

III

The same promise and the same magic charge were kept by the paintings of the places the tourist had been. More than that. The paintings named the stations on which subsequent tourists must stand and admire the prospect, and of which they must acquire further paintings, or else paint their own versions for themselves.

I have said that each tourist carried a Claude glass through which they could shape a landscape as the great Claude Gellée of Lorraine taught them to see it in the landscapes of the Virgilian Campagna which he painted between 1630 and 1670 or so (he died at a great age, much revered, in 1682). As like as not, the glass would be tinted the golden, dusky brown which Claude's own taste as well as his varnish made part of his signature, and which Turner was at such admiring pains to transcend with the fresh colours of true nature.[27]

The Grand Tourists turned first to the topographical painters of the day to paint their mementoes for them. Topographical painting had its origins in the military garrisons established by Britain and France as the march of empire began in the early eighteenth century. Such painters painted the lie of the land as aids to the military defences. They learned the trade, as one would expect, from a convenient eminence and they effected panoramas of harbour approaches or battlefield by sticking together their elongated curves of cartridge paper. They painted in water-colours and were therefore responsible for that medium retaining its lower status on the market until the present day. When the Society of Water Colour Painters founded itself in London in 1804, its members expressed anxiety that to call themselves *painters* might smack of presumption!

But water-colours were easily portable and so was cartridge paper. Antonio Canaletto's panoramas of Venice had won enormous success among the British, much encouraged by the painter's major patron the British consul, Joseph Smith, and this had done much to promote the standing of topographical or 'landskip' painting rather than copies of Nicolas Poussin in the classical mode. Professional painters of all sorts turned their hands to landscape work, excellent caricaturists like Thomas Patch doing a decent panorama or a mountain prospect in no time. But the big patrons wanted big pictures, so Richard Wilson, Thomas Jones, John Robert Cozens for the British and Louis Ducros or Jean-Honoré Fragonard for the French stood on behalf of the tourist in front of the stations of the Tour and painted: painted St. Peter's, Rome from afar (Wilson, now in the Tate); Tivoli and the Temple of the Sibyl (Wilson, now in Dublin or Fragonard in Besançon); the Bay of Naples (countless examples, but Jones, now in Cardiff); Lake Avernus, where Virgil went down into Hades (Wilson, now in the Tate); Vesuvius in eruption (countless examples – Dickens made the trip to the top and passed out in the fumes – Joseph Wright of Derby in the Tate is a fine one); the Colosseum, of course (Cozens, now in Edinburgh). Nor could any painter remain unaware of the gothic magnificence of the work of Giovanni Piranesi whose etchings of classical Rome commanded the market and were consciously intended to match new theories of the beautiful and sublime to the ruins he found about him. His *Vedute di Rome* which came out during the 1740s contained 135 views and his training as an architect, his father's craft as a stonemason, allied to his own self-taught command of ancient history combined to make him the aesthetic didact of Roman tourist and painter alike.

Piranesi's influence was enormous but his monumentality couldn't do everything. The charm of the water-colour is not only its readiness – painting in the open air is swift and easy; it is also that the water-colour so gracefully encompasses a quick glimpse of things or the sort of slight but pretty scene for which the grander effects of classical oils would simply be too much. In other words, it is the tourist's best medium. Its mobility, its modesty, its pastel colours and its quick effects made it into the tourist's own art-form and especially the tourist who simply didn't have the money to commission the big names, as Boswell did Hamilton, for 200 guineas a time.

Not only that. The *size* of the water-colour has its own recommendation. Even in the powerfully worked-up water-colour effects of a master like Cozens, Francis Towne or John Smith (nicknamed 'Warwick' because the Earl bought so much of his work), the usual size of a sheet of paper would be 20 by 15 inches. This was a size to fit happily on the walls of middle-class drawing rooms in the tall terraces of Bath, Brighton and Scarborough. That was also the class which, following the path marked out by the aristocracy so turned the poetry and painting of landscape into the teaching of its heart, that it required the craft of water-colour painting to be taught to its children as part of the curriculum of the new, genteel schools it founded. In London, the Society of Water Colour Painters kept itself consciously and conscientiously subordinate to the Royal Academy, where the real work was done in oils, and its members made a living as much from teaching young ladies the genteel art as they did from selling their small masterpieces.

The water-colours of Francis Towne are early signs of this change in patronage, although it was Wilson who lived and worked long enough really to make his fortune out of it.[28] Wilson, however, continued to paint more or less in the grand manner. His famous views of Rome, of the Tivoli villa, of Castel Gandolfo were so easy on the eye of the New Man of sensibility and the dutiful wife he, at times, had by him, exactly because their frames and distances, their golden haze and restorative shadows sustained the picture of nature devised by his severe masters, Claude and the brothers-in-law Poussin. Kenneth Clark writes of 'Claude's gentle poetry ... his wistful glance at a vanished civilisation and ... his feeling that all nature could be laid out for man's delight, like a gentleman's park', and he concludes that Wilson, understanding Claude's lessons, 'is a true minor poet, a sort of William Collins, writing his "Ode to Evening" in classic metre and with fresh perception'.[29]

The aesthetic judgements from here are less important than the formative social power such paintings possessed then and for which Wilson stands as the most distinguished producer of the moment at which the new mercantile class began to commission him in a large way. What we are looking at, in considering these paintings, is a moment of correspondence between the shape of a landscape, the framing power of a sociable way of seeing, certain conventions about what to feel in the presence of aspects of nature, all this as orchestrated by the painter.

Our own environment is so saturated by imagery, above all by the imagery of advertising, that we have got out of the way of the extended contemplation of a picture, whether framed by a Claude glass or on a canvas. But during the second half of the eighteenth century, habits of landscape-viewing and looking at paintings combined to establish certain deep correspondence in people's sensibilities. We endorse both habits still, glancing at advertisements repeating Claude's forms three centuries later on television and in the lifestyle magazines.

Richard Wollheim sketches a theory to express this correspondence (his term). In doing so, he indicates how we may write a history of the feelings to which in its turn this book intends a contribution. Wollheim imagines somebody in a transport of happiness; just having fallen in love, say. This person *projects* onto the landscape corresponding feelings; its wintry cold and hard frost express her keen sense of the world as sparkling and delightful. This other person, however, just rejected, it may be, by a lover, sees the same scene as bleak and chill and desolate.[30]

Conversely, the scene *tells us* what to feel. Caught by the toils of overwork and anxiety, a sublime or beautiful landscape instructs us in the sense of awe or peace which corresponds to such a prospect. The movement of expression is both ways. We feel strongly for the view because of our projected feelings *and* the view is lovely of itself, and we feel its beauty accordingly.[31]

John Ruskin used to refer to this Romantic attribution of expressive qualities to a natural scene which could hardly express things for itself as 'the pathetic fallacy'. He meant the phrase rather pejoratively, though he loved its practice. But Wollheim claims something different; something which gives us more of a hold upon what Wordsworth meant when he wrote, 'Let Nature be your teacher' and in doing so underlined the pedagogic force of a new and popular curriculum of experience which came into being with the assorted careers of painters, poets and Grand Tourists. Wollheim says that, sure, we *project* our feelings onto a scene, but that they are in turn modified by our experience of the particularities of the scene. We see the terrific and awe-inspiring properties of the storm as expression of our own angry excitement; but we see its beauty also, the brilliance with which the lightning cuts open the purple clouds and on the horizon, at the edge of darkness, the lovely pale blue of the calm skies on their way. Projection and experience move into a balance; the storm enlarges and deepens our feelings. It takes us, as we say, 'out of ourselves'. The good painter – Richard Wilson, John Robert Cozens, mighty Turner – the great poets – Wordsworth, Keats, Coleridge – teach us both expression and response, projection and reciprocity, passion and experience. They leave this residue as the inheritance of subsequent generations. This is the history of learning-to-feel.

This little detour nonetheless stands close to my theme. Taking a vacation is anticipated as being such a pleasure because it will renew that broken connection with nature, where nature may be the kind old sun, the shining sea, the dark groves of fruit, the blue remembered hills. Remembering is part of the point: vacations summon up childhood happiness, when our connection with nature was quite unforced and taken-for-granted, when nature and beauty were synonymous, even down by the beautiful mucky pond with rusty barbed wire in it.

The water-colour was, of its nature, much more a *glimpse* of the scenery (even in the elaborations of Towne). It presaged a decidedly more modern sensibility and scheme of values in which a battered, lovable, nondescript but faithfully depicted housefront in Naples is as much to be valued as the set pieces of the Via Appia or Hadrian's villa. Thomas Jones broke from his grand topographies of the Bay of Naples to paint the washing hanging outside the broken shutters and crumbling stucco of Neapolitan tenements. In doing so, he announced a different kind of vacation remembering, and inaugurated a new memento.

These are the little and cherished memories of childhood and vacations which turn them into the talismans of past and future happiness. They take their place as jewels in

Figure 2.3   Thomas Jones, *Buildings in Naples with the north-east view of Il Castel Nuovo*
Source: National Museums and Galleries of Wales

the crown of a rather more personalised aesthetics than Burke proposed for the Sublime and Beautiful. Such an aesthetics is less classical than domestic; its beauties are homely and lovable rather than sublime and beautiful; its details are shaggy and broken instead of manorial, sculpted and resplendent. Its occasions, however, mark the places of fierce loyalties, never more so than when the locale moves from Virgil's homeland to Shakespeare's.

IV

For there was a slightly less Grand Tour of Britain established over the same period as fixed the road to the Alps, Venice, Florence, Rome and Naples. These were, after all, the same years as those which saw Britain launch its empire and its industrial revolution and emerge as the world's first superpower, whatever the French thought about it.[32] No-one can doubt the sincerity of the classicophilia which fired the scholarly ardour of Sir Horace Mann or the great Edward Gibbon, but there was a competitor feeling abroad that the picturesque stations and conveniently noble ruins left by the dissolution of the Catholic monasteries under the edict of Henry VIII two hundred years before were more than a match for the best that Tuscany or the Roman Campagna could do.

The 'picturesque' was the thing, and the term, transcribed straight into English from the Italian during the early part of the eighteenth century, was effectively made his own by the best-known of British travel guide-writers, William Gilpin, whose earliest essay of 1768 was called *An Essay upon Prints: containing remarks upon the principle of picturesque beauty*. Each of his subsequent, many times reprinted guides, to Wales and the Wye Valley, to the Highlands, and of course to the Lakes (Gilpin lasted well) used the signature phrase 'picturesque beauty' in its title, and by picturesque he then meant, as we mean now, 'like a picture', although in Gilpin's case he pretty surely meant a picture by Claude or Wilson. He also meant 'picturesque' as word-painted by the best known of the English poets-of-landscape, starting out from Milton's famous duo *L'Allegro* and *Il Penseroso* (the cheerful man and the pensive one), taking in Alexander Pope on *Windsor Forest*, for sure, but quoting most from James Thomson's *The Seasons*, a long, agreeable, descriptive poem in classically iambic pentameters (the English ten-syllable, five-stress line) which Turner was to learn by heart.

Gilpin was accompanied by a large troop of guidebook-writing rivals, among whose favourite scenery the Lakes of Cumberland and Westmoreland came out top, as they still do. If you compare the celebrated and innumerable Wainwright walks of the past thirty years with Gilpin, with James Clarke's *Survey of the Lakes* (1787), William Hutchinson's *An Excursion to the Lakes* (1774), Thomas West's *A Guide to the Lakes* (1780) and, in print from that day to this, the poet Wordsworth's *A Guide through the District of the Lakes* (in five editions by 1835), you will find the same routes faithfully trodden into the same paths from the outset.

After the long haul from the south, the tourists stopped in Kendal, braced themselves and went by Windermere to Ullswater, round Keswick to Derwent Water and came back to Grasmere and Coniston Water. From the appropriate spot, they admired the splendours of Helvellyn behind Thirlmere, Skiddaw behind Derwent Water, and Scafell over to the west. Hutchinson noted their progress with some amusement:[33]

> As a gentleman said to Robin Partridge the day after we were upon
> Windermere, 'Good God! how delightful! – how charming! – I could live here
> for ever! – Row on, row on, row on, row on'; and after passing one hour of
> exclamations upon the Lake, and half an hour at Ambleside, he ordered his
> horses into his phaeton, and flew off to take (I doubt not) an equally *flying*
> view of Derwent water.

Beholding the great curve of the waters exquisitely placed beneath the majestic mountains was the tourist's business. He and she chimed together in the thrill of seeing
rocks, trees, lake and sky as they ought to be seen, as Thomas West instructed they
should be seen:

> The change of scenes [being] from what is pleasing, to what is surprising;
> from the delicate touches of Claude, verified on Coniston Lake to the noble
> scenes of Poussin exhibited on Windermere-Water, and from these to the
> stupendous romantic ideas of Salvator Rosa, realised on the lake of
> Derwent.[34]

This is the education of the feelings which we have had Richard Wollheim codify for
us earlier. There is a *correspondence* between attributes of the landscape (wildness,
peacefulness, etc.) and between the inarticulate but expectant feelings we bring to it.
The one is balanced against the other and adjusted for fit. Feeling and form (the view)
then match one another with pleasurable fullness.

Just as in the guides to Italy, West halts his travellers carefully at the exact station
which commands the picturesque picture to gaze on which is the point of the outing.
Here by Coniston – 'Look for a fragment of dark coloured rock on the margin of the
lake, and near it will be found the best stand' – one may assemble for oneself the
perfect composition, the waterfall correctly off-centre pouring between two swelling
bluffs. Andrews points out that each guidebook warns against too high a vantage-
point; right composition demands a foreground and 'wings' or *coulisses* (e.g. trees,
slopes) which serve to enclose and frame the prospect. The artistry, first, of the great
landscape gardeners and then of the painters had done the work of transforming
picturesquerie into picture, and as one fitted the other, so they opened into full feeling.

As the Lakes developed into tourism, so the new middle classes, expanding with
great draughts of energy from industrial and imperial profits, captured themselves bits
of ground and built summer-houses with picture-windows to shape their prospects
and their feelings for them. The little tale of Joseph Pocklington points the moral. It
has a familiar form.

Pocklington, a Nottingham banker, bought Derwent Island in 1788, demolished its
only building, a peasant hovel (picturesque, naturally) and replaced it with a fine,
square but unignorable mansion in plain Georgian style and surrounded with smooth
turf. The locals, including Wordsworth, were appalled and a long-familiar emotional
trope was founded, in which too-wealthy newcomers come from the city and ruin the
countryside with garish new buildings. Such choruses surround the history of tourism.
The roads to and in the Lakes were improved. Then one found that one's solitude was
being violated by numerous kinds of ruffians who had taken advantage of the new
roads one had rather thought would remain empty for one's own greater convenience.

Figure 2.4   Joseph Wright of Derby, *Rydal Waterfall*, 1795
Source: Derby Museums and Art Gallery

The same arguments recur, with unstaled virulence, at the coming of railway passengers, bicyclists, car-owners and package-tourists-off-the-charter. All true, of course.

The Lakes, like the Highlands, were all Nature. Dr Johnson had been to the Highlands with Boswell in 1775 and taken in the Hebrides as well, but being the stout city-dweller and rationalist he was, had found the landscape overwhelming but barren and the people simple but rough. The Highlands really found their moment when they were reinvented by Sir Walter Scott, together with the whole paraphernalia of Scottishness, including the clans, the kilt, the claymore, heather, malt whisky, the Jacobite rebellion and the grim grandeur of the mountains.[35] Scott, in point of fact, wrote his best descriptive prose about Edinburgh and the Lowlands, where he lived, and his courteous, urban, irresolute Tory heroes fare a lot better than his wild Gaelic chieftains.

Between Johnson and Scott the tourists put in the Scottish signposts from Edinburgh to Stirling, north by Perth to Killiecrankie and the Trossachs, pausing to tremble at the ghosts of Glencoe, moving southwards by Loch Lomond. The poet most quoted in their guidebooks was the spuriously rediscovered old Gael 'Ossian', in fact a fraudulent piece of pastiche work playing on the chords of the new Romantic mood. The effects of this poetry taught Scott, the first runaway bestseller, his bestselling lessons and, apart from the mountains and lakes, the other pieces of important *mise-en-scène* were the medieval castles at Edinburgh, Stirling, Dalhousie.

Old stone, piled in impressive walls, ramparts, choirs and pillars, scattered in gracefully improved patterns upon thick turf, mown by pastoral sheep, this was the stuff of picturesquerie and the trail of ruins which runs due west and due north through England and Wales filled that taste then, and fills it now, to repletion.

In 1798, as I noted, Wordsworth and Coleridge published their famous collection, *Lyrical Ballads*. Wordsworth was then 28. In 1797, aged 22, the young Turner set off for his first extended trip round the north of England.

Wordsworth, of course, started life up there. Born and raised in Cockermouth, he made and was made by the Romantic revolution. The argument of this chapter has been that a general movement of feeling swept people into its current across the second half of the eighteenth century. This feeling matched ontology to geography, passion to landscape in a wide, rich hierarchy of vision and experience. It was the genius of Wordsworth, however, to capture and express this colossal surge of sentiment with such merriment and majesty that every contemporary British person is in part his creation. It was he who took his opportunity and turned the seasons and ceremonies of a little market town into the imagery which taught his countrymen and women a love of nature which was also the ground of both an honest patriotism and a longing for a lost and neighbourly companionship. He saw plainly enough what was happening. It was no accident that along with his poetry, he wrote his famous *Guide to the Lakes*. There he says roundly:

> A resident in a country like this which we are treating of, will agree with me, that the presence of a lake is indispensable to exhibit in perfection the beauty of one of these days; and he must have experienced, while looking on the unruffled waters, that the imagination, by their aid, is carried into recesses of feeling otherwise impenetrable.[36]

This is the teacher's voice, instructing by way of a textbook what he has himself made actual in his poetry and in doing so, made it possible for others to feel the same. In Wordsworth's great poem of 1798, 'Lines composed a few miles above Tintern Abbey on revisiting the banks of the Wye during a tour', he shaped for two centuries and beyond the central experience of European and American landscape tourism.

It is a wonderful poem, too long and too lovely to treat here in a brief analysis. But I cannot resist these incomparable lines:

> These beauteous forms,
> Through a long absence, have not been to me
> As is a landscape to a blind man's eye:
> But oft, in lonely rooms, and 'mid the din
> Of towns and cities, I have owed to them,
> In hours of weariness, sensations sweet,
> Felt in the blood, and felt along the heart;
> And passing even into my purer mind,
> With tranquil restoration: – feelings too
> Of unremembered pleasure: such, perhaps,
> As have no slight or trivial influence
> On that best portion of a good man's life,
> His little, nameless, unremembered acts
> Of kindness and of love.

This is the noblest holiday prayer: that our restoration to the comity of nature in August will make us better people in November. It transposes the site of popular education from Claude's Campagna to Wordsworth's and Turner's Tintern. Wordsworth took his copy of Gilpin down the Wye Valley to find and to have these feelings. The splendid nave, the choir and arches of the ruined Cistercian Abbey set in the deep and peaceful greens of the river valley were, you might say, made for it. It would be hard to over-estimate the importance of the poem in the making of the many meanings of the vacation.

What Wordsworth did in words, Turner did in paint. His sketchbook for 1797 is the diary of his tour, of the famous Cistercian ruins, every one of them placed in a remote (but defensible) valley or a comparably inaccessible height, congenial alike to Christian prayer or Romantic meditation, to solitude, to an ardent admiration of all natural things, as well as (for Turner) the antique reminders of old bloodshed (the castles) alongside a present, keen fearfulness at the ruthlessness as well as the sublimity of nature (the shipwrecks). So he journeyed from site to site, up the Great North Road from Kirkstall Abbey to Bolton, from Fountains Abbey to Richmond Castle and Barnard Castle, from Durham to Dunstanburgh and Lindisfarne, until he turned south again at Norham Castle on the Scottish border and painted the first version of what became in 1845 one of his most strange and celebrated paintings.[37] Then, following many painterly predecessors and rivals, especially Tom Girtin at the Falls of Lodore, he came south by way of the Lakes and returned to his patron, Edward Lascelles of Harewood House, with an amazing haul.

V

So far, this is a history of holidays as charted by artists. Wordsworth and Turner are its leading actors. But from the beginning of Grand Tourism there were, of course, tour operators who set themselves up to arrange the passage of the bright young things to Switzerland or Italy; to fix deals for the acquisition of classical fragments by the serious collectors; at the higher removes, to wait upon the true grandees, of royalty, ex-royalty and the like, Electors of Saxony, Dukes of Cumberland and Old Pretenders, as they took the waters and hired the portrait-painters. In some cases, the painters or the archaeologists themselves ran the tours; at lower levels, the family hired a courier (the 'bear-leader') to arrange transports and stop-overs and to point out sights and sites.

The last hero of this tale of the tour is one such entrepreneur and impresario. His advent marks the full-dress entry into this benevolent history of the holidaying of the middle classes, large and small. Claude François Denecourt, as resurrected by the immortal Schama, known as *Le Sylvain* (of which I suppose the best English translation would be 'the green man') was a sort of enterprising founder-rambler.

Denecourt turned the forest of Fontainebleau into the Parisians' Arcadia. He found Fontainebleau in the early 1830s much like Windsor Forest a century before, the home of peasants, derelicts, highwaymen and romantics (including himself) competing for the game of the wild with the wealthy classes hunting there. He set himself, quite literally, to chart the forest, singlehandedly mapping *all* its paths, landmarks and picturesque stations. He left blue blobs of paint on relevant tree trunks to mark the paths. He effected little improvements to the countless grottoes and cavelets he found, opening up the entrance a little with his pick, shovelling out drifted earth, easing the passage of air and light in order to adorn the recesses. As Schama puts it, Denecourt 'invented the trail'[38] and having thwarted the neurotically suspicious authorities with his complete guilelessness, opened his walks to a new class of promenaders who, after 1849, took the excursion trains from Paris and, clad in highly self-conscious walking-boots, gaiters (the men), woollen leggings (the women) and thornproof coats, tramped Denecourt's trails to gaze at the right prospects, crouch in the grottoes and take themselves a little *déjeuner sur l'herbe*.

Denecourt's career completes this tour of the Tour. His peculiar, unself-seeking dedication created for France that happy blend of sufficient effortfulness, limited daring and self-edification won from modest doses of the beautiful. These treasures lie close to the heart of grand tourism.

The meaning of the tour is mobility. The tourist moves on. The original grand tourists had plenty of time, because they had plenty of money. The younger ones were in any case studying at the open university of antiquity. The middle class and its embarrassing consort, the smaller-middle class, had less time to spare from making money. They went to Fontainebleau for the day or to Central Park for the afternoon. They also went, in a neologism of the 1860s, *to stay*. They holidayed, sojourned, took a vacation in a *resort* and watering-places.

From the beginning of this ceremony, a resort was beside the sea.

3

CONFECTING SEASIDE

Watering-places provided the waters; resorts provided the sea. As the domestic affections enlarged the space they occupied in everyday life, and as households no longer included every employee of the master's trade, so the number of people living there diminished and the earliest beginnings of privacy – a room of one's own – began to make themselves felt. With better glass in the windows, better lighting technology and the new leisure made possible for the new mercantile classes by the long mid-century boom[1] starting to show itself in the comforts of their pleasant terrace houses in the towns, the money and the time were spare with which to concoct occasions for ostentatious display; for social assembly and encounter; for indicating that one had the position and the income to do nothing elegantly; for dedication, away from the squalid exhalations of city sewage, to one's health and longevity; above all, for giving oneself over to the new enlargement of the range of feeling, to the 'renaissance of wonder' which Romanticism inaugurated.

This rich interplay of aspiration and opportunity found its ready-made locale beside the sea. Until the middle of the eighteenth century nobody wanted it. Landowners had no interest in it for investment. Only fish grew there and were harvested by the poor. The seaside offered everything: free access, natural beauty and sublimity (as per Edmund Burke's recipe), medicinal properties, the chance of solitude and, once John Nash and company got cracking, the certainty of fair sociability.

Not surprisingly, since they started it, the French are the historians of the beach. In the opening pages of *Sur La Plage*,[2] Jean-Didier Urbain improves on the half-dead old traveller–tourist distinction. His archetypes of beach life are, instead, Phileas Fogg, hero of Jules Verne's *Round the World in 80 Days* and Robinson Crusoe. Fogg is much the more attractive of the two; forever cast as David Niven, he is the reckless English clubman-gambler-gentleman, an eighteenth-century figure really, ready to throw away all his money with a fine munificence in pursuit not so much of a wager as simply winning the game and being in the right. In all this, as well as in his literal geography, he moves on the extremity of the social world in order to circle the globe and, in doing so, in and out of hot and cold water, he lives the tourist life, befriending and helping strangers he would never otherwise have met, travelling light and light-heartedly, taking the weird world as he finds it, which is to say with the Frenchman's caricature of English *sangfroid*. Fogg lives at the social limits, always on the move. He is liminal man. The beach is the ultimate limit and the joke is that he is always getting beached.

Robinson Crusoe, by contrast, is going nowhere once he gets there. Admittedly his unchosen destination is that most unlocatable of seafaring termini, the desert island. The provenance of desert islands is to be found in the earliest travel books and poems, in *The Tempest*, *Mandeville's Travels*, Columbus's *Diaries*, Hakluyt's *Voyages*, Vasco da Gama, Marco Polo. The rush of such writing, quickly translated in English, which comes out of the beginnings of empire, Defoe, good journalist and interested in science as he was, turned to such amazing account in his crazy bestseller. In a literature as populous with magic refuges, edenic isles, marvellous possessions and utopias as is European poetry, desert islands have always provided an indispensable trope. The Mediterranean had lots of them, and Odysseus was their first, best-known visitor. When the explorers of the seventeenth and eighteenth centuries set off to find El Dorado and the North-West passage, and found instead the archipelagos of Polynesia and the Caribbean, first Defoe and then Jonathan Swift were well set for their masterpieces. Crusoe and Gulliver stood out as ideal types of the splendid new ports of Bristol and London. Gulliver went to chat with the locals, an early anthropologist.[3] But Crusoe, intending to remain on the move, found himself forced to stay and settle, an involuntary but enthusiastic colonist.

As Ian Watt points out,[4] Crusoe is all bourgeois capitalist. He collects everything he can from the wreck, what he might need and what he couldn't possibly, and arranges it in a fecund and plentiful order, nature and his own resourceful acquisitiveness combining to provide what would abundantly prove to be the child's view of paradise. Having made, grown or found everything he wants, Crusoe rediscovers the amiability of society, and Man Friday becomes, for Defoe and three hundred years of child readers, that perfect sort of friend, who doubles as servant, sure interpreter of the unknown and no less obligingly fearful, obedient and admiring of oneself.

Crusoe makes the ideal holiday home of his settlement and Friday is the perfect local housekeeper. Alexander Selkirk, Crusoe's celebrated prototype who recounted the story of his exile to the eager journalist sitting in the shiplike snug of the *Llandoger Trow* on the Bristol waterfront, had a much harder time of it. He longed, of course, to be saved. Crusoe is much more of a holidaymaker. Ineffably self-referential and exploitative, he stays long enough to make his home in a strange land, happily balancing the exotic (delicious fruits) against the domestic (goats), agreeably fearful nature (storms, cannibals) against satisfyingly ingenious gadgetry (the treehouse). He makes himself snugly nested; he explores his island in order to see the sights; he enjoys the strange and is reassured by the familiar; he comes safely home.

Defoe's prosy, cheerful, matter-of-fact fantasy-classic frames the form of the good vacation-under-capitalism. He works to make things work, but he is his own master, and no one can dispute his possessions. At the same time, the little empire he so easily acquires is only held on sufferance. When finally he leaves it, it reverts to nature. While he lives there, nature makes herself free, open, liberal to him. That is how she is, beside the seaside.

II

The seaside is one complementary settlement to the Grand Tour's deliberate perambulations. The other is the spa. Alike inventions of the eighteenth century, they resembled each other closely. Where inland spas lacked the splendour of the sea, they made up for its absence with the rugged cliffs which encircle Matlock, Malvern, Buxton. They shared architects and architecture (Nash made the huge fortune he later lost in Bath and Brighton), and the two-and-three storey terraces threading down to a seafront crowned by the affection of royalty at Salcombe Regis, Lyme Regis, Bognor Regis, Deal and Weymouth settled into that easy vernacular of cobbled streets, neat shops and the big sky and sea which was completed a century or so later by the grand hotels.[5]

In either spot, spa or seaside, our tourist, a traveller in antique lands when on the Tour, pauses to *dwell* for a little. In this season, exploration starts out from the temporary 'home' of the vacation. It must, for the success of the sojourn, metamorphose itself into a 'home from home'. (The highest praise of the seaside boarding house was, as we shall see, that it was – in the English turn of phrase rather than the American – 'homely'.) The explorer-on-vacation goes down to the sea, because only at the seaside can he or she walk the thrilling line between domestic propriety and that licentious spontaneity for which the sea is the inexhaustible and commonplace metaphor.

Like the origins of holidays in holy days, when the rules changed into misrule and during which the brief excesses of the potlatch or the carnival served as a guarantee that after the discipline and sobriety of winter, plenty would come again, the lure of the sea[6] goes deep into the European past. Antique myths of the cruel origins of fecundity and sexuality, of the birth of Venus out of the foam of Neptune's severed testicles,[7] stir yet at the back of our cultural memory.

The memory slept for a millennium or so and began to rouse as more and more men and women went down to the sea from the 1650s onwards. Antiquity and Christianity joined together in the symbology of divine rage and retribution as read in the tumult of the storm. The beach was the line drawn by the finger of God between land and water. In the ancient premonitions of the theory of evolution, the beach is where the monsters of the deep move momentarily onto the land and terrify humankind with its own abominable development. Scylla and Charybdis devour sailors at the edge of the land; Poseidon rears up offshore sending vast waves to swamp those who live on the limits of the land; Andromeda is chained naked to her rock, her rich tresses flowing down her body towards the sea; the Sirens sing to Odysseus from their rocks just off Sorrento; Polyphemus shoulders his way in from the sea to abduct Galatea. These tales were keenly present to the classicist heroes of the Grand Tour but they were also sedimented in some much less conscious way for those who, not working or living there, began to repopulate the beach in the eighteenth century. Their painters began to paint not just the topography but the 'unplumb'd, salt, estranging sea' its very self. And the sea in turn enlarged its character. Having been so much the occasion for pious thoughts on the anger of God or the gods, the Virgilian prospect over the Bay of Naples gave rise to different meditations on the serenity and tranquillity of the blue, and Claude obliged with his *veduti* of coastal scenes on the Virgilian route. Sometime after 1700 the wonderful variations of sounds and surfaces which the sea plays to the human eye and ear became the stuff of both scientific and aesthetic re-imagining.

Corbin may be used to extend the little theory of correspondence which Wollheim initiated for us in Chapter 2. He says that:

> Landscapes put out images which facilitate the movement from the conscious to the unconscious realm; topographical analysis provides symbols to which sensitivity responds; but to my mind these operations occur as a function of mechanisms which can be dated.[8]

Our way of turning the sea to new imaginative uses coincided with and takes formative energy from the first moments of Grand Tourism. When Vanburgh designed his small but magnificent baroque mansion at Seaton Delaval in Northumberland in 1720, he turned the building's back upon the sea, plainly visible a few hundred yards away. By the time the developers got going in Brighton fifty years later the maritime horizon defined every prospect and in those landscapes where there was no sea, the landowners hired their men – Brown and Repton – to dig out the middle distance and install a large lake. The grand tourists had gazed upon the Swiss and Italian lakes from the mountain slopes and, Virgil and Homer in hand, looked across the Bay of Naples from Pozzuoli and stared out from Sorrento at the isles of the Sirens. The sea swept plenty of classical poetry in on the tide, and the Navy of the day was just beginning to give rise to epic tales of incipient empire with which to fire impressionable imaginations to new activity.

Not only imaginative activity, physical ones as well. As the discipline of medicine began to shape itself out of the advance of natural science in the seventeenth century, writers with a physiological bent began to recommend the airs, liquids and environs of mother nature as a source of cures freed from superstition. The literature of the Renaissance, especially in English, long counterposed the country to the city as the domain of healthy and natural longevity; the lesson was there to be picked up from the Latin rural and gardening classics, from Horace, Catullus and Pliny as well as great Virgil and Cicero.[9]

These writers, however, took the balmy air of the Tyrrhenian coast and laved themselves in the warm waves of the Mediterranean. An enthusiasm for the health-giving potency of the Channel or the North Sea demanded a much sterner and more medicinal regime. It took 1700 years or so from Pliny's artless guide to a healthy body to the construction of bathing machines at Brighton, Scarborough and Dieppe.

The novelist Tobias Smollett was an early, ardent advocate of a cold, early morning dip, much to the consternation of the locals in Boulogne who watched him at it on a sharp May morning in 1763. He was only a vociferous celebrity, however, announcing the change of social habits[10] among the well-to-do such that the sea in virtue of its tonic chill and the bracing smack of the waves restored lost energy, cured feebleness of both body and will, daunted tumescence in particular and sexual desire in general while *also* making men manlier, and brought discipline and grip to those of debauched life.

Plenty of Englishmen still alive will recognise these as the commonplaces, only yesterday, of boarding school and military life. Given the deep and plausible human belief in the intertwinedness of body and soul, once sea-bathing took hold in northwest Europe it became equally as moral as medicinal and, either way, at times miraculous. Dr Richard Russell made a fortune with which he eventually purchased the finest house in Brighton from spotting the antiseptic properties of salt seawater, its 'saltiness, bitterness, nitrosity and unctuosity', generalising these into the prescription of doses inside and out as protection against the body's entropy and decay and packing his nostrums into a bestselling primer for his well-off patients.[11] Since his contemporaries suffered torments from skin infections, seawater was as likely to do some good as none at all, so Russell flourished while brother-doctors in Boulogne and Bordeaux extolled the happy consequences, especially for those of a hysterical disposition, of *really cold* bathing.

A mere sousing in cold water would hardly do. From the turn of the nineteenth century and the triumph of Romanticism, swimming entered its still-universal phase as the exercise of the middle classes. It was joined to all kinds of weird but still prevalent beliefs. 'Ozone', the peculiarly healthful sea air, would clear congestion of the sinuses ('but it *does* ...') and put colour in pale faces. Promenading beside the sea and along the cliffs would combine exercise of the body and the spirit together as walkers watched the majestic sea while taking its air. The beach itself, cleansed and smoothed by the tide would softly, even suggestively receive the print of their feet and when those feet were bare in preparation for swimming, beware the transports of suggestion.

Swimming was a luscious contradiction, lived in the body. It still is. It was cold, bracing, a medicinal shock of a self-improving kind; it was also abandoned, dangerous, a thrilling plunge into the realms of rulelessness where, under the buffets of the waves, strangers might touch, might even catch you up in their arms as the breaker swept you over.

Nor were things very much safer on the beach, the uncertain liminal. In the sea you might become someone else, someone freed from propriety. On the beach, laughing with the excitement, breathless, pouring with cold water, you were in hardly better case. Anyway, the beach was a spontaneously egalitarian place. Anyone could go there. Fishermen lived and worked there. Tramps slept there. Policemen did not patrol it. People ate and drank there without regard for table manners, because (mostly) without a table. No doubt as, across the nineteenth century, watering-places turned into seaside resorts, a limited architectural respectability was invented with which to formalise the strand. The graceful promenade with its stout iron railings offered a boulevard to the *flâneurs* inhaling the ozone. Neat little pavilions with dashing strips of barge-boarding round their topknots provided shelter from showers. Cafés and stalls and handcart vendors turned the boulevard into a little urban throng.

III

Urbs in rure. But seaside isn't quite countryside. The emerging rules of social conduct were always opaque, changeable, ambiguous; they veered unpredictably between discretion and spectacle, abandon and containment, land and sea. The delightful architecture invented on location symbolises, as architecture is meant to do, all these fulfilling, strange inversions. Hence, first William Holland then John Nash designed for the commonplace seaside debaucheries of the Prince Regent his amazing royal pavilion at Brighton (formerly Brighthelmstone), with its Indian stables and Muscovite minarets, its glass arcades, ogee arches and exotic flora.

The pavilion expressed and invited excesses. A town was built to match. Brighton took some of its lead as well as its chief architect from Bath.[12] So its development was

Figure 3.1   Brighton Pavilion
Source: Hilary Britland

marked by grandly encrusted stucco-rococo houses along the seafront and pretty little rows of plain white terraces punctuated with larger crescents and parks running up the slopes behind.[13] This is the moment of English Georgian, one of architecture's best-loved styles, sunny, stylish, humane.

These developments followed the discovery of seabathing. The sea, after all, required no pumprooms. Its waters excluded no-one. By the 1760s, Brighton, like Scarborough, had built bathing machines, cumbrous, trundling engines wheeled into the waves so that the bather could slip into the water from its wooden steps without exciting the large, appreciative crowd which turned out punctually to watch for the excitement. But of course it was the Prince Regent, during his interminable wait upon his father for his crown, who made Brighton fashionable. By the time he finally climbed fatly onto the throne, the fast coach from London pulled up at the Pavilion only five and a quarter hours later. In 1837, the records say, 50,000 people made the coach trip. When the railway came ... ah, then the whole world changed, and in 1841 there were 20,000 visitors staying in the town at once. But there was much to do before they steamed in.

All along the south coast of England, fishing villages became watering places. Starting, roughly, in 1770 the speculators and builders shook hands and transformed a beach, a harbour and a few scruffy cottages into Southend, Margate, Ramsgate, Hastings, Brighton, Hove, Worthing, Bognor (collecting the dignified suffix 'Regis' on the way), Lymington, Bournemouth, Weymouth (where the King approved his statue),

Bridport, Lyme (also Regis), Torquay, Paignton, before making a temporary halt at Salcombe (the last Regis for a while). The same thing was happening on the other side of the Channel, from Ostend to Deauville. The two littorals sprouted a rich, ornate, crenellated waterfront with assembly rooms, cafés, promenades, parks for summer and, a little later, for winter also, once the new glass technology had been copied from the Parisian *Arcades* of 1822.

Development was naturally uneven. It followed the Prince Regent and then the King. The railways then pursued him. Brighton came first, with Scarborough and Cromer further north on the much colder east coast. There were still only 700 people recorded in Bournemouth by the 1851 census and Yarmouth, as we learn from *David Copperfield*, was still a straightforward trading and fishing port in the 1850s. Sidmouth and Salcombe, both Regency resorts, started off with a bang but were back to resident populations below 1,500 by 1860.[14] Effectually, however, over the half-century the south coast of England became an unbroken line of resorts, infinitely varied and infinitely the same in their social timetables, their topography and architecture, their pleasures, theatres, flora and foodstuffs.

The pier and the promenade together fix, in their dramatic right-angle, the topographical syntax of the watering-place. Each mimics or, rather, anticipates the decks of the great liner of which Brunel's first ocean-going steamship, *SS Great Britain*, became at her launch in 1843 the harbinger. Like them, the pier is a plank walkway with stout iron railings along the side. The ladies and gentlemen take their morning *touche* along the pier in order to feel the sea winds blow in their faces, tug at their clothes, with a bit of luck blow away somebody's straw benger into the agreeably tumultuous waves tumbling beneath the heavy cast-iron struts and pillars below. With the taste of sea-spray on their lips but immune to the disgusting possibility of *mal de mer*, the *ton* of the town beheld the force of natural circumstance in what Schama happily calls 'protected terror' and 'measured doses of alarm'.[15]

Even measured doses could be hard to digest. When Charlotte Brontë made her first, much reported visit to see the sea, she was described by her companion as:

> quite over-powered, she could not speak till she had shed some tears – she … made stern efforts to subdue her emotions … her eyes were red and swollen, she was … trembling … for the remainder of the day she was very quiet, subdued, and exhausted.[16]

Pier and promenade were at once the decks of a ship at sea and the playgrounds of the urban boulevardiers who had come to the seaside in order to conduct themselves in more liberal, not to say licentious ways than they could at home. Social stiffness and severe urban respectabilities were put off. The model for behaviour was the aristocracy and the rich at play, and yet seaside behaviour *was* a play, far more so than ordinary life could ever be. When the fashionable carriages turned out from Pozzuoli and Posilippo in order to behold the bay of Naples in its deep blue magnificence, the slow passage, wheel to wheel, along past Mergellina beside the water was a ritual of mutual admiration and denigration by all those, wearing their gayest off-duty clothes (pale colours, frills, loose, unbuttoned) and with their shiniest pair of horses on show, who came to see and be seen at their leisure.

This was the coming of a new kind of ritual: the social spectacle, and it was

Figure 3.2   Clevedon Pier
Source: Hilary Britland

imitated in every European resort to which holidaymakers travelled in order to work so hard at being leisurely, and so insouciantly to be the object of others' envy. These are the origins of modern glamour, one of the strangest as well as most familiar values to feature in, as well as to cause, the rise of consumerism.

There was a lot to do, down on the promenade. Apart from the arduous business of being fit to be seen, there was the seeing itself to be done, especially by men of women. They came flocking down to watch the bathers, and to see the loosened hair and the sweet curves of hips and bottoms outlined by wet bathing suits in a way forbidden by the full dresses and firm chignons demanded by polite sartoriality. Much genteel discretion could be exercised by the judicious use of a spyglass or telescope and young women sported at being self-consciously unself-conscious, both as they were watched and as they were carried piggyback by broad-shouldered fishermen the few yards from bathing machine to water. By the time the century was elderly and the seaside resort fully founded, Henry James could with endearing coyness speculate not on the improprieties of long-distance girl-gazing but on very much more daring approaches to the water.

It is 1876, and the great novelist, still in his thirties, is lying on the beach at Etretat, Claude Monet almost certainly painting at that moment on the cliffs behind him. Propping himself on one elbow, tilting back his white flannel fisherman's cap ('these articles may be extolled for their coolness, convenience, and picturesqueness') he watches a well-known Parisienne actress show off her diving.

> She wears a bathing-dress in which, as regards the trousers, even what I have
> called the minimum has been appreciably scanted; but she trips down,

surveying her liberated limbs. *'C'est convenable, j'espère, hein?'* says Mademoiselle, and trots up the spring-board which projects over the waves with one end uppermost, like a great see-saw. She balances a moment, and then gives a great aerial dive, executing on the way the most graceful of somersaults. This performance the star of the Palais Royal repeats during the ensuing hour, at intervals of five minutes, and leaves you, as you lie tossing little stones into the water, to consider the curious and delicate question why a lady may go so far as to put herself into a single scant clinging garment and take a straight leap, head downward, before three hundred spectators, without violation of propriety – and why impropriety should begin only when she turns over in the air in such a way that for five seconds her head is upwards. The logic of the matter is mysterious; white and black are divided by a hair. But the fact remains that virtue is on one side of the hair and vice on the other. There are some days here so still and radiant, however, that it seems as if vice herself, steeped in such an air and such a sea, might be diluted into innocence.[17]

The actress and Henry James tell us much about what happened to the coastline on either side of the Channel over the previous hundred years. They tell us of changes in decorum and manners and, as we shall see, of changes in the correspondence between the scenery and the feelings people had for the scenery. In a little time, Claude Monet will tell us in addition about the organisation of memory as effected by the paintings the visitors liked to take home.

What brought James and Monet to Etretat was, in a general way, the fashion, and fashion is never a trifle but always a complex interplay of desire and value, habit and ceremony, impulse and need. What brought them more literally was the railway.

The railway packed the watering place with visitors from the lower classes. It did this rapidly in southern England and northern France, more slowly in the Mediterranean and on the eastern seaboard of the United States. But the *form* of the resort was pretty clearly and stoutly built before the railways began their amazingly rapid colonisation of the countryside.

Pier and promenade life brought the city stroller and cosmopolitan *flâneur* to the seaside. They added the thrill of closeness to the sea without actually being at or on it (even down to the deckchairs). The larger the throngs, the more leisure apparatus: a town band playing in a pretty little rococo-cast-iron bandstand at the far end, and a small theatre at this one. Nor was it the raucous classes who brought firework sea-battles, magical extravaganza or mechanical monsters to the seaside. All the delights of pleasuredrome and ghost train started life in the hands of the aristocratic and landowning classes, when they first put their estates on show (for a price) after 1760 or so.

Prince Leopold of Anhalt-Dessau, for example, devised an imitation volcano on his estate at Wörlitz, where visitors in a state of agreeable terror wandered underground past scenes of 'fearsome horror', flames, molten lava, boiling waters and whatnot (the lava, ingeniously, being water flowing over illuminated red glass panels). Sir Francis Dashwood, Satanist, welcomed at West Wycombe paying visitors to hellfire caverns beside the River Styx, in Paris tourists found an artificial thunderstorm machine (large sheets of oscillating tin for thunder) while on Windermere they could watch, by kind permission of Joseph Pocklington and Admiral Crosthwaite, an imitation naval battle, with cannonading echoing off the rock faces and miniature men-of-war ablaze and sinking gloriously beneath the waters of the lake.[18]

The commercialisation of leisure started early, as freebooting capitalists (many of whom went bankrupt on the way) spotted this unprecedented social space in which both time and money were going spare. The seaside was the obvious place for such antics to become habitual. The technology of the spectacle became as much part of the prom as it now is part of Longleat. By the time Wordsworth wrote his famous *Preface* to the second edition of *Lyrical Ballads* in 1800, he could say disapprovingly:

> For a multitude of causes unknown to former times are now acting with a combined force to blunt the discriminating powers of the mind, and unfitting it for all voluntary exertion to reduce it to a state of almost savage torpor. The most effective of these causes are the great national events which are daily taking place, and the increasing accumulation of men in cities, where the uniformity of their occupations produces a craving for extraordinary incident which the rapid communication of intelligence hourly gratifies.

No doubt he was right, and would be even more right two hundred years later. His malediction, I suppose, is spoken over the invention of the entertainment industry and if he thought it was bad then … But it was not (and is not) all bad, and the seaside, which became its busiest location, in offering entertainment of both natural and artificial kinds, was at once the site of its manufacture and its consumption.

I have already hinted at the limits of the metaphor 'consumption'. Within pure economics, the term is part of a finite algebra. Goods are made, sold, used, finished. Within the cultural economy, things have a more complex life. The life of the seaside partakes of tranquillity (the stroll to the view) and thrills (a visit to the play or to the end of the pier). That life is genteelly licentious (watching the diving beauties) and it is vigorously disciplined (cold swims and glasses of sea water). It is deliriously libertarian (windswept walks along the Cobb, dancing with strangers, eating in the street); it is sternly puritanical (carriages to the seafront at eleven, bonnets and stays, and as the heroine of John Fowles's great novel, *The French Lieutenant's Woman*, well knows, no walking by yourself, young woman, in the Undercliff at Lyme).

It is the exquisite mixture of pleasures and prohibitions which made Brighton and Scarborough, Boulogne and Dieppe so enticing and successful. The townscape, naturally, symbolised resort life. Its architecture is equally prefigured by the crazy minglings of more-or-less oriental exotica at Brighton Pavilion, the gothic and baronial magnificence of the Grand at Scarborough, the deliberate prettification by bargeboarding at Cape May, the cliff paths and belvedere at Etretat, the palatial baths at Dieppe. That same environment everywhere causes the vivid overlapping of classes, customs, livelihoods, so that fisherman, leisured nobility, dancers, mountebanks, middle classes with only temporary leisure. pedlars, buttered crumpet salesmen ('beignets, chocolat, abricot, sucrés' they still call along the Mediterranean beaches), chestnut stalls, *children*. All this rich orchestration of jostle and tranquillity, the grand style and the small street, was an unprecedented, enchanting, rapidly contrived *cultural* confection. It still is.

IV

Topography and architecture were all laid out and stylised before the coming of the railways; their form dictated the content of pleasure and the direction of the traffic. Over here, we find social and sociable life, the taking of tea, the easy contemplation of the labour of others (seafarers, fishermen, farriers, harvesters), a little dancing (the *thé dansant* arrived in the 1830s and lasted, to my certain knowledge, until the 1960s), the sipping of coffee and chocolate, the flirtation, the match-making, the sexual display. Over there, the site of strenuous solitude and engagement with nature (a little fossil-hunting at Lyme or Bournemouth, a taxing walk up to High Force on the Tees or down from Rokeby to the meeting of the waters), the encounter with the sublime on the cliff edge at Cheddar or below the cleft rock of ages in Burrington Combe.

It wasn't that the railways swamped all that, or that the coming of the working classes brought a quite new range of consumer satisfactions. It was, more simply, that the railways vastly extended such practices throughout Britain and, as revolutionary ardour turned into reactionary gentility, in France. On the other side of the Atlantic the people of Philadelphia boiled over the top of the city and poured down the coast until they halted in Cape May.

In Britain, there were 100 million railway passengers in the year of 1848, twenty-three years after George Stephenson's Rocket officially inaugurated rail travel on the line from Darlington to the Tees at Stockton; by the turn of the century there were 1,000 million.[19]

The vehicle came out of the needs of industrial capital. Coal was hauled at first manually in tubs along iron rails from pithead to canal, then by immobile traction engines, and finally by locomotive. The locomotive turned into the emblem of the new industrial age. Investment capital poured in, far more than the railways needed for development (£240 million by 1850), for the country was by mid-century awash with surplus savings looking to be spent and a populous new leisure class ready to spend it. By 1870, Hobsbawm tells us, there were 170,000 *rentiers*, 'persons of rank or property',[20] without formal occupation, a surprising number of them single women, and all ready to take the train to the seaside.

It was such a short journey. In 1830 London to Brighton took four and a half hours, London to Exeter nearly seventeen, London to York twenty, London to Holyhead (for the ferry to Ireland) twenty-seven. In 1855, London to Dover or to Brighton took just over two hours, to Plymouth seven, to Holyhead eight. The glut of capital meant that the railways were lavishly too expensive in construction and in detail – 'capitalisation per mile of line in England and Wales was five times as high as in the USA'[21] – but the money gave the whole development such colour and glamour, made its journeys such a focus of collective excitement, all set off by the thrilling size and black magnificence of engine and rolling stock, that a rail journey provided the perfect counterpoint to its vacational destination. Britain was the virgin land of that unprecedented wealth capitalism had made possible, whatever the filth and injustice it also brought. New mass transport was ready to launch the amazing new phenomenon of mass leisure life.

V

It was a point not lost upon perhaps the most famous single entrepreneur of the coming of the age of the vacation. Thomas Cook, born in 1808, was a mission worker for the Baptist Church and a vehement campaigner against alcohol and on behalf of the Temperance Society, editing in the cause, I'm happy to say, *The Children's Temperance Magazine: a cabinet of instruction and amusement of little teetotallers.*[22] He earns his place as premier innovator of the age of mass tourism. John Murray, no doubt, sold the earliest guidebooks to be written and produced under a mass imprimatur, and the railway companies quickly spotted the returns likely from chartering the new invention. But when Cook's first excursion train followed the new line from Leicester to Loughborough on 5 July 1841, he opened an era. It was only a modest start, having been organised on a non-profit-making basis for Baptists and other signatories of the Temperance pledge, exactly because Loughborough was dry and the whole family could go on a day's outing without fear of meeting drunks. The short trip cost one shilling and sixpence return.

There is, however, no injunction placed upon a teetotal Baptist to avoid making money. Seaside excursions were more appetising than jaunts to Loughborough. Cook fell to arranging trips to the seaside, starting in 1845 with an outing from Leicester to the Mersey's very own imitation of the south coast at New Brighton, with a visit to the centre of Liverpool thrown in. Next year he took his excursioners from Leicester to Fleetwood where the lines ended, put them on an overnight steamer for a choppy lift up the coast, before picking up the railway again at Ardrossan and being greeted by the city brass band at Glasgow and fêted in the City Hall.

Cook was not the only person to grasp the possibilities of the excursion. The railway companies themselves cut their prices below his with special offers of cheap accommodation in the magnificent, new, three or four hundred bedroom hotels they had built at the edge of their own stations. The splendour of these compounds fairly dwarfed even the magnificence of the promenades and piers which gave shape to the resorts, never more so than in the great new cities, surely the crowning aesthetic achievement of the age. The vast, airy curve of the glass-and-iron canopies arched over the terminus of the main lines into the capital, for example at Paddington, St Pancras, King's Cross, Euston, and adjoined the grandiloquence of the Doric arch at Euston or the amazing gothic of St Pancras, all set off by the railway hotels whose foyers and dining rooms echoed the space and display, the brass and glass and marble which adorned the station itself. After the big cities, the same drawings served for the sea front.[23]

Building a special industry to sell the happy wonder and leisurely gaping evoked by such palaces of the people was a natural corollary of the age. The nineteenth century was the day of the entrepreneur, and Thomas Cook, with his Baptist puritanism and philanthropy, his indefatigable hard work, his dash and imagination, his lack of education and his innocent belief in the edification brought by travel, will stand well enough as its typical, English representative.

For twenty years, after that first epic trip to Glasgow, he concentrated on the seaside and on London. The Great Exhibition of 1851 was his opportunity in the capital, and cutting his original price of fifteen shillings to five in the nick of time in order to beat off competition from Great Northern, he took 165,000 people in the year to wonder at Paxton's Crystal Palace. The day or the week excursion brought prosperity to the beaches of England; Cook took the people overseas as well.

Four years later he did the same for Paris and its exhibition as he did for Crystal Palace, the stoic British bearing the crossing of the Channel gallantly. The mainland lay open to Cook's imperial design. In 1855 he followed, naturally, the routes of Grand Tourism, once he had negotiated a route past channel ports blocked to him by hostile railway companies. To begin with, he had to use the Harwich–Hook of Holland route and his tour began at Antwerp before heading down the Rhine as far as Strasbourg and coming back up to Paris. Once the tunnel was dug under the Alps, however, beneath Mont Cenis, and the French, Swiss and Italian networks had linked up, Cook could make his excursion arrangements to Switzerland and Italy. By 1863, and Cook's first trip to Geneva, the petit bourgeoisie could behold the mountains their ruling class predecessors had colonised for admiration and sublime effects a century before.

The tale of Cook's tours is nearly done for us, though nothing did for him. He brought the people to Blackpool and the middle classes to Cairo. After Mont Blanc and walks to the glacier, Lauterbrunnen and walks to the falls at Staubbach, Cook wrote grandly, 'France and Switzerland now present to me new and almost unlimited fields of human endeavour.'[24] He had sold 140 tickets for the tour, the majority first class. Rome and Naples were to be his next stops. He and his no less energetic son John Mason made the trip first, hired a palace in Rome because the hotels were all full, lost a bit of money on the first tour, but never again, and polished off the 1866 season with a mammoth picnic in the amphitheatre at Pompeii, 'chickens, tongues, sandwiches, cakes, fruits of various kind and drinks for all palates', cognac and *Lachrimae Christi* for those on the wrong side of the pledge, essence of lemon for the allies of temperance.

Cook had offices in London and couriers in his mainland cities. In 1869, with considerable daring, his excursions reached unvisited sands in Egypt on the heels of the Prince and Princess of Wales. The new travelling class had caught up with its rulers. Improbably, Cook knew de Lesseps and had been invited to the opening of the Suez Canal. The canal moved Egypt into a central place in the British imperial imagination (it remained there until 1956). It was adjacent to the Holy Land. It was the birthplace of civilisation: Isis and Osiris the ancient deities of Europe's formation, even before Greece. It was the hinge of Empire on which, now the canal was open, the soldiers and administrators would swing south in order to take care of the profits coming back from India and Africa.

Just like the classical travellers through that geography, Cook could turn the rough into the passably smooth. No hotels in Palestine; he took tents topped with a Union Jack and carpeted with the best Arab throws, saddle horses for each member of the party (65 in all), pack horses, mules,[25] John Murray's *Guide*, Bibles, guide dogs, shotguns. The party picnicked in the desert and swam in the Nile. They stayed, of course, at Shepheard's Hotel in Cairo where Cook shortly opened an office. They climbed the Pyramids and, pretty soon, they took Cook's own Scots-built steamers down to Luxor: 100 guineas for ten weeks, out and back.

By the 1870s, Cook's clientele was as wide, in class terms, as the railways upon which he depended. He had opened up the Grand Tour to a wide fraction of middle classes, and by that date, the lower classes were pouring into the seaside resorts by way of his excursions. With *SS Oceanic* in 1872, he had opened the route across the

Atlantic to what would quickly become one of the most powerful images of tourist life, forever fixed in the imagery of the *Titanic* and the tale of Phileas Fogg. He and his son had an office at 362 Broadway and, after long and nervous procrastination, in 1894 the firm agreed to issue cheques in dollars to travellers making a deposit in New York. By then, their clients had included the Dukes of Clarence and York, the Kaiser and his Empress, the Empress Eugenie, the Shah, Kipling, Rider Haggard, Cecil Rhodes and Gladstone. Cook's son John had twice been an emissary of government and the great company dealt busily in troop movements to the Middle East and India as well as moving those same soldiers' families to Blackpool and Scarborough, Margate and the North Wales coast.

VI

In *The Whig Interpretation of History*, Herbert Butterfield made elegant fun of that account of British history which teaches, in the accents of the old Whig progressives who took their theories of progress, reason and democracy from the Enlightenment, that, since 1832, Britain has become more democratic, more prosperous and more content as Parliament has become more representative, industry more productive and domestic life more comfortable.

The history of 'the Englishman's holiday'[26] fits this picture. But the fit is made both neat and ragged by the horribleness of old British snobbery, the very slow unclenching of its grasp on common freedoms by its employer class, and by the protean capacity of capitalism to turn defeat into victory, as when its productivity diminishes slightly because of paid holiday time for its workforce, until it spots that leisure itself is a huge new and unoccupied market ripe for exploitation. The natural history of Blackpool will serve to illustrate these commonplaces.

If you took Cook's cheap excursion to Scarborough on Monday 12 September 1859, returning on Thursday, the journey would have cost you 14 shillings from Birmingham and 10 shillings from Derby. Scarborough, however, was long established as a watering-place; it had a spa, pump rooms, a pavilion and, by that date, fine terraces and crescents built out of solid bourgeois success.

The town split in two as the century progressed. The ten-bob trippers from Derby filled the north bay beside the harbour and the old streets. Their betters were up on the south cliff with the spa below them. In the south of England, Brighton still stood high in the hierarchy. For Blackpool, these were the models. But Blackpool in 1859 was comparatively formless. It had some attraction as a respectable middle-class resort while the invention of the seaside took place, but the gentry didn't go there (not a single title in the 1841 census record[27]). Their local gentry developed Lytham and Southport to the south for their own class. The Local Board of Health, inaugurated in 1851 and pretty well the sole regulatory authority, had no leadership accustomed to looking beyond small profit and private interest. The railway branch from the main line to Blackpool had opened in 1846 but without large capital or landowning inter-ests in the town itself, all developments – for example, of a wide promenade – foundered on the patterns of small-time and small-minded ownership.

It was a critical moment. Liverpool and Manchester were taking their sea-air in Southport, Blackpool lacked everything: a pier, a prom, municipal buildings, baths, big houses.

By the late 1870s it had acquired them. *Three* piers, eventually, then a tower – *the* Tower, Blackpool Tower, a metonymy to match the Eiffel Tower – together with a building development company and, in 1876, a full-blown Town Corporation. The money came mostly from Manchester as investors watched the rail excursion numbers climb, by 1865, to 285,000 per year[28] and went towards new assembly rooms as well as the first (northern) pier with its penny toll to keep out 'the undesirables'. The only grandees of the region, the Clifton family, backed a coastline railway to Lytham that helped to spread respectability along the front and, after much local quarrelling, the promenade was started, almost went bankrupt, but ended, as much for geological reasons as any other, as the widest, finest boulevard of all the northern resorts of England, with wide flat beaches and the wild Irish Sea below it.

These looked like the standard developments towards 'a specialised and well-equipped resort catering mainly for the expanding middle-class family holiday market'.[29] But the unevenness of that development and the comparative absence of a local bourgeoisie determined to keep Blackpool for itself left it helpless before the invasion by railway of the largest, most self-confident working class in the world. That same class lived and worked a very short way down the tracks in south Lancashire. Its arrival in its millions after 1850 turned Blackpool into the eponym of the working-class holiday. Other resorts, on the south coast for instance, were at pains to keep the railway coaches and their contents at bay. The 1855 *Guide to Bournemouth* was large upon the topic:

> At a time when the pretended humanity, but really unprincipled cupidity, of railway companies has provided extraordinary temptations to Sunday travel-ling – so that termini of railways do not even enjoy the grateful peace and propriety of the Sabbath day, one of the greatest sources of gratification and pride to the Englishman – it becomes a matter of the greatest importance in seeking a place of retirement to find one sufficiently far from a terminus to be relieved from this source of annoyance, yet without being so far distant as to occasion inconvenience in travelling. This is happily the case with Bournemouth. There is a regular communication by omnibus several times a day with Poole, the nearest railway station ... only five miles distant; from hence to London is five hours.[30]

Blackpool, on the other hand, had the railway at its heart and the populace a three shilling and sixpenny excursion ticket away.

This was long before legislation for official breaks from work – holidays from Rochdale, vacations from Jersey City – was even tabled. The British, with a stronger and more organised working class, were first with these. The 1833 Factory Act enforced two full days and eight half-days of holiday per year. It was only in 1871 that, in Britain, the Bank Holiday Act was passed four years after the legalisation of trade disputes and strike action. In the USA, Wisconsin, the first social democratic state, started things off in 1905 but the Americans had to wait until the New Deal in 1932 for any kind of Federal legislation on behalf of official holidays, and even then it was a weak creature. It took the war to enforce the furlough.

The British Act of 1871 stipulated fixed full public holidays at Christmas, Easter, Whitsun and (at that date) the first weekend in August. Day trips by excursion trains became a matter of course at Whitsun and in August: trippers were on the beach by nine o'clock in the morning. But the long-standing 'wakes weeks' of the wool and cotton trades had deep historical roots in the dedication of parish churches and were recognised perforce by the employers. The Durham coal miners had held their galas at the centre of a week off work[31] since the turn of the century and the Welsh miners had done the same. Shipbuilding, iron- and steel-making, all the traditional heavy industries whose skilled and well-paid artisans had won, by way of solidarity and sheer economic indispensability, the most strategic victories in Britain's long and genteel class struggle, counted their unpaid vacations as one of their battle honours. Overwhelmingly, from the 1870s onwards they took them at Blackpool. They went to the new Raikes Hall 'pleasure gardens' (a neologism of the day) to see the fireworks, the dancers, the freak shows, to climb the treewalk. They went, as the immortal Marriott Edgar and Stanley Holloway testified, with young Albert, his Pa and Ma, to the seafront and the zoo.

> They didn't think much to the Ocean:
> The waves they was fiddlin' and small,
> There was no wrecks and nobody drownded
> Fact nothing to laugh at at all.
>
> So, seeking for further amusement,
> They paid and went into the Zoo,
> Where they'd Lions and Tigers and Camels
> And Old Ale and sandwiches too ...[32]

and Albert was swallowed whole by the toothless and amiable old lion, Wallace. On the beach, their children shouted themselves hoarse at the antique rituals of the Punch and Judy shows and took tuppenny rides on the scruffy and indomitable donkeys, still surviving their mange and trotting in and out of the next century. There were stalls with queues of anxious girls to see the fortune-tellers; mountebanks with swords to swallow, fire to eat and pennies to bend in their gums; clowns on stilts and hurdy-gurdies creaking out their sweeping, circular waltzes; there were performing fleas and, by 1895 or so, there were little picture houses with seven or eight minute films in jerky black-and-white of ordinary street scenes or very vaguely erotic flashes of nakedness, and just-as-jerky peepshows ('what the butler saw') for a penny a time in a small arcade outside the picture house. There might be a performing bear with a chain through its muzzle; there would certainly be monkeys in boleros and a man on a platform preparing to saw his wife in half, she in a long box with her head and feet poking out. On the beach and on the promenade, there were increasing numbers of very mild thrill machines, carousels and roundabouts with music to match, Big Wheels, helter-skelters, so many that by 1900 they were all rounded up and moved into a special, enormous enclave still Blackpool's biggest thing, and beautifully caught in the new word, 'funfair'.

All this crowded, noisy, fretting, chafing, colourful world was a long way from Brighton's Regency saturnalia. This was working-class culture, exactly because of its abandon, noise, laughter and carnival and if the class had invented this corner of its tradition in a generation, its components went a long way back.

It was not genteel. It was intensely gregarious. Its population came from skilled labour and repeated in its play assorted negations of its work: crowded non-productivity; collective unself-protectiveness; joint indolence; financial carelessness; unrewarded effortfulness. All these reversals of the normal thrift and mutuality were embodied in the Building, Friendly and Co-operative welfare societies of their north of England origins in Bradford, Leeds, Burnley, Halifax and Rochdale (to say nothing of informal saving coupons sold as dividends from the grocer). The conduct of the Blackpool holiday was as regular as the labour of the class: the family was turned punctually out of its boarding house by nine o'clock, not to return until the evening meal. The uniform of pleasure was as fixed as that of labour – the men in three-piece suits, solid boots and watch chains, the women in slightly stiff, full-length bombazine or stuff dresses, softening later for the more youthfully daring, into leg-of-mutton sleeves, white blouses and straw hats, the children in sailor suits.

These were the numerous best-paid representatives of England's industrial masses, and looking at them now from over a century later, as they make their boisterous, respectable vacation on the promenade at Blackpool, it looks all the more unlikely that they would ever fulfil Marx's predictions for them, and trade the solid gains and keen satisfactions of their seaside Augusts for the mad uncertainties of revolution.

> My husband, Herbert, is a railwayman himself, so we travel free. His pay these days is steady, generally about £3.15s and I do a little extra work myself. We take the children and go for a week. We share the bedroom, and bed and breakfast comes to five shillings a day. We're lucky, we can come in and go out of the house whenever we like, and the landlady will make sandwiches for us. We sit on the beach and rent a deckchair. Ice cream cornets are a halfpenny each for the girls. Then Herbert goes up for a beer, and we go to watch the beach races. This year the sun shone nearly every day …[33]

They came in steady hundreds of thousands, even when slump and the cotton famine hit hard in the early 1870s. Two million a year arrived at Blackpool by 1890, mostly on excursion trains. The cotton holidays were by then extending to a full week, although these enormous numbers included not only wool-making competitors from Yorkshire but plenty of Cook's customers from the potteries and industrial Midlands.

Nonetheless, they were predominantly Lancastrians in Blackpool, brought there by the forces of propinquity and the deep ties of custom. They came *en famille* and from the mills, parties of close friends and relations for whom the holiday was an extension of home life in home towns and blessedly without the inexorable summons of factory bells and hooters. Blackpool was, with the full force of the adjective, *familiar*, made in their image and then idealised – a much grander, cleaner, fresher, sunnier home town, 'the immaturity of the social product transcended' as Benjamin had it earlier. So they behaved in Blackpool as they would have done at home, only more so.

It was this familiarity, as Walton points out, which gave the Blackpool landlady, doyenne of the boarding houses where the millions stayed, her power and symbolism. At her best she was an ideal mother – cheerful, welcoming, generous, resourceful, a good cook of well-loved dishes, keeper of a hygienic household; at her worst she was mother's just as necessary negation, queen of the music hall joke and seaside postcard, the demon mother-in-law, tyrannical, mean, avaricious, permanently enraged. She stands out as a popular symbol of that essential half of vacation life which imitates the perfect homecoming.

Outside her little kingdom, Blackpool was, as the maxims require, at once homely and exotic. The Winter Gardens, a triumph of Arcadian architecture in glass, iron, sub-tropical greenery, gilded cafés and chocolate shops, and its sumptuous dance-hall effects, held out the promise of foreign scents and airs as well of the perfect stranger with whom to dance. The South Jetty, deliberately constructed in the 1860s to keep the poorer classes away from the more fashionable North Pier with its full orchestra playing Strauss, became instead the place to embark upon steamer trips up and down the coast ('the sixpenny sick') and to dance in the open air.

The English working class danced its holidays away, in quickstep, waltz, foxtrot, as well as in those curiously stately and collective circlings which ensure that one changes partners each round so that no-one is left unsuited, the Valeta, the Gay Gordons, the Sir Roger de Coverley. They danced on each pier, at the Winter Gardens, at the Empress Ballroom. After 1890 they danced at the Alhambra (another exotic piece of tropicality, not for the first time with a Moorish savour) and, grandest of all, at the Tower, which brought in big London investment for the first time.

There was, as all those who loved it said as they trooped regretfully to Central Station on the way home, nowhere like Blackpool. Indeed, there wasn't. It had terrific style. The formlessness of its dull brick terraces, themselves so reassuringly familiar to the people of Bury, Preston or Wigan, were given definition and direction by the splendour of the piers and promenade, and by the studied opulence of the spectacular pleasuredromes – the Winter Gardens, the Pleasure Beach, the Big Wheel, the Tower and the rest – which lent the town its grand horizon and were to be so dramatically unified at night by the brilliance of the Blackpool illuminations after the coming of electricity in 1902.

VII

This has been, as well it might be, a song of praise of Blackpool. But it is worth bringing out, alongside its singularity, just how general this making of El Dorado for the respectable working classes was in the second half of the nineteenth century and how completely their architectural symbolisation of luxury and magic and their juxta-position in the heart of the vacation still shape our imaginations. Indoors, the signs of vacation luxury nowadays reach back beyond the austerities of the Bauhaus and quote, in postmodern abandon, the obsidian and bronze glass, the heavy fretwork, the greenery and bargeboarding of Victorian cafés and winter gardens. Outdoors, the jewelled magic of the moment is once again signified, in new hotels and malls, on restored piers and rehabilitated town centres, by heavy flagstones and granite setts, by classical statuary and cascades, by terraces, solid stone stairs, iron capstans and balus-ters and heavy cast gates.

These images have risen again at Blackpool, indeed universally: in France, Italy, the USA. There is a key to our mystery somewhere in here. Cast-iron piers, lovingly restored fretwork pavilions, broad plank platforms, granite setts signify something durable from the past. The purpose of such restoration is to quote to the present the imagined safeties and certainties of the high Victorian moment. The past is surpassed but mythologised. In other words, in the present we have put behind us the deformations of old industrialisation, the misery and poverty, the horrors of class, but we have retrieved (as Walter Benjamin foretold) this idealised spectacle of its greatest successes: its picturesque leisure, its dependable craftsmanship, its pride in solidly grasped artefacts matching its sureness in solidly grasped moral truths.

These retrievals are as reassuring as a big plate of well-made sandwiches. They are part of the power of kaleidoscopic repatterning which seasides have always proved to have. The seaside is weirder (those ghost trains), more festive (kiss-me-quick hats), more contradictory *and* more old-fashioned than piety allows.

Bloody old social class, its cruelty and snobbery, is everywhere, of course, on both sides of the Atlantic, and the ceremonies of the seafront announce its ubiquity. But the way of life of the seaside and the buildings which symbolise that life have, in all their boisterous vitality and variety, much more going for them than the offices of status and superiority. Their 'deep play'[34] speaks for a life of happy, magical and sociable luxury; almost, you could say, a good life. John Betjeman, Britain's most popular poet ever, thought so and once exactly caught that goodness, with a touch of plangency excusable, I would say, given the date.

> Margate, 1940
>
> How lightly municipal, meltingly tarr'd,
> Were the walks through the Lawns by the Queen's Promenade
> As soft over Cliftonville languished the light
> Down Harold Road, Norfolk Road, into the night.
>
> Oh! then what a pleasure to see the ground floor
> With tables for two laid as tables for four,
> And bottles of sauce and Kia-Ora and squash
> Awaiting their owners who'd gone up to wash -
>
> Who had gone up to wash the ozone from their skins
> The sand from their legs and the Rock from their chins,
> To prepare for an evening of dancing and cards
> And forget the sea-breeze on the dry promenades.
>
> From third floor and fourth floor the children looked down
> Upon ribbons of light in the salt-scented town;
> And drowning the trams roared the sound of the sea
> As it washed in the shingle the scraps of their tea.

A large social class, now on the wrong side of fifty, can still catch an echo of Betjeman's seaside in its bosom. Brown sauce and orange squash still decorate the tables laid in many thousands of the sometimes faltering, reassuringly continuous hotels along the sea fronts in Hastings, Weymouth, Bude, and Lynton; in Prestatyn and Aberystwyth; and on up the west coast of England to indestructible Blackpool, or the east by way of Margate herself via Cromer to just-as-unkillable Scarborough. The picnics, the rock, even the dancing, so lovingly commemorated in the poem, survived 1940, survived cheap travel to the Balearic Islands as well. I don't really doubt that children in England now abed will still be touched with the same recognition of this blissful townscape when they too cross to the wrong side of the decades.

4

THE MEANING OF LUXURY

I

It will be our axiom in this not-really-historical chapter that the whole of culture was pulled up and replanted in a different order between about 1830 and 1880, never more wholesale than in planting the new fields of leisure pastimes and the taking of vacations. There are three classical locations for the vacation: first the City, with all it entails of multitudinous strangeness, richness of size and squalor; second, the Country, with *its* powerful presences of Nature herself, the simple, even primitive living that goes with her, a certain asceticism enjoined by solitude and meditation; third, the Seaside, a mixture of the two, where fashionable urbanity on its promenade dissolves suddenly along the pier into awed contemplation of the sea, where the rules of polite dining-out and taking of tea are so daringly overturned by food eaten with the fingers and in the open air, and where chance encounters at the *thé dansant* may turn into love affairs before the waltz is over.

These straightforward distinctions intertwine themselves as the meanings of the vacation accumulate over two centuries. Each of the three realms – city, country and the hybrid which is the seaside – must lose familiarity and take on estrangement in order to glow richly as a holiday locale. Thus, we cannot go to the city we know well because it is the place of work and grime and anonymous multitudes trudging bent-headed home. Vacation cities must be unfamiliar, characterised by all those qualities missing in our own which in the strange city we can breathe in, as we say, luxuriously; for here time is free. That's what we paid for.

So too with the countryside. It is not this site of peasant labour – or only if, as we also say, a picturesque kind. It is the object of our free, restorative contemplation. This is the luxury of a recovered simplicity of living, of a steadying of time (again, because 'free'); it is a clearing of one's gaze, the luxury of ease.

Third, the seaside is a veering, slightly crazy blend of both. Disneyland and Club Med are attempts to corral and enclose the craziness *and* the quiet within a single perimeter, so that whatever one wants, one doesn't have to go anywhere else to pay for it. The consumption of precious spare time, for which the leisure industries must compete so fiercely,[1] is cut almost to zero. All the same, such places, whatever their commercial success, are still rather thought of as somewhere to take the kids and in themselves a bit artificial. The seaside resort, for all its contrivance, is spacious enough to satisfy the taste for unforced luxury in either its voluptuous or its ascetic guises.

City values invert country ones. As a cluster of holiday values, each is a negation of daily routines. Seasides contain both in miniature: a bit of city here, a bit of country there, both freely savoured; both luxurious.

All future holidays, let us say, will be subdivisions of this simple scheme. The dangerous vacation at the world's end is an intensification of the trip to behold Nature; the City is always the Eternal City, whether the towers of paradise glimpsed on the turnpike or Moloch and Gomorrah, promising sinfulness on an agreeably abandoned scale, limited only by the length of the tour. The seaside mediates the two, now crowded, now lonely, *urbs in rure*, *rus in urbe*, polite and civic and raising its hat on the Spa, naked and bacchanalian at the water's edge where men and women take their clothes off and shriek and splash. The ideal type of seaside is the Mediterranean where gods, poets, painters, film stars and fishermen congregate their weird history. The ideal city is as various and as uniform as its eponyms – Paris, Cairo, Bangkok, Melbourne, Venice, Manhattan – when we get there, it will unite the best parts of every Baedeker. It was John Murray who first conceived of mass-produced guidebooks in a brand-name series, but it was Thomas Baedeker who started off the first, Europe-and-America-wide best-selling guidebooks in a dozen languages in 1848. They were small and pocketable. He devised the neat system of marking the best sights to see with a star or two, and after writing the first few himself, carefully setting out the best walks and permitting himself agreeable little paragraphs of general encomia on the local landscape. By 1860 the volumes were institutionalised across Europe (Henry James is careful to keep his by him in Italy[2]), Baedeker had had to recruit a team of writers and had joined John Murray as the object of Ruskin's detestation.[3] In 1898, prescient to the great changes brought by the bicycle and the motor car, Michelin invented a different order of guidebook, benignly presided over by their portly tyre-man Bibendum, one adjusted to a tourist more swiftly on the move than ever before, purposeful, directed, destined.

The new tourist would see much of the chosen scenery through the windscreen of an automobile. City and country are, for the time being, alike framed as travelling spectacle.

> The expressway turns to cross water full of the redness of the sky, and there, floating on the horizon above the shining red water, are the clustered towers of the inner city, purple with distance, lights shining in a million windows – exactly as he has always known they would be. Now other freeways are converging upon his, passing above and beneath, wheeling and turning all round him. He follows the Downtown postings, up, round, through, and over; one of a thousand particles circling the orbits of a complex molecule.

The hero has driven straight from his fatal car accident to the Eternal City. When he gets there, the City is, as of course it will be, both strange and familiar. The hero is the perfect product of contemporary English liberalism; the vanity, egoism, the remorseless brightness and the generosity of *The Guardian* compressed into one pair of trousers. At the hotel, he finds the ideal porter to whom he can speak fluently in the porter's own language. The next morning he goes out for croissants and coffee and to see the perfect buildings, the product of heavenly collaboration between Brunelleschi and Mies van der Rohe, praised in the celestially stilted prose of the *Michelin Guide* to Paradise.

The list of things to be seen goes on for several pages, and most of them have three stars. It's suggested that you should linger on the great avenues and squares in the morning and afternoon, to see the swarms of officials and experts who administer the universe hurrying to and from their offices; or sit for a while in the shady walks of the various public gardens, and watch these same officials' wives proudly taking the baby out for an airing. There are certain bars where artists and writers are always to be seen, talking animatedly as they set the world to rights. The pageantry surrounding the court is a feast of spectacle and venerable tradition.[4]

He books in without anxiety to the hotel which combines with heavenly exactitude the luxurious and the domestic.

So, too, does the city (it is Heaven, after all). It is old and new in equal, perfect proportions; it is terribly beautiful and completely familiar in a way adjusted with great accuracy to the taste of the English *bourgeoisies* of assorted sizes as they have entered into their inheritance over the past thirty years.

Luxury is as much the key to understanding the long duration of consumerism as is homeliness.[5] It is one large claim of the doctrine of consumerism as propounded by its parent system capitalism that it provide a plenitude of luxuries, and that these luxuries are nothing to be ashamed of.

Luxury has a long history as the object of moral detestation. Once Christianity had fashioned a new version of old asceticism[6] towards the end of the fourth century, opulent display was, notwithstanding a few jokes from Chaucer, dedicated to the service of God until the Italian Renaissance, when the Venetians and the Florentines made so much money they couldn't confine it to the churches. London and Amsterdam followed in the sixteenth and seventeenth centuries,[7] and by the time the Grand Tour opened its books what Christopher Berry[8] notes as the 'de-moralization of luxury' was well on its way.

Berry's view is that luxurious satisfactions may usually be gathered under one of the following four headings: shelter, food, clothes and, allowing for the elasticity of the concept, leisure. We shall take shelter (in the form of hotels and cottages) first; then food; finally leisure, here defined as bodily exercise (sex and sport). Berry points out that luxury stands in tension with the idea of necessity. You don't, by definition, *need* a luxury. But the definitions move. What was once luxurious, as in the cases of the water-closet, the sprung mattress, the television and the motor car, may readily become necessities as they are absorbed into the rhythms of everyday life. Nor is this absorption always a matter of the inevitable progress and increase of material welfare. In this connection, Fred Hirsch[9] has (famously) coined the idea of a 'positional good' to indicate that the increased availability of certain luxuries removes them from the category of luxury and turns them into something quite different. A country cottage used as a holiday home no longer *is* a country cottage if it is surrounded by hundreds of other such homes.

Hirsch pursues his argument into the economics of sex and it is odd that Berry doesn't find a place for sex in his classification of luxury, given that the word itself in usages easy to find in Shakespeare is at times synonymous with abandoned (and, generally, male-tyrannical) sexuality. I am at pains in this book to recommend a way of thinking about individual life in relation to 'consumption' as its dominant feature in which our satisfactions ('utility' in the jargon) are themselves 'derived in some *combination* from characteristics of the goods or services themselves and of the relevant environmental conditions'.[10] This is to think holistically about 'consumption'. Such analysis refuses the traditional economic theory in which consumption is the name given to the acquisition by the buyer from the seller of a commodity whose utility is then deployed to the buyer's satisfaction.

To understand exchange and consumption as inextricable from what is being exchanged gives us more of a grip on luxury and its key significance in our holiday-making. It establishes for us what looks like a moral truism, were it not that consumerism in its crudest versions will have it that human welfare is simply identical with material satisfaction and personal advantage. It will be the argument of this book, as it is of Hirsch's pioneer work, that built into the dominant meanings of consumerism we will find strong residues of earlier moral values, and that these continue to insist that pleasure itself is also compounded of love and mutuality. The deep drives of economic productivity and the monetary policies which go with them,[11] however, make it increasingly difficult to live and symbolise those values. Mutuality and love don't get much of a place in the small narrative of the television ad, even though tourism and the luxuriousness it seeks themselves depend on those old presences.

The luxurious vacation, in other words, confirms and restores deep familial values; the fact that these values are, as we say, 'personal', doesn't mean that they aren't social and economic as well. The mistake, as John Stuart Mill understood, is to suppose that economics is simply defined by pecuniary self-interest; it is *not* a mistake, however, to suppose (as Mill himself said) that certain virtues may become weaker because they have no customary means of expression. Mill remarked (of altruistic conduct) that 'the only mode in which any active principle in human nature can be effectively cultivated is by habitual exercise'.[12] Practice indeed makes perfect.

Surprisingly to the ascetic view, luxuries encourage the virtues. Berry tells us, as we heard, that luxury may be classified under the four heads of food and drink, shelter, clothing and leisure. To each of these, in its many forms, I add sex, a leisure pleasure (or luxury) which is also a necessity.

Sex, in other words, is imbricated in each, and each carries its luxurious charge *when it is leisurely*, which is to say, when it is freed from time and commodification. A luxury is a commodity one does not need. It is chosen. It may be transformed into a gift. Certainly, one may give away what one needs, and doing so betokens not so much one's asceticism as one's generosity. But then one remains in need oneself, and there cannot but be a reproach in this.[13] To make a gift of a luxury, on the other hand, is to admit the other person to the realm of abundance. It is to make them free, as the phrase goes, of plenty, and thereby to surrender one's own claim upon it. As one does so, ushering one's lover into the hotel bedroom with a gesture of pure magnanimity, one renews the civic virtues.

This breezy moral detour is intended to stand up in a small way against the brutally foreshortened appeal to luxury in the advertisements, as well as to put this more large-spirited and re-moralised case for luxury as a core meaning in the structure of consumerism in general and vacationing in particular.

Each of the headings identifies a basic human need (or, if you prefer, an abstract universal). We have to eat, find shelter, wear clothing of some sort, make a bit of spare time. Luxury then arises when we find and delight in a surplus beyond the satisfaction of basic need. Subsistence no longer oppresses us; we have marked the margin of indulgence and, Berry says, *refinement*.[14] The refinement of need into luxury is an infinite gratification. Nowadays one can say quite plausibly, 'I not only want, I *need* a holiday' and indeed this need is recognised as some kind of legal right by the existence of legislated holiday-with-pay. But if there is such a thing as a *basic* holiday (a few days away with no domestic labour), then luxury finds its realm as we adorn the need (days in the sun; someone looking after the kids and mother; a glass of wine with the evening meal; a new dress; your own bathroom ...).

II

The dream of luxury is at the heart of the holiday. The power of its spell over everybody, even during a fit of puritanism such as any sensitive person might fall into given the present riot of consumer self-indulgence, plays lustrously over the holiday and its paradisal imagery. Given that it was the genius of French and British capitalism to invent mass vacationing as the necessary refuge from the horrors and tedium of industrial work-discipline, that genius found its fullest expression, as you would expect, in the most sociable of the arts, architecture. Genius was distinctively of the place, and if pavilions, piers and promenades came first to the watering places and gave them their characteristic and lovable topography, their pleasant, open-air and sauntering sort of symbolism was quickly surpassed by the invention of the hotel.

There are two ideals of holiday locale, the grand hotel and the holiday home. Of course, the immense weight and complexity of class structure in the first industrial and holidaymaking societies immediately interposed their bulk between us and that simple formula. The boarding-house, the small hotel, the farm which takes in a few summer visitors, the caravan site and the camper, the tent and the tavern, the *pensione* and the monastery all betoken a much wider variety of sojourn than can neatly be set on either side of the binaries. All the same, one can see that simple scheme beckoning behind all vacationing, find its outline in the advertisements, and clearly detect its usefulness to those universal industrial processes which, even in the day of niche marketing, seek to reduce and clarify all leisure and cultural life in the name of lower unit costs and the marginal rate of profit. The vacationer looks for solitude in the cottage or for urbanity and sociability in the hotel. The luxury of the cottage is familiar, rural, anachronistic; the luxury of the grand hotel is modern, extravagant, conscientiously indulgent, too much.

Capital city hotels appear at the same time and in the same idiom as the banks and the railway terminus. All over Europe and North America, at what seems to have been the identical moment in 1850, capital cities and then, a very short time later, their faithful parodists at the seaside, sprouted an amazing crop of hotels in the splendid vernacular of high Victorianism.

In large part, of course, these colossal buildings were intended to house the hundreds of thousands of comfortably-off new and old *bourgeoisie* as they poured out of the railway stations into the capital. The soaring eight storeys of the Grand Hotel at Brighton, designed by one J. Whichcord in the Italianate manner of 1862 is an easily visitable example of the sheer capacity of these places (nearly four hundred bedrooms in its day) and its massive towers at each end of the façade, its florid balconies and heavy pediments above the windows, its solid classicism finished off with a long glass conservatory walk in front, all prefigure the universal rhetoric of Victorian hotels and declare a new kind of relation between the individual figure and the city.[15]

That relation still holds. It can be studied anywhere such hotels flourish, and they have proved strikingly durable. Tested by the technology and the productivity economics which have reduced a once-teeming staff to an insufficient minimum, struggling in the competition brought by the motor car and the consequent reduction in railway passengers, bending under enormous maintenance, heating and modernisation costs, the big hotels have shown themselves, on the whole, capable of impressive self-renewal. Telephones, televisions; private bathrooms; squash courts, swimming pools, sweatrooms and saunas, have all been hospitably accommodated and the hotel dining room has remarkably survived the extraordinary multiplication of cheap places to eat.

For a hundred and fifty years these buildings have borne witness to the powerful and ubiquitous dream of luxury and the delight of closing the gap between desire and actuality for just a few nights. Their very names speak the nursery talk of luxury: the Grand, the Imperial, the Waldorf, the Dorchester, the Palace, the Queen's, the Royal, the Erzherzog, the Kaiserin, the Regency, the Plaza; the nomenclature rings out a medley of ruling class and regal tintinnabulation; the appointments of the hotels were in keeping. As in the banks and the clubs, the grand entrances with their flight of steps, their pillars and porticos combined solidity with swagger in a way that took

Figure 4.1 The Grand Hotel, Brighton
Source: Hilary Britland

some nerve to breach and enter. A person's self-assurance had to match the building's, let alone brave the terrifying commissionaire with his epaulettes and uniform great-coat, his medal ribbons and his white-gloved underlings.

Once inside, the customer – expertly reclassified by nineteenth-century management technique as the guest – entered a complete, endlessly renewed and recreated social system. Given what a gift this miniature society is to those novelists always seeking a microcosm for their theory of human bondage, it's surprising that there is no Great-Novel-of-the-Hotel in English. After all, the leading characters of Henry James in Boston and Venice, of Proust in Paris, are forever walking in evening dress into splendid glass-and-gilt-and-marble foyers in order to begin love affairs. So one would expect better of the form than Arnold Bennett's effort *Grand Babylon Hotel* of 1926. The nearest thing that comes to a hotel classic is the Berliner novel *Menschen in Hotel*[16] in which the novelist Vicki Baum indeed sees just how complete a society was invented by hotel life, with its bars, tea rooms, afternoon dancing to the Palm Court orchestra (of four players), its conference rooms, kitchens, bellhops and receptionists, chambermaids and managers, its sleepless activity and mountains of waste, its elaborate front-of-house ceremony and ostentation, its squalid and labyrinthine backstairs haste and improvisation.

The narrative life of such an emporium brings to birth its instantaneous clichés: the lonely tears of the ageing ballerina; the deathly illness of the book-keeper; the illicit, idyllic passionate love affair glimpsed on the balcony of room 70; the cashiered officer barely keeping up appearances; the lady world-traveller with reservations in the Imperial in Prague, the Bristol in Vienna, in Rio, Rome, Paris, 'an endless perspective of hotel rooms with double doors and running water and the indefinable scent of restlessness and strangeness ...'

What Baum and Bennett miss out, but Henry James, of course, puts in, is not only life outside the hotel, but the natural life people bring into them. Baum's mysterious figures are cut off from any membership one of another, but the so-called family hotel, still going strong at assorted levels of luxuriousness from seaside Grands to country house grandeur, thrived in terms of its cheerful, sedate vitality of the sort Betjeman celebrates in 'Margate 1940'.

That same vitality, moving along the axis of luxury from lavishness to homeliness, lives also, as it has done since the writers and painters of Bloomsbury all went down together to St Ives in about 1890, in the holiday home. Holiday luxury must partake of the enormous consolations of safe shelter. In one shelter – the hotel – servants (who must become friends) keep you safe. All definitions demand an opposite. The other luxurious shelter is the holiday home.

I suppose its provenance is to be found in the yearning prompted by the Romantic movement for solitary communion with Nature and for space uninvaded by the demands of work, the presence of other people and the squalor of the industrial city. It all goes back much further[17] than that, no doubt. Wordsworth's *Tintern Abbey* fixes the essential feelings, and Henry David Thoreau's *Walden Pond* turns Wordsworth's little walk into a refuge where deep feeling and Romantic metaphysics were confirmed by the material nature of the cabin, the fauna, the paths and the light-hearted simplicity of the living.

This is luxury as reduction. What a relief! Thoreau lectured to packed audiences on 'Walking' and by insisting to genteel New England on the sweet restoration of natural airs and aromas (the fragrance of nectar, of wild animal odours, of human sweat) injected a strong dose of sanctimonious self-improvement into the good life of vacationing. Thoreau turned his great landlord and mentor Ralph Waldo Emerson and his grand All-American doctrine of self-reliance into vacation self-improvement and natural cleansing. 'Sauntering' (Thoreau's favourite word) beside the still water, rowing on its glassy surface with only his flute to summon Pan for company, Thoreau transformed Emerson's precepts into action and showed how on vacation we (meaning men) can recover the godlike innocence of boyhood.

> Independent, irresponsible, looking out from his corner on such people and facts as pass by, he tries and sentences them on their merits, in the swift, summary way of boys ... But the man is as it were clapped into jail by his consciousness ...
> These are the voices which we hear in solitude, but they grow faint and inaudible as we enter into the world.[18]

Wordsworth put this thought into circulation in his famous *Ode on Intimations of Immortality* where he, too, had placed a boy (himself of course) around whom, as he grows up, 'shades of the prison-house begin to close'. Emerson turned this ghostly feeling into a metaphysics. Thoreau transformed it into a scheme of practical experiences, based on the cabin he hewed for himself out of the forest (with a certain amount of local help) and the plentiful epiphanies of Nature he arranged to have.

> [I]n the midst of a gentle rain ... I was suddenly sensible of such sweet and beneficent society in Nature, in the very pattering of the drops, and in every sight and sound around my house, an infinite and unaccountable friendliness all at once, like an atmosphere, sustaining me ...[19]

The cabin, isolated from humankind but surrounded by the blessed neighbourliness of countless natural forms of life is a place of new, rough luxury. The stale luxuries of the Grand Hotel and Fifth Avenue are put off, along with the noise, the traffic, the tense timetable of work and sociability. The truly luxurious life bids goodbye to all that, for the set period of the vacation. The countryside will provide the peace which the city destroys.

This, as we know, is an old song. *Walden* is a main signpost pointing the way to the holiday home. Thoreau himself would have been confounded by the *agriturismo* which he inaugurated. After all, he *lived* (for a while) by the Pond. But he taught a large generation of American middle-class New Englanders that even if you couldn't make a life like Thoreau's, you could imitate it once a year. If you were wealthy enough, you could buy a cabin and live like Thoreau every weekend. Either way, the holiday home became part of the leisure of the theory class, and presidents, thriller writers, prominent Leftists and physicists joined the throngs of millionaires, robber barons and chief executives of banks and insurance companies in clapboard houses silvered by the sea all the way from Martha's Vineyard to the Keys at the southern tip of Florida. The ascetic lessons Thoreau taught have been learned wonderfully well by the holiday home industry of today. The converted barn behind the farmhouse, the fisherman's terrace above the harbour have had their plank floors replaced in blond ash and loudly clicking metal latches fixed to their doors. Their unused ranges are black-leaded and their brass handles polished. Their thick white Amerindian rugs are spotless, and their gaily pastel-coloured curtains still stiff with sizing. Their stone walls are snowcemmed a dazzling white and all the woodwork smells sweet and scoured from recent planing.

The past of these places is, as I put it earlier, surpassed and mythologised. Such simplicity comes damned expensive. But it matches a taste in which Emerson and Thoreau over there are compounded over here with Wordsworth, William Morris and the Arts and Crafts movement, to say nothing of the noble Lord Armstrong who made millions out of machine guns and built the wildly Romantic, lavishly simple Cragside in Northumberland.

Virginia Woolf's *To the Lighthouse* of 1922 is, one might say, the great novel about the holiday home. The fraction of the middle class in question is the scrupulously non-mercantile, cultivated and intellectualising membership of the ancient universities in which Virginia Woolf herself grew up. Her father was a distinguished historian of ideas, her sister became a well-known painter, she is now a revered ancestor of public-spirited feminism. The Stephen family's actual holiday cottage was in St Ives, the first artist's colony to spring up on the economy of seaside vacations. The pervasive influence of Woolf's Bloomsbury group – those glittering prizewinners who included John Maynard Keynes, E.M. Forster, Dora Carrington, David Bomberg and Virginia and Leonard Woolf – served to confirm and enrich Thoreau's naïve rhetoric and lend an unpretentious grace to leisure time.

In the opening of the novel, set in a summer just before the First World War, the Stephen family (transposed as the Ramsays to the Hebrides) plans a trip to the lighthouse. They have several university friends to stay, a not-very-well-off (woman) painter-friend, as well as the about-to-be-fiancée of the eldest son. Mr Ramsay talks philosophy to his chums. There is (what else?) an impoverished, rather snuffy bachelor hanging on the fringes of the family. The little boy James is desperately looking forward to the lighthouse trip, but the weather dooms it. Mrs Ramsay is the calm, loving, capacious and all-seeing centre of the life of the house.

This picture of the good life as lived in the holiday home spreads wide and goes deep in the Anglophone and European imagination. Virginia Woolf didn't invent it. But her novel canonises it, even as she explodes it from inside, abruptly killing off Mrs Ramsay and two of her children (childbirth, the war) in three devastating and laconic parentheses. Mrs Ramsay returns as a ghost. The bereft family repair the house when the war is over, and finally make the trip to the lighthouse.

The dinner party *daube*, French cricket on the lawn, philosophic chat, painting, stolen kisses, the rowing boat to the lighthouse are classical elements of the perfect vacation in the temporary home-from-home (which is, because of its rusticity and improvisations, more completely one's real home than one's real home back there, at work, in the city).

The drive of this family life is its children, Mrs Ramsay its hub. The awful anguish the novel so vividly represents takes the measure of just how near a miss life at the cottage was. The sadness is that it was all but blissfully happy. This is its grownupness. Consequently, it is no surprise to find that way of life turning into the subject-matter of a new and flourishing literary form, the popular novel for children, exactly because children can take their luxuries straight. A couple of names will have to stand for this widely welcomed innovation.

Arthur Ransome is a fine novelist; Enid Blyton is – well – an amazing literary phenomenon. Plenty of people turn up their noses, as well they might, at her petty vengefulness, neurotic offendability and small-town English snobbery. But she brought unrivalled happiness to millions of readers and did so by her simple-minded celebration of the sunny summer and snow-filled winter holidays in which a group of perfect childhood friends find safe adventure without benefit of parents. Ransome did the same, but was a far better writer. He did for his sailor-children on the Lakes and the Norfolk Broads what Blyton did for a much more mythological landscape, with an uninhabited island within easy reach of an idealised Perranporth of the 1920s, which was where the rest of the action took place. These two children's novelists initiate what has been well praised as a golden age of children's literature. They serve for our purposes to recall that there should be something preciously childish to find on vacation and if we miss it, the disappointment will be as bitter as it would have been in our lost childhood and as it is for the Ramsays.

Luxury in these places comes close to being synonymous with freedom; it is, for adults, the rediscovery of innocence experienced as a luxury. With a lucky childhood on holiday, memory itself may be kept safe to be taken luxuriously out in moments of free time. Ransome himself wrote of his own childhood holidays on a farm at the south end of Conistonwater that he and his brother and sister

> adored the place. Coming to it we used to run down to the lake, dip our hands in and wish, as if we had just seen a new moon. Going away from it we were half-drowned in tears. While away from it, as children and as grown-ups, we dreamt about it. No matter where I was, wandering about the world, I used at night to look for the North Star and, in my mind's eye, could see the beloved skyline of great hills beneath it. *Swallows and Amazons* grew out of those old memories. I could not help writing it. It almost wrote itself.[20]

III

Virginia Woolf, Arthur Ransome, Enid Blyton are iconographers of the informal, sandy, irregular and untidy luxuries of the holiday home. Inverting the splendours of the Grand, they affirm the same pleasures. For the rules at the Grand were made to be broken.

Hotels, clubs, banks, department stores came to the capitals and the big resorts at the same moment just after the railways, and they came to stay. Their heavy stone structure pierced by deep windows, their baronial entrances and castellated rooflines declared for the solidity of the money they conserved and consumed. In their massiveness and durability, the hotels combined the irresistible ingredients of the holiday. They were familiar. Whether one was in Rio or Rome like Vicki Baum's heroine, their geography and iconography wore the same style and signature, the heavy, ornate, complacent style of Louis Napoleon's Paris and Prince Albert's London. They were exotic: neither Blenheim nor Schönbrunn were so unremittingly lavish. They were vast and permissive: one could hide most misdemeanours from one's class if not from the servants. They invited excess and suborned all defences against indulgence. The full works of the show *table d'hôte* dinner at the Carlton in 1903 when served to the President of France ran to eleven courses: caviare, soup (clear or thick), trout, chicken, lamb and peas, shrimp suprème, champagne sorbet, savoury quail, asparagus tips, peach, parfait, chocs.[21] No doubt not everybody ate everything but the sheer scale of eating leaves today's dieticians reeling. Such scrumptiousness was and is the point of the grand hotel and even if one comes several notches down the social scale, eating big remains at the centre of the good vacation life. Food, with gluttony always lurking under the table, is as big a luxury as shelter.

It was the second half of the nineteenth century which saw the coming-to-dominance of French gastronomy over all Anglophone cookery books and recipes belonging to the cultivated middle classes. Theodore Zeldin tells us that the French cuisine was yet another invention of the century which founded the culture of the present, and the product of joint labour by the professional male cooks, the restaurateurs, self-conscious gastronomers emerging from the new Parisian bourgeoisie, and women cooks employed by the same people. The legendary Antoine Carème, Baron Rothschild's own, is designated by Zeldin founder of the tradition. He died in 1833 but by then had canonised the stately sequence of *mets* and *entremets* which mark élite French cuisine. First the *potages* and *entrées*; second, the roasts and *entremets*; third, the desserts; each stage offered many choices, at Carème's hands on occasions up to forty-eight in all.[22]

Carème was succeeded by Georges Auguste Escoffier, who lightened the brute weight of the food and, simplifying the overdone lusciousness of the *fin-de-siècle* sauces, taught the purity of the precept 'food should taste of itself'. He ruled at the Carlton and the Savoy, organised a division of culinary labour in the kitchen so that dishes were prepared by components and only brought together on completion, and *haut-cuisinier* though he certainly was, devised the essential stratagems of the modern *grand chef*, the speed, the dexterity, the intelligence, the hot, fresh dishes. By the end of Escoffier's career, the most famous restaurants of Paris – Café Anglais, Café Riche, Maxim's, Lapérouse – set the standard for London and New York, reversing London's pre-eminence of the previous century.[23] A conscious, 'de-moralised' greed expressed itself, as it were, innocently in the groaning, lavish adornments of the French *table d'hôte*.

The French élite enjoyed a perfect hegemony over the culinary arts. France was, as one would expect, the first country to publish journals for the intellectual discussion of food. *L'Art Culinaire*, which first came out in 1883, was to begin with a supplement of a literary and artistic review, and others – *Le Progrès des Cuisiniers* among them – quickly joined it. Like all French movements, this one had a programme, which was to promote (naturally) the social standing of the profession at home and abroad by formal association and by establishing the annual conferences and competitions or *concours culinaires*[24] in 1882. Escoffier will serve – still does – as the hero-ancestor of a new social group, and one rising rapidly in social standing. The French were the first by a long chalk to confuse the category of art with other, more long-lived forms of cultural expression, and with food and wine they did so comprehensively. It was their wine industry, after all, which classified wines according to social classes – 'premier cru', 'cru bourgeois' – and by the end of the nineteenth century possession of the taste and experience to discriminate between wines as to their grape, region and age was a key badge of status.

The dream of luxury migrates into art, Adorno said. Escoffier fixed dinner as a work of art, balanced between tastes within and across the courses, matching wine to dish with a terminology borrowed from the critical vocabulary of the performing arts.

Figure 4.2   Claridge's restaurant, London, 1905
Source: The Mary Evans Picture Library

Escoffier and his associates aimed not to include a profusion of strong flavours in a single dish, but to achieve a perfect balance between a few superb ingredients. The fact that these ... might well still include expensive and 'rich' items like truffles and crayfish sometimes makes the modern reader fail to perceive Escoffier's objectives and his simplification. But his aims can be seen most perfectly in his use of only a few of the most ordinary ingredients and in the simplest way to create one of his most celebrated dishes, the Pêche Melba. In its final form, this involves the inspired addition to the original peach with vanilla ice cream of the counter-balancing tartness of puréed raspberries.[25]

Escoffier's daring simplicities must be played off against meals of the day vast in terms of brute size and vast also in their sometimes grotesque effects – Mennell illustrates this with an example of a vast dish of *poulardes à l'anglaise* the size and shape of a fountainhead, topped with cherubs, its stem thickly encrusted with asparagus, langoustines and sliced lemons. But the culinary divas allied to the new journals and the competitions conferred the final adornment upon Paris and secured the city as capital of urban vacationing and its cuisine as *the* type of hotel luxury. When César Ritz founded his eponymous hotels, his biggest coup was to entice Escoffier to London as visiting chef.

Like the first Renaissance in Florence, the giant of the day was surrounded by great rivals. Between 1882 and 1914, Phileas Gilbert and Prosper Montagné are only two of the names whose menus drew the fashionable crowds to the most famous restaurants. Luxury in food, of course, may be thrown into even sharper relief by a deliberate dowdiness in décor and furniture. Thus and thus is finesse brought to refinement while snobbery is as snobbery does, even to the gastronomic and lifestyle magazines of the present.

IV

The luxurious pleasures of *haute cuisine*, however, like those of *haute couture*, may be sampled less austerely as well as in much more improvised a style. If my two types of holiday locale – Grand Hotel and country cottage – will hold, one opposite of dinner at the Ritz-Carlton or Maxim's is the abundant picnic served by the Rat to the Mole from 'a fat wicker luncheon-basket' beside the River some time during the summer of 1907.

'There's cold chicken inside it,' replied the Rat briefly;

'coldtonguecoldhamcoldbeefpickledgherkinssaladfrenchrollscressand-
widgespottedmeatgingerbeerlemonadesodawater –'
   'O stop, stop!' cried the Mole in ecstasies: 'This is too much!'
   'Do you really think so?' inquired the Rat seriously. 'It's only what I always take on these little excursions; and the other animals are always telling me that I'm a mean beast and cut it *very* fine.'[26]

The Rat's choices for lunch are no doubt the preference of Kenneth Grahame's first listener, his small son. But they are eloquent of the way the picnic in all its lavish informality becomes the mirror-image of the splendid dinner in the Hôtel Splendide in the capital. It observes Mary Douglas's famous rules, formulated on behalf of all British social classes (and, she suggests, most comparable societies). They require that the main course includes one strongly stressed and savoury item (meats and pickles) flanked by two lightly stressed blander items (in the Rat's luncheon-basket, french rolls and salad).[27] To be a meal, there must be 'at least one mouth-entering utensil per head' and the variety of taste and texture must go beyond the 'bland-sweet-sour dimensions' (which may be covered by a single party snack like a small pastry with shrimp and mayonnaise on it). A proper meal 'incorporates a number of contrasts, hot and cold, bland and spiced, liquid and semi-liquid, and various textures. It also incorporates cereals, vegetables and animal proteins.'[28]
   Mary Douglas, as a good anthropologist, is looking for the rules of the social order which concentrate meaning in certain practices and disperse it in others. These practices, above all, set boundaries, arrange classifications, as a consequence of which we know where we are in time and place. The definitions of Parisian *cuisine* were rapidly codified by the new order as Paris assumed its position, revolutions notwithstanding, as *the* capital of the nineteenth century. At the same time the commanding heights of the new wine economy loomed over all social life, and authorised the sequence of dishes on its own terms: steely white wines from the north to join the soup and fish at the outset; heavy old reds from Burgundy and the Rhône to partner the blood-heavy

dark meats; a meal hinged on the cheese and the lighter, clearer red of the claret; then the succulent Sauternes alongside the sweet dishes. Luxury lives in freedom, but to be luxurious and free, there must be rules.

The massive culinary architecture corroborated the luxury of the Hôtels Splendides, Magnifiques, Ritz and Royaux where it was built. No doubt, it didn't run menus all its own way. A + 2b in English county hotels meant, until recently, roast beef, Yorkshire pud and two sodden veg. But the Parisian menu stood and stands as the dominant type of gastronomic luxury, even though the tides of kitchen globalisation now erode it as they flow from many oceans, the Chinese, the Southern Mediterranean, the Caribbean.

Meals define and quote other meals; each meal is a congeries of tastes and meanings folded upon itself in many layers and allusions. The Rat's picnic is a strongly English affair and a picnic is at once echo and subversion of *haute cuisine*. Inexplicably the Rat has omitted the strawberries and cream and the Bakewell tart anybody else would have packed in 1908 (sweetness plus dairy products or cereal), while he correctly observes the other gastronomic balances as a young gentleman-about-town-or-country. But this is also a meal eaten sitting on the grass and as such is a deliberate refusal of the proprieties of the table. That's the fun of it. You can stretch across the cloth in a way forbidden at the dining table; you can mix up courses and drop bits of food with impunity; you can use a teaspoon to finish off the paté and your fingers to fish out a gherkin; and you can pile together all the thrillingly different meats in the hamper and simply gorge away.

Picnics are part of the grand reversal of things which happen on vacation, never more so than at the seaside. At the seaside, after all, the visit to the harbour[29] was required of any devout admirer of Poussin, Vernet and Claude. Down at the harbour, one could watch the fishing fleet bring in its catch to the quiet quays on the other side of whose walls the great seas banged and ran. Down at the harbour one can eat any old how; one can eat *on the move*.

By the harbour the everyday snacks of its labour force became the casual refreshment of the conscientiously idle visitors; oysters had always gone down a treat in the city, both cooked and raw; the seaside turned them into a dish to be eaten in the open air or at the inn counter. Beside them appeared the pintpots of pink boiled shrimps, the whelks, mussels, miniature clams and saucers of cockles which are the diminutive shellfish of the British coastline. Over on the western side of the water, of course, the shellfish, like all the fish and all of life, were vaster by far, and up and down the coast of Maine and on the eponymous Cape of Cod itself, eating fish with one's fingers became a staple of the boardwalk.

Even so, the imperious order of things held. The British quickly made a meal out of the newly disembarked fish. They whipped a batter of eggs and milk, flour and fat, dipped the amazing plenty of cod[30] in it and fried the result with a handful of sliced potatoes. The cooked combination was then soused in salt and vinegar and turned into a full-blown main course with a dominant bland and savoury protein, accompanied by a cereal and vegetable content and placed upon a tablecloth made of newspaper. Fish and chips were incarnated as the favourite dish of the English working class and the leading invention of the industrialisation of its cuisine. It was fast and easy to cook; it could be prepared in large quantities for long queues of hungry people; it was very cheap. You ate as you walked. From the 1880s onwards, fish and chip shops sprouted up and down the coastline of England but most especially in the North where the working class worked and took their vacations and had their pride, *and* didn't give a curse that this great staple of their sojourn in Blackpool and Skegness would not be thought of as quite the thing by the genteel promenaders on the front at Bournemouth.

For some years, fish and chips lacked a dessert in order to make up the full meal. Ice cream filled the bill. It was sweet, cheap and filling. Like all sweet and milky foods, it had a childish taste and colour to it, especially with the addition of strawberries or chocolate, and as we have noted, on holiday childish pleasures play best.

Ice cream has a surprisingly long history,[31] although it had to wait for mechanical refrigeration in order to find its industrial processing. The essential instrument, ice, was traded as a commodity in second millennium BC China. Although it only turns up in early modern European ledgers in the fifteenth century, it was cut and hauled to the homes of wealthy Romans in Augustus's day. The Italians devised dishes of crushed ice served beneath soft fruits – peaches, summer berries – and by the end of the seventeenth century had learned to freeze the contents of an iron bucket placed inside a wooden one packed with ice and saltpetre.

It is a pleasure to know that the Italians are indeed the original ice cream merchants and that by the beginning of the eighteenth century, brand leaders the Neapolitans had learned to combine vanilla, strawberry and chocolate ices in their famous trinity. But the mass production of ice cream was, as one would expect, part of the development of a world cuisine[32] which is another of the all-shaping inheritances we take from the nineteenth century.

It was in the United States that refrigeration was most largely pioneered. The Chicago stockyards had to preserve their meat on the long railroad east and the first rail car chilled with natural ice had brought butter from Ogdensburg to Boston in 1851. The year before an expatriate Scot in Australia had vapourised and compressed ether to contrive a mechanical fridge. Ten years later a French engineer called Carré did the job better with ammonia. Before the end of the century, Joe Lyons had set up his enormous teashops in the Strand and Regent Street and was serving ice cream as well as chilled cucumber sandwiches to full houses. As usual, warfare accelerated innovation and production much more rapidly than peacetime and after 1919 Thomas Wall and Lyons sent their busy tricyclists along the seafronts of every suitable town while the same thing happened down the New Jersey coastline, and a penny cornet could be purchased wherever one cared, in Wall's slogan, to 'stop me and buy one'.[33]

Vacation food is luxurious in virtue of its bulk and stateliness (the ceremonious bringing together of society to worship at the gluttonous shine of the Grand), and is equally luxurious in the happy jumble of categories and flouting of good manners as you eat with your fingers on the beach front. In all this, the unignorable precepts are that the food must be filling; must mix sweet and savoury; must be tasty; must provide something to drink ('lemonadesodawater … Chardonnay, Champagne'); must include company. Richard Hoggart, as ever, is both shrewd and affectionate in the way he catches from his own memory the distinctions of value made by the poor about their own food in the northern England of the 1920s, by which time canned goods were fully established as a staple of a working class battling to feed itself better than its predecessors. Even in the grimmest days of slump after 1929, the class enjoyed much more bulk and choice than its grandparents.

'Something tasty' is the phrase in feeding: something solid, preferably meaty, and with a well-defined flavour. The tastiness is increased by a liberal use of sauces and pickles, notably tomato sauce and piccalilli. I used to notice that in the flusher early years of married life my relatives were often frying at tea-times – chops, steak, kidney, chips... The emphasis on tastiness shows itself most clearly in the need to provide 'something for tea', at week-end if not each day. There is a great range of favourite savouries, often by-products – black puddings, pig's feet, liver, cowheel, tripe, polony, 'ducks', chitterlings (and for special occasions pork-pies, which are extremely popular); and the fishmonger's savouries – shrimps, roe, kippers and mussels... At the week-end we lived largely, like everyone else except the very poor, and Sunday tea was the peak. By six on that evening the middens up the back had a fine topcoat of empty salmon and fruit tins. Pineapple was the most popular because, in that period of what now seems extraordinarily cheap canned fruit, it could be bought for a few pence (there was a recurrent story that it was really flavoured turnip). Peaches and apricots were more expensive and needed something approaching an occasion – a birthday or a sudden visit by relatives from a few miles away. The salmon was delicious, especially the red middle-cut; I still find it far 'tastier' than fresh salmon.[34]

Pretty well everything about the home (and homely) cooking of a whole class is in that splendid paragraph. If tastiness wasn't there in the original, it was added by way of spicy bottled sauce. If we stick to 'tastiness' as one measure of satisfying food (where tasty applies to savouries) and what one might call 'thick sweetness' of that intense, glutinous kind to be found in all canned fruits or the orange tea made with a very strong brew allied to condensed milk, then one is close to the class gastronomy in hand and the meals it looked for in Blackpool.

Canned meats made for easy, flavoursome, tender stews; canned puddings for saccharine-sweet heavy puddings; condensed milk for almost chewable mugs and cups of tea. Fish and chips provided the outdoor convenience lunch or late supper to which 'high tea' of fried meats from Hoggart's menu or stew built out of Heinz famous 57 varieties was the day's holiday centrepiece. The great abstracts of nineteenth-century history – industrialisation, urbanisation, democratisation – find their precipitate in the big eating of the new industrial working class beside the seaside. The menus formed in England at Blackpool and Scarborough, Margate and Yarmouth became set for the better part of the long century of which the little report in Hoggart's great book is barely the halfway mark. You can still eat these meals in Weymouth or Redcar; you can eat them in Boulogne or on the Costa Brava.

The lubricant of this massive shifting of bulk food was, in Britain, tea. Beer made its menfolk drunk on one, perhaps two evenings a week. Tea was what fuelled the labouring body's need to sweat, and having become abruptly cheaper with imports from India during the nineteenth century (replacing the Chinese product which continued as a refined taste), thickly sweetened tea became the symbol of hospitality between strangers and the gift of welcome to friends. Even when the sign of the café began to appear in Winter Gardens and the like towards the end of the old Queen's reign, tea and teas were what cafés mostly sold in Britain. And it continued to be so until only yesterday.

PORT NAVAS, Cornwall **TREWINCE COUNTRY**
near Falmouth   **HOUSE HOTEL**
         Constantine 268
This hotel is still a rather happy-go-lucky country house.
You may even be late for dinner; and dinner may be late for
you. When Mrs. Myers is cooking, as she usually is, the food
is very good. Among her specialities are flambé pineapple,
tournedos Béarnaise and a fish dish called Rizzi Pizzi. Lunch,
8/6 to 10/6; dinner, up to 15/-, including crêpes Suzette;
if you want à la carte it can be arranged, but consult Mrs.
Myers beforehand. Among à la carte items at 8/6 have
been duck Bigarade, casserole of pheasant in wine and fillet
steak. Good coffee. Small dining-room, so telephone.
Club licence; brief wine list, starting with red ordinaire and
Beaujolais at 10/-; among dearer wines the Piesporter (21/-)
and Pouilly (15/6) have been tested and approved. Wat-
ney's draught bitter. Bed and breakfast from 25/-; full
board from 11½ guineas. Normally closed October to
March. (*App. G. Smallwood; J. M.; G. A. Briggs; V. & A.
Mitton; R. S. Brewer; John Engleheart; P. & C. Hannam; A.
G. L. Shaw.*)   **Map 8**

Figure 4.3 Extract from the 1961–2 *Good Food Guide*

This is a structural history. The dream of luxury goes back a long way and finds its embodiments according to different times and places. Renaissance luxury is not ours, although ours retains its traces of that gilded gorgeousness. Class history is what we have to inherit from the days in which the early railway trains disgorged into Brighton and Atlantic City. The industrial food of capitalism and its voracity for profit brought the dishes I describe, and local culture, opportunity, time and chance did the rest.

Globalisation, we say, will make all dishes the same. But if we look around us, it has made them all different, never more so than in the last twenty years. And if we go back to the moment at which, so to say, the past traditionalised itself at the very moment of its inception, the moment which is the parturition of the present, almost exactly when Thomas Cook's Temperance picnickers set off to Loughborough in 1841, then we find that, as ever, globalisation must pass through the filters of localism and issue as what culture makes of it.

It is a cheerful story, this one of the making of the vacationers' menu, its plenty and flavour. It is a tale defined by social class as well as by nation and location. As told here, it misses out the extortion and meanness of restaurateur and boarding house-keepers, as it also misses out the ruthlessness with which the 'paying guests' were expelled from shelter after breakfast into the worst seaside weather could do until readmitted for high tea or evening meal. Cafés and chophouses were places to stay out of the rain and places in which visitors might once again be squeezed for every penny saved for the vacation by a local people all of whose annual earnings must be packed into a few weeks' uncertain sunshine.

The tale of luxury food is, however, a tale told by that necessary angel inside all of us who cherishes the dream of paradise and the good life lived there. And so, after the perfect picnic or before the edenic supper …

V

… why then, enjoy a little heavenly recreation …

In the terrific earthquake of cultural reformation in the nineteenth century, new money, old corruption and class struggle jostled to devise the cultural forms which would contain and express this unprecedented rout. The novel wall space upon which the crowded fresco of the day was painted was no longer housed in the apse and chancel; it was lived, danced and written in the kingdom of leisure. Leisure, marked off and counted as vacations ('vacant' space and time) was the realm won by labour, conceded by capital, always open to the rich, where men and women could inscribe the shapes and rhythms of a corner of life they could call their own.

Luxury is the dance of leisure. As we have seen, luxury is compounded in the dwelling, its food and fashion, and in something vaguer and more circumambient which I shall call, a bit uneasily, ecstatic freedom. Ecstatic freedom is a *game* (it may be dangerous but mustn't be lethal) and the good life seeks out the luxury of games as a picture of perfect correspondence between the social order of the match and one's own impulse to expression. Social role and personal identity coincide and, if we are lucky, open at their centre into happiness. The greatest games codified during the defining half century of early capitalism made and still make this transfiguration feasible. Thus football, most potent of all games, so cheap, so simple, catches in its figures the social divisions of labour (each player has a special task assigned), repudiates economic rewards and transmutes work into creation, regulation into spontaneity, resentment into delight.

For nearly a century the economic rewards of sport were merely equivalent to the local wages. The reward for the stars was symbolic and passionate: they were admired in the streets of their town. Then capitalism, as ever, broke into the sanctuary of sport and turned everything into gold.

Games and sports still retain some residue of their formative values. Plenty of people pour capital into sports clubs without any expectation of a dividend. In that special enclave of leisure time marked off for vacations, in the realm of freedom and spontaneous making, games are like works of art.

As one would expect, the games themselves were shaped out of the vernacular iconography of their context. Golf courses reproduce the sand, the whin, the water and the perfect turf of the Scottish seasides where they were born. Football was the game closest to reproducing industrial processes: the huge stands *looked* like factories; the huge crowds looked like men going through factory gates; the endless data produced by the game – goals, spectators, points – were analysed like industrial statistics. The game itself, by happy chance and creative genius, came to signify the spontaneous expression of men joined together in friendly antagonism for strictly non-productive, gleefully pointless activity. Football, like art, once embodied a critique of capitalist values even while it grew out of them. It had the edge on art as well because it created no product, could not be bought for any price, and retained the coarseness and excess of antique festivity long since smoothed out of aesthetics. Hence its luxuriousness, which of course one can rarely afford.

A similar development can be seen in the other great sporting inventions of the century, as they assumed their special place in leisure and vacation time: cricket, tennis, baseball, horse-racing. Each had its prehistory; each was necessarily remade out of practices already there; each took its characteristic form and features from the joint creative effort to turn competition into holidays and killing work into living play.

The happiest seaside work of art in England is the game of bowls. It brought together in the smallish space preferred by the elderly who contrived it a tiny garden with a perfect lawn of a kind made possible by heavy rollers and mechanical mowing machines. To this they added a little bargeboarded bungalow-pavilion of 'Seaside Queen Anne' design (red brick, white gables, a wooden cupola) and the grave, stately rhythms of a game adjusted to the creaking knees of the players. Cheap ebony of empire made the bowls themselves easily available to those sometime skilled artisans with Friendly Society insurance policies, and the same men, joined in 1910 or so by their wives, wore the leisure uniform celebrated by Manet and Renoir, white flannels and panama hats, as they went through their gentle rituals on the little green with its bright herbaceous borders. Slow grace; quiet sociability; perfect turf and bright flowers, a white pavilion; this is the scenery of life's last holiday, retirement.

The same sort of elegy could be written in a grander vein to celebrate the establishment of the mighty golf courses of the USA once the Scots had effected their export after 1880 or so. But there is no need. Their gorgeous prospects and attire speak their own poetry and are in any case built deeply into the self-congratulatory rhetoric of a nation's politics hardly separable from its advertising. Either way, the game of golf is a synonym for vacation and never more so than in the sun belt paradises arranged in California for the well-upholstered and vociferous elderly.

VI

Games unite the holidaymakers' two realms of sociability and solitude. In either location, the play's the thing. It sets off the luxurious moment by being freely chosen; by *not* being work; by being self-forgetful; by being physical and unrehearsed; by throwing off propriety. Games also have other, sometimes risky additions; they may admit strangers; they may be dangerous; they may be cruel.

Games, that is to say, are a formal, rule-governed family of practices, the meaning of which is to deny the rule of rules and to enjoin irresponsibility. They are presently taking a terrible pounding from the invasions of capital and its innate, destructive drive to turn innocence into investment and enter the gleeful irresponsibility of luxurious waste in the margins of profit. The consumer-and-vacationer fights back, as we saw, battling to do nothing and not pay for it, spending free time cheaply, turning early thrift into late luxury.

One would instinctively say that capital and luxury were made for each other. But it isn't so. Luxury, as we know, is compounded of its own long history, once sinful, subsequently blithe; always excessive, sometimes envious; tinged with danger; inherently a lark. These contradictory qualities resist the control, predictability and demand management capital must of its nature seek out. It is a surprising conclusion to come to but lessons about luxury learned from Renaissance princes, nineteenth-century grand hotels, Parisian cuisine, fish and chip shops and the local bowls league turn out to make a strong redoubt for the protection of our souls from absolute possession by the last enemy, totalitarian consumerism.

5

MAGNETIC DANGERS

I

We learn to feel from the past. Where else? Or perhaps it would be better put to say that we learn to feel by entering one of the many stories society offers within which we can live our lives.

These are stories in the most literal sense. Your parents, your teachers, all those whose immediate task it is to bring up children tell us in our childhood dozens of stories about what to do, how to be good, how to succeed, how to live as this, that, or the other kind of grown-up when the time comes: as student, lover, parent, wife; as doctor, shopkeeper, farmer, scientist; as leader, solitary, matriarch, sportswoman, playboy, hero, neurotic. Each of us learns to live a medley of the lives open to us and to inflect each narrative in our own way in order to match it, so far as possible, to what seems to us to suit ourselves.

Feeling in all this is then a matter of giving a form to experience by finding a feeling to go round it, and adjusting it until it fits sufficiently well. This is rarely a very certain business. Most of the time we have to work out what we truly feel quite slowly, and even then, as often as not, the feelings don't always fit, or are ambiguous and contradictory. The irresistible beauty of spontaneous feeling is exactly the rush of certainty it brings, carrying us over into action. Most of the time, the narrative of our society which we seek to enter and the feelings we seek to match to it are on rather wavering terms and only find a settlement out of habit. Unless you are very lucky, you learn, on the whole, a certain needful resignation to the feelings suitable to your job, your home, your friends.

This little sketch of the reciprocity of feeling and experience has been implied throughout this book. We take a battery of feelings towards an event; the event moves towards us, collides with us, and our feelings enfold it and make it intelligible. Sometimes the event is too much for the feelings, and their structure is blown open. We don't know what to feel.

This is the natural history of the passions. But they have of course a social history as well. The social history of the passions is also a history of evaluation: these feelings good, those feelings bad, and both evaluations change. Courage and heroism are cherished values, patriotism less so, and less so as well the military versions of courage and heroism. As redemption has faded as a value, so has the passion of religious devotion; happiness has replaced it. It's said that the pursuit of happiness is absurd; happiness is a by-product of absorption in experience. But an awful lot of people go looking for it, never more so than on holiday.

The social history of the feelings[1] is a new kind of thing. Its evidence is largely the narratives of the past, especially a nation's official literature. But of course some of that literature is fictive and those parts which are purportedly objective records, like reports, diaries, journalism, logbooks, news broadcasts, are all pretty liable to local distortion and partiality. The point of this commonplace reminder is that if we are going to use the literature of the past as evidence of the making of the feelings, it will be as well to remember also that people use those stories imaginatively, which is to say experimentally, and in order to try out what it would be like to have such feelings as the narrative in question reports; whether one would have them oneself; whether one *ought* to have them (but didn't).

Such play is, as much as anything, the function of literature. Literature is a record of how to match feeling to eventuality, and an invitation to play with the record. There we can see the jostling current of feelings, as some begin to fade into residue, as new kinds of feeling (for the landscape, for instance) begin to come through, and as a certain range of feeling settles in as normal and predominant in a given epoch.[2]

As the urgency of subsistence retires for the wealthy half of the world's population, and the global game of tourism becomes so inclusive, it is possible, I believe, to understand the uses of tourism in something of the same kind of way as the uses of literacy. Tourism becomes a way of experimenting with feelings without having to live them too fully. Like literature, it offers a variety of alternative events around which we may seek to wrap feelings unfamiliar to us, and enticing in virtue of that very unfamiliarity: awe, perhaps, vertiginous excitement, gregarious gaiety, solitary rapture, homesickness, terror. (It should be obvious what a very long way such experiments are from anything usefully to be comprehended by the idea of 'consumption'.)

Like other games and like literature, vacations may be used to provide us with versions of ourselves we would like to try out for various reasons (the libertine, the glutton, the painter, the lover, the life-and-soul-of-the-party) but with longer-lasting consequences removed. You put your sobriety back on, back home.

In some such games, in the movie or the novel, or on the vacation, we can experiment with 'a powerful rendering of life as we most deeply do not want it'. The phrase is Clifford Geertz's,[3] and he applies it to the wild and playful ritual of the usually composed and correct Balinese when they hold a cockfight:

> The cockfight enables the Balinese, as, read and reread, *Macbeth* enables us, to see a dimension of his own subjectivity. As he watches fight after fight, with the active watching of an owner or a bettor (for cockfighting has no more interest as a pure spectator sport than does croquet or dog racing) he grows familiar with it and what it has to say to him, much as the attentive listener to string quartets or the absorbed viewer of a still life grows slowly more familiar with them in a way which opens his subjectivity to himself.
>
> Yet, because – in another of those paradoxes ... which haunt aesthetics – that subjectivity does not properly exist until it is thus organised, art forms generate and regenerate the very subjectivity they pretend only to display.

And it is so, I shall claim, on vacation. But in this case, the subjectivity which one finds (or seeks, or invents) for the vacation has even less of a proper existence than the aspect of Macbeth or of the demented gambler at the cockfight which one has lurking in the dark inside one. This, no doubt, is something to do with modernity. The picture people have of themselves is, the theorists of modernity tell us,[4] more fluid and provisional than it used to be. The discussions about identity are quickened by a keen sense that identity is partly there to be invented, that an individual's choice may have something to do with it, that the past has not fixed it for ever. And so, in 'free', leisure or vacation time, now more than ever, people turn to the variety of human experience and speculate on how to sample some more of it for themselves.

II

They can only do so by trying out upon themselves the tales of the past which catch their eye. This may not be a single such tale. It is more likely to be what might be called a 'value-realm', in which a number of similar sorts of story have gathered and concentrated into an essence, laying down a kind of deposit, like veins of ore, in the geomorphology of culture. The deposits remain there, glowing, until somebody picks up this imaginative radio-activity and turns it again into energy.

Consequently, when a present-day tourist plans a vacation, the first point of which is that it *not* be luxurious (or, as it might be put, one which rediscovers the unadorned luxuries of nature) and the second, that it not be safe either, he or she hunts for models in the past who were, at first sight, deadly serious and certainly not enduring the ravages of the North and South Poles, the Capes, the Sahara or the rainforest for fun.

As is often the case, however, popular mythology is capable of subtle affinity and when otherwise well-to-do and comfortably-living tourists go off in search of difficulty, discomfort and more or less serious danger, their cheerful combination of temerity, foolhardiness, larky high-spirits, moral resourcefulness, cheek and genuine bravery is not so very far away from George Mallory, Robert Falcon Scott, Amy Johnson and Wilfred Thesiger, whose books they put into the back of their ancient transport.

There have always been such people on holiday, since holidays began. The danger of the Alps or the Mosque was as much part of their delights to Boswell and Lady Mary Wortley Montagu as was their sublimity. But it is worth speculating that the sharp rise in their recent numbers represents a deliberate searching out of certain feelings-and-values made residual by the comforts of modern technology and its well-upholstered security systems. The experience of immediate physical danger, even on a bad day for urban muggings or guerrilla irruption, has vanished from most lives. Beyond that pub truism, there is a more pervasive absence in everyday labour of efficacious physical action. It is increasingly difficult, in the absence of war, to find out a plausible narrative in which purpose and physicality combine in a fulfilling kind of way. This surely is the explanation for the sharp rise in those kinds of tour vacations expressly undertaken to sample one or more of the immediately natural kinds of danger and of nature's violence, as rediscovered (naturally, and by exaggerated contrivance) well outside the limits of conventional safety.

Such safety is conferred by the softnesses of culture; by the social order and its legislation; by the comforts of technology and its subjugation of distance; by the steady diminution of the unknown world. The slopes of Everest became, notoriously, so littered with the garbage of half a thousand successful and fatal ascents that in 1997 a party went almost to the terrible summit, tidying up. By the same token, the subject of anthropology became, for a season, so irresistible that remote and solitude-loving people, far from being surprised and curious at visitors from upriver, began to ask them to go away. And as for the Seven Seas, or for the trackless deserts, there is no corner of them but washes up and down the banal picnic rubbish of human travel upon its watery or sandy waves.

There are countless dirges sung about human pollution and the suburbanisation of the wilderness. This book must, for truth's and duty's sakes, sing a few. But the globe remains pretty big and nature herself, as we shall see, still plentifully supplied with the power to awe and annihilate. So when our contemporary tourists reach for their intrepidity along with their knapsacks they catch up for re-enactment a school of narratives from not so very far back and still capable of active and convincing embodiment. They set out to find action, physicality, danger and discomfort, as well as reminders of ardour and of desperate glory, along the outer limits of the globe, its ultimate *Thule* and the peoples who live there. They go to the jungle, the desert, the mountains, the ice and the ocean. They go deliberately unprepared, with the simple, even primitive equipment of predecessors two, three or four generations ago, in order *not* to win the easy victory over the elements which modern technology can (nearly) always promise, and they go so artlessly in order not to poison the wilderness with rubbish which bio-chemistry cannot degrade. They go to sea under canvas and in clinker-built boats; they go to the highest mountains without oxygen and in twos; they cross the desert once again by camel or in an ancient Land Rover; and they try (and fail) to walk across the Antarctic.

There is something touching and admirable in this determination to dissolve the tourist role back into the traveller's. Indeed, as I suggested earlier, it isn't a distinction which ever holds very fast. We heard Schama speak a bit sarcastically of the 'protected dangers' of the trampers-after-nature in Fontainebleau, and he would say the same no doubt of whale-watching vacations off Cape Cod at the present time. But the whale-watchers, Melville in mind, are paying a small, imaginative homage to the great novelist's terrific commemoration of his subject, while no doubt keeping themselves as well as keeping the whales safe, as all part of the package. At the same time, vacation sportsmen and women, tourist explorers of the desert and jungle botanists on their holidays, even weekend sailors out of Pin Mill and Hyannis make unwritten poems of their experiences and the feelings which shape them. They copy a bit of life out of the records of their ancestors whose books, as like as not, they keep in the cabin.

There's a penetrating remark in Francis Spufford's splendid study of the way the Antarctic[5] has worked upon our imaginations since tourists first followed explorers by way of the explorer's stories. Spufford writes:

> Implicit in [his book] is the assumption that ideas lose their form when they decay, yet do not necessarily lose their place in the mentality of an age. They turn to imaginative compost. Complex reasoning lives on, perhaps, as a couple of self-evident maxims. A taste it took a book to establish, and many more to justify, becomes the single word 'attractive' in a tourist guide. Schools

of thought, life's works, artistic endeavours, all find their ultimate destination in a habit of vision scarcely worth discussion.

Kant's *Critique of Judgement*, Burke's *Essay on the Sublime and Beautiful*, the eighteenth-century's guidebooks to the Lakes together made for the habit of vision which finds a view of Coniston beautiful. *The Boyhood of Raleigh* is the nineteenth-century painting depicting the young explorer listening to the tales of adventure which fired him up to make the fearful ventures himself.

Our danger-hunters have been shaped by the five centuries of tales of exploration since Columbus set out. More particularly, in Britain they have been shaped by the colossal enterprise of Empire, and in North America by the comparable scale of possession and colonisation. The same passionate stories were also circulated, with surprising success, by the British in those extensive territories to which they carried their civilising mission, as so many post-colonial writers have unironically testified.

More particularly still, as literacy became universal and the habit of reading general from the 1820s or so onwards,[6] the passions and associated values of an English élite assumed formative power in the literature of Empire, in the national ardour which subtended it, and the making of a highly peculiar, localised version of heroism which turned out to have remarkable purchase as a cultural export.

No heroism (then) without brave manliness, but no heroism either, it emerged, without more than a touch of such womanly attributes as tenderness for others, a keen sensitivity to the awesomeness of nature, a recognition (even) of the limitations of English manliness, which gave rise in turn to a recognition of what may be preferable in ways of life very different from those lived in English boarding schools.

The danger-hunting holidaymaker grows out of this compost. It was laid down in the seafaring stories of Joseph Conrad, a Polish Master Mariner of the Mercantile Marine whose third language was English. In the same stuff we find the mountaineering biographies and attitudes of, say, Edmund Whymper, first up the Matterhorn, and of George Mallory, who may or may not have been the first climber to reach the summit of Everest. In the mulch, we shall detect the spoor of Richard Burton and Montague Speke, trekking across Africa through a mixture of the densest jungle, desert and bare mountain in the walking attire of the well-prepared English gentleman-botanist – stout boots enhanced with puttees, a Norfolk jacket with deep, well-loaded pockets, waterproof cape, wide-brimmed hat, spyglass. Burton punctuates his expeditions with compulsive copulation, Speke, sleeping on the ground in torrential rain, wakes to find a medium-sized beetle well into the channels of his ear and chewing its way audibly towards his tympanum. After trying several times to sluice it out with a solution of melted butter and hot water, in desperation Speke twists the point of his knife deep into his inner ear, puncturing it as he does so, and skewers the beetle on the point, subsequently washing it out in bits. Thereafter his troop of African bearers, laden with the expedition's baggage, is reduced to helpless giggles every time Speke, smitten with an awful cold after the rain, blew his nose so that the air whistled shrilly through the punctured drum.

It is of course Speke himself who tells the tale, and helps initiate the sacred tradition of the travelling English explorer and his impregnable *sangfroid*. Compounded of nonchalance, understatement, resolution, courage, pitilessness and the crazy toxin of imperial romanticism, an eerie ghost walked the century from 1850 to 1950 and took over the minds and hearts of as varied a bunch of public and elementary school Englishmen and women as Robert Scott and Petty Officer Evans, George Mallory and W.H.R. Rivers, Wilfred Thesiger and D.H. Lawrence, Peter Fleming and Gertrude Bell, Robert Byron and Freya Stark. These remarkable men and women move in their turn as ghostly presences in the lives of a new generation of traveller-tourists, still lending to their heirs their expressive combination of cheerful wonder and curiosity allied to deadpan understatement.

It is a complex attitude towards the world and one can see that it can hardly be shared with even the most sympathetic holidaymaker. For it involves a repudiation of all the luxuriast goes to find: self-indulgence, indolence, homeliness, even good weather and balmy nature. The old explorers and their ascetic followers reject all this, as they must, in the name of their very opposites. Even in their opposition, however, the iron system of ethical difference holds, and in virtue of this very opposition, asceticism collapses into luxury, austerity becomes a riot of extremism. A value is only defensible in terms of its opposite. Left to itself, in other words, any moral value turns into an excess. That is why the Ancients made so much of the Golden Mean.

That there are therefore moral lessons in this antinomous rapture is a relief to us moralists. They rescue this chapter for relevance and, thank goodness, pit it against the outright hedonist. After all, even the laziest tourist takes a travel book down to the beach at Amalfi, and there, amid the charred bodies and bikinis laid out on canvas strips to barbecue in the sun, he and she read raptly of the extremes of heat and cold, monsoon and torrid sun, exposure at the edge of life and death, starvation voluntarily tempted. They read such things, there and then, to keep sobriety in reach and the scarey side of life in view.

III

This is the source of the irresistible charm of the bad weather book, especially on vacation. Protected absolutely from danger and terror, one longs to taste them.

> Perhaps the place is the foot of a cliff in the dark, so cold and still that the breath of the travellers crystallises and falls to the snow in showers, so cold that their clothes will freeze at impossible angles if they do not keep their limbs moving ...[7]

Perhaps the place is the fishing boat caught in the perfect storm[8] when two massive disturbances of the heavens coincide off Cape Cod in 1991, and we watch in horrified entrancement as 90-foot waves stove in the windows, pour through the fastened hatches, flood the dreadfully tiny spaces below, rush upon nostrils and throats and crush them with water until consciousness drifts upon the darkening flood, and perhaps the six sailors discover that the end of things is not so bad after all ...

... Or perhaps we face the Arabian desert with Wilfred Thesiger, a mere fifty years ago. Driven by his relentlessness, akin to Burton's, Scott's or Fleming's, we have set out to cross the enormous wastes of the Empty Quarter of Arabia in the company of a handful of the Bedu who are our guides. Water will be ten days away, and in temperatures of up to 120° we will have at most a quart a day of horrible-tasting, warm, salty, brackish, dirty liquid to drink. After shitting, we will use the sands as an astringent for our arms and douche our hands in a sudden cascade of camel urine. We will chew dry dates and eat a smelly little ball of baked flour. And we will lurch on our camel's back three, four miles an hour for seventy days, dismounting to haul and shove the bellowing beasts up the steep, soft sides of 70-foot dunes, treading gingerly over the deadly crust of the Umm al Samim quicksands, glorying at last in a banquet of oryx meat, once the beast has been shot and butchered with blunt knives and no water, lying on the gritty blood-soaked sand under a thick fur of black flies.

Those who follow Thesiger in fact and those who merely follow him in imagination put on the guise of the original and find in it an aspect of their subjectivity. Objectivity also, perhaps to their surprise, They learn a little of why Thesiger did it. They may sharpen the pleasure by *not* journeying quite as he did – the actual traveller looking for trouble today in the Yemen may have a jeep, the imaginary one shudders at the thought of the Bedu toilet, puts down the book and goes for a drink. In either case, however, the power of comparison forces home its truths. For the reader, the comparison is made by discrepancy, and *that* is the pleasure. 'What effort, what stamina, what terrible patience, what *constitutions* those men had!' For the follower, the satisfaction is one of respectful emulation. One simply couldn't relive Thesiger's journey step for step: the place is busier. The positional good of firstness is lost for ever. But one can get close enough. The climate is as hostile as ever, the roads bad, food scarce, the people strange. Charles Taylor, philosopher puzzling out the moral force of comparison, its capacity to reveal truth, observes:

> other-understanding is always comparative ... We only liberate the others and 'let them be' when we can identify and articulate a contrast between their understanding and ours ... We embark on the comparativist enterprise ...

Figure 5.1   Desert sands at sunset

because of some deep intuition about the equal value of culture.[9]

Reading Thesiger or retracing his footsteps in actuality bears this out. Not only does he teach us about and recreate the magic of the desert, he leads us close to the Bedu, whom he loves. They in turn teach us about – as they say – the politics and the ethics of difference. They teach us the natural history of difference as well. For Thesiger brings out beautifully how the barrenness of the desert, its heat and aridity together bake the moral as well as the visible features of the Bedu men (this being the Kingdom of Islam, we never even glimpse their women).

The geography requires their endurance. The deserts exact their hardiness. The struggle for food and transport creates their courage in battle. The arbitrariness of tribal membership defines and purifies their altruism, loyalty and vengefulness. No wonder that the desert church, the harsh and stoical creed of Islam frames this experience of the world in its finished vision. No wonder, even, that Thesiger scarcely grimaces at its savage justice, an adulterous woman beheaded, a stray shot in the palm of a hand avenged by blowing away the fingers of a captured boy guilty only of the right, the wrong relatives.

In Paul Fussell's study of travel-writing,[10] already praised in these pages, he has a chapter entitled 'I Hate it Here', in which he assembles a little scrapbook of quotations from his chosen authors – W.H. Auden, George Orwell, Evelyn Waugh, Christopher Isherwood, D.H. Lawrence – in order to show how deeply the fashion went to denigrate England (rather than Britain) as filthy, damp, grey, dreary and so forth, thus requiring those who thought like this always to be at the ready for off, for getting to France (at least), or better, to somewhere more remote, more exotic but also more elemental in its way of life; more natural, naturally, because simpler, less industrial, freer, more dignified, permitting one to lose one's ghastly conventionality and other people's even ghastlier pretensions and inauthenticity.

The attitude was powerful. There was, there is, plenty of truth in such attitudes. It also sorted easily with something of the same kind in a more general modernism. The modernism which shaped itself into a critique of its world immediately after the First World War was deeply pessimistic, as well it might be. Its most lasting works of art – T.S. Eliot's *Waste Land*, say, or Stravinsky's *Rite of Spring* – sentimentally combined an intense dislike of modern city life, its sterile meaninglessness, with an urgent longing for remote ways of life and their ritual grace and shapelessness.

Thesiger shares fiercely these feelings of revulsion and attraction. He has been through another world war of even more terrible slaughter, this time including millions of civilians. The machinery for which he expresses such loathing turned out to include the nuclear fissile bomb and the gas chamber. He abhorred the coming of modern technology, the search for oil which would, he knew, bring with it petrol-driven transport, movie-houses and awaken the ferocious avarice of poor sheikhs.

> Here life moved in time with the past. These people still valued leisure and courtesy and conversation. They did not live their lives at second hand, dependent on cinemas and wireless. I would willingly have consorted with them, but I now wore European clothes. As I wandered through [Dibai] I knew that they regarded me as an intruder; I myself felt that I was little better than a tourist.[11]

For all but a few pages in the book, Thesiger has worn the minimal Bedu clothes, gone barefoot, slept on the cold desert floor with a single blanket, carried his loaded .303 rifle by its muzzle, walked and ridden with his Bedu comrades and friends. He has come to revere their extraordinary endurance; when it rains heavily his youthful friend (and equal), the faithful Bin Kabina, tells him:

> that he only remembered three springs in his life. Occasional springtimes such as these were all the Bedu ever knew of the gentleness of life. A few years' relief from the anxiety of want was all they ever hoped for. It seemed to me pathetically little and yet I knew that magnificently it was enough.[12]

Thesiger, in the manner of the good anthropologist (he describes himself as an explorer), comes also to understand and condone the savagely retributive justice of the Bedu, for in a country with no settled system of law, the doctrine of a life for a life is the only way to conclude a conflict and satisfy hatred.

Finally, he decides that in spite of empire, in spite of his official endeavours on behalf of map-making and locust control, he had gone

> to find peace in the hardships of desert travel and the company of desert peoples. I set myself a goal on these journeys, and although the goal itself was unimportant, its attainment had to be worth every effort and sacrifice,[13]

worth it also, one might add, for the Bedu who happily risked their own lives for Thesiger's goal because they had nothing better to do and because, in Thesiger's words, 'the harder the way the more worthwhile the journey'. He is the more relieved that he brought it off by camel and not by car because cars made things too easy, yet 'to have done the journey on a camel when I could have done it in a car would have turned the venture into a stunt'.[14]

'Turned the venture into a stunt'. One sees a little what he means. All the same, plenty of people might make his journey by car and feel the journey to be worthwhile. So, too, plenty of people, sharing an aversion to machinery or luxury, might refuse the easy way for the sake of the sport without cheapening their satisfaction. Thesiger can afford his absolutism. As he recognises, he is himself harbinger of an automobile future, but he goes on nevertheless, last exactly because first. In making his journey his way, however, he ties together the experience, the values and the feelings. You could go now by Land Rover, much easier than by Thesiger's camel but still damn difficult, and you could feel you'd done *something* and done it, in part, the way he did it; felt and seen for yourself the freedom of the desert, its incomparable array of colours, the majesty of the dunes, the thrilling, bitter water-hole.

There were, after all, numerous young men and a few young women like him. Peter Fleming rode from Peking to Kashmir in the company of a handsome Swiss woman called Kini, and while there were stretches of his road on which he and she travelled by truck, the *Daily Telegraph* reviewer praised his book of the trip[15] in the classical trope that 'no modern traveller had made so romantic a journey before, none has made one since'. Romantic journeys are always on the point of vanishing and the way of life the travellers encounter is always on the edge of extinction.

Fleming himself fairly glows with romance. Ian's brother (but a much better writer), foreign correspondent for *The Times* (on six-month leave during which he makes his journey purportedly to see what is happening to modern politics where revolutionary Russia meets imperialist Japan), later married to the world-famous actress Celia Johnson, Peter Fleming carries off his tale in a decidedly more vacationing spirit than Thesiger's agonised renunciation of Europe. Maybe he is more frankly a tourist, which is to say he sees privation as temporary, sharpening the pleasures of the comforts to which he will return. Thesiger is an all-Englishman who nonetheless disappears completely into the sunburned skin and loincloth of a Bedu. He is close kin to John Buchan's clubland hero, Sandy Arbuthnot, Lord Clanroyden.

Fleming stays English all the way. He plays patience all the way, setting out the cards on his upturned trunk. He is laconic, amused, caustic, overstatingly understated.

> A semi-circle of scrofulous children screamed with delight outside a butcher's shop where a sheep was having its throat cut. On the summit of a cliff over-looking the village a small and presumably devout party beat enigmatically and monotonously upon a gong. Rumours began to run about that we should not leave until the next day.[16]

The rhythm of the day is marked only by the rhythm of Fleming's notation, a dying sheep here, a gong-bashing there, here today, gone (maybe) tomorrow.

The likeness to Thesiger is more than passing. Along with Fleming's mild exasperation, there is the same easy-goingness with the ways of life through which he moves, the same contained sense of the sublimity of his surroundings, the same tolerance of the awful, exigent and only diet (fatty, watery stews, rice and tea with rancid butter in it, in his case). Triumph and disaster are not even impostors to either man; they are abstractions from the always *interesting* dangers to hand, now mud, now snow, now being lost on the vast, stony plain of the Borodishin, now calmly meeting the local Consul-General, with whom he had of course been at Oxford, high in the mountains, learning from him that the Foreign Secretary had been inquiring anxiously of their whereabouts ('It was news to us that we had been lost. We had completed the course in bogey or under …'[17]).

Unlike Thesiger, however, Fleming keeps his English distance from the Mongolians. Thesiger, like so many of his predecessors, craves identity with his utterly other people, the Bedu. While he is with them, clad like them, as like as they are to die on the journey, he dissolves into their otherness even while remaining an English officer. Fleming, an inevitable pipe clenched in his teeth, watches all that there is to watch as an occasion for combining endurance with amusement. These people are foreign – as foreign as one can get. The context of their life is theirs. Be phlegmatic but find it funny (making us laugh as he does so). That'll see you through.

Such men are scattered about the pages of the literature of imperial travel. Robert Byron went driving beaten-up cars over broken roads to behold the sumptuous lapis lazuli in the great Friday mosque of Isfahan. Patrick Leigh Fermor first walked clean across Europe at the age of 18, and then went back, after a war spent in liaison with the partisans of the Greek islands,[18] to travel in the English tradition across northern Greece. Like Thesiger, like Fleming, and Byron, Leigh Fermor walked alongside ways of life said to be vanishing, and paid lavish tribute to their colour and variety.[19] All of them Oxford-and-Cambridge, gentlemanly English, they figured out a still-living style in which to visit foreign lands and come home again.

Not that their tributes were just occasions for courtesy. Each writer plays, in spite of himself, the scholarly guide. How else shall we find out about the world? Fleming and Byron made their explorations sixty years ago; Thesiger fifty; Leigh Fermor thirty-odd; the day before yesterday. Each found a new history and geography, glimpses of a new aesthetics. Each fashioned these into a sequence, and presented the sequence as a story about a humankind needing a new understanding because of its antique and unfamiliar way of life (we'd say 'culture' now). Each taught an English kind of tolerance, and tolerant curiosity. Each relished hardship and played up the playing down of danger. Each loved the landscape they had passed, and passed it on for others, even tourists, to find for themselves.

IV

'Fare forward, traveller,' the poet has told us already, and he goes on:

> There are other places
> Which also are the world's end, some at the sea jaws,
> Or over a dark lake, in a desert or a city -
> But this is the nearest in place and time,
> Now and in England.[20]

T.S. Eliot was looking for sacred places, places which concentrate sanctity, partly because of where they are and how they appear, partly because of what happened there and because of a long narrative tradition configuring the place. The guidebooks of desert places and wilderness already visited in this chapter mingle with the loneliness they found and loved the gritty certainty of *other people*. The mountains and the deserts proved surprisingly and reassuringly populous.

It is in this sense that these guidebooks are classics of everyday anthropology. But there are far more solitary dangers that draw men and women into a narrative tradition of an even more absolute kind. In some versions, the story may place them in danger on the most commonplace Sunday afternoon. The weekend sailor or mountaineer may risk or lose a life in full view of the picnickers. But for the moment we shall stay with those who seek what they shall find at the world's end. They have been fired and inspired by books of eschatology of a sort our homespun ethnographers are at pains to avoid. The story of travel, however, is not complete without them, they learned their passions from men (and in this case, men only) for whom the gesture was as much the thing as the dread solemnity of the place which insisted upon it.

The place in this case was the Pole, either one but, because colder, the South for preference. As Thesiger showed, it could have been, at a pinch, the desert but the absoluteness of the desert was unavoidably qualified by its being jolly well *home* to the Bedu. The only intelligent way to find it was the way they had found, and to ignore that would be to kill yourself. Of course, you might die in any case; but not out of ignorance or solitude.

The case with the Pole was different. Inuit apart, there was no-one to help; in the south, no-one at all. The Norwegians knew enough about the cold to fare better than the English, but nobody knew much. Ice, in this light, is better because even more ultimate and absolute than sand. Getting to it and across it is harder.

Spufford's study, already noted, of the imaginative power of ice is impossible to improve upon. Ice serves at this juncture of holiday history to name a completeness of sublimity, where nature is utterly untouchable by culture, where danger is synonymous with her terrible indifference. This cannot fail to magnetise any imagination not immune to the ideal of heroism. Heroes also take holidays. And if you take the right kind of holiday, you may find a touch of heroism in yourself.

Something like this must be the reason why a few people pay £40,000 to be taken by experienced guides as far up Everest as they can climb.[21] Something more openly competitive drove a group of women to make the trek to the North Pole in 1997. But it is not just a matter of emulation. Everybody knows the story of Odell looking up as the cloud cleared momentarily and seeing Mallory and Irvine, without oxygen, 'going strongly for the top'. Everybody also knows the terrible tale of mistakes and disasters which left Scott and his party dead and mutilated in their tent only eleven miles from refuge. Some writers blame Scott, for unreadiness, for incompetence, for bad temper, for misjudgement;[22] many more admire, even worship him for leadership, tenacity, resolution and, when it came to it, such written steadiness in the face of death as it looked at him from only a pace away.

I have known those last lines of his pretty well by heart since I was a little boy, and still they seem to me, for their mild provincial patriotism, their gallantry and grace, their not quite believable resignation and making-the-best-of-things even in such straits, unbearably fine and moving.

> We are weak, writing is difficult, but for my own sake I do not regret this journey, which has shown that Englishmen can endure hardships, help one another, and meet death with as great fortitude as ever in the past. We took risks, we knew we took them; things have come out against us, and therefore we have no cause for complaint, but bow to the will of Providence, determined still to do our best to the last.

And then, the last faltering postscript, 'for God's sake, look after our people ...'.

The world's end looks a long way for a vacation. But there are straight lines of feeling which still come through, by way of Fleming and Thesiger, the mad jokes and dry understatements of physical endeavour in two world wars, from that idealising Edwardianism. People who take two, three or four months off work nowadays to feel the amazing dry cold air of Himalaya or Antarctic sear the depths of their lungs and unfold their furthest warm-blooded tendrils with an involuntary gasp, have gone to see what *it was like*, like for the first men there, for Amundsen, for Scott, for Mawson, for Mallory and Irvine and then for those who came back later in triumph, for Edmund Hillary and Vivian Fuchs.

This is a visit to the very edges of regulated danger. You look down beside Niagara and cannot help searching for the places where, if you went over, you might just conceivably be safe. There isn't one. The imagination recoils at the moment at which the water drives you thunderously below the surface, and the eye takes over in relief, caught by the lovely rainbow iridescence hanging over the solid torrent.

After Niagara, it's easy to walk away down the path. For those who take the rather greater trouble to travel across Nepal or to McMurdo Sound, the physical facts are harder to turn your back upon. That, after all, is one good reason for going. It is 50°

below zero and even the modern parka cannot keep out such cold. One's lips split and eyelids freeze together. It's not as bad as Scott's face when the frost snapped its purple bites at the cheekbone ends, but bad enough for a reminder. The snow buggy won't die like his ponies died and become dog fodder, but it might break down. The solitude is immense; sometimes it stupefies, sometimes it inspires rapture. The colours of the ice are wonderful, 'Cambridge blue,' said Wilson, the expedition's water-colourist, but indigo, cobalt, emerald, pink, blood-red, blinding white-no-colour as well. 'The worst journey in the world,' said Apsley Cherry-Garrard who came back safely; 'surely the most dreadful place on earth,' said Scott.

The tourist turns away and comes home. But she has seen something about the ends of the earth, and learned something, too: about the natural sublime, and its awfulness; about the unignorability of physical facts as well, of cold, dazzle, terrible distances, all sobering ones in any case.[23]

As it happens, there is a very good novel about a polar holiday. In Arthur Ransome's *Winter Holiday*,[24] his celebrated seven children aged between about ten and sixteen, named after their sailing boats, Swallows, Amazons and the two Ds, are caught on an extended stay beside the English Lakes by the quarantine rules then strictly enforced by private boarding schools. With keen childhood memories of his own from the famous winter of 1895 when a coach and horses was driven across Coniston with horns blaring, Ransome equips his ideal team of friends with a perfect winter frost, days of high pressure and then a splendid blizzard. The climax of the novel is the search for the North Pole, and it is noticeable not only that Scott, by then a dependable item in *The Boys' Book of Heroes*, is never mentioned, but that the great Norwegian explorer Nansen, whom Scott visited for advice, gives the name of his famous explorer vessel the *Fram* to the houseboat similarly locked in the ice and belonging to the Amazons' wonderful Uncle Jim (Ransome's own persona in the book).

Uncle Jim has appointed a spot north of the lake to be the Pole. There is a race to be first there, not without a touch of real danger when the two children least versed in the ways of snow capsize their improvised ice-yacht and, with broken specs and mild lacerations speckling the snow, still win the day. Anxious adults, following the tracks, find all seven children warm and safe, a fire lit in the holiday cabin serving for Pole, the picnic hampers cached there thoroughly sampled. 'Shhh,' says Dorothea half-waking and immediately concerned for the others' sleep, 'shhh,' say the quiet-voiced elders reassuringly in reply.

The moral of all that is that children's games replay the deadlier serious games of grown-ups so that when they are grown up they will have learned those lessons and be able to apply them. Crudely put, perhaps, but about right. Ransome was very intelligent about children and about life (he was, by the way and among many things, foreign correspondent for the London *Daily News* throughout the Russian Revolution and married Trotsky's secretary). He knew that lessons are not 'applied' like this. But he saw, and wonderfully recreated, the happiness of children on holiday, with an ample space cleared of adults, when they have a really full, satisfying, not quite predictable story to play out.

Like children, of course, adults suffer a lousy holiday when the story of the game in hand doesn't have enough in it. Hence the magnetism of danger. Hence the grip of the game or the hobby which becomes a passion such that its pursuit invites dangers, and the dangers are at the heart of the game.

This is obviously true of sailing and of mountaineering. Both of them may take those who love and practise them to the world's end, the sea jaws, in full view of more domestic lives. Even the tyro off Dartmouth for the first time feels a grain of terror leak into his blood when the sky darkens, the squall hits a boat carrying a bit too much sail, she heels over and the fearful sea crosses the gunwale and fills his shoes.

There are more people pottering about nowadays in boats than ever there were when the Royal Navy was at its biggest wartime strength. One look at the marina at Key West or Nantucket would convince anybody the same is true for the USA. The potterers under sail live perforce the narrative tradition rehearsed (and added to) by Joseph Conrad, who made himself ardently into an English sailor larger than any English sailor was in life. They would hardly put things as he did, no doubt, but in the way they pick up their moorings, come alongside another craft, move down the estuary in the still dawn, reef in a squall, or conduct themselves in fog and a crowded channel, they enter as a small cousin the same tradition as Conrad's ship's captain when he sees himself in the mirror of his new command as:

> this representative of what for all intents and purposes was a dynasty; continuous not in blood, indeed, but in its experience, in its training, in its conception of duty, and in the blessed simplicity of its traditional point of view on life … he had his place in a line of men whom he did not know, of whom he had never heard; but who were fashioned by the same influences, whose souls in relation to their humble life's work had no secrets for him.[25]

To disregard the tradition is to put others' lives at risk. The years of a sailor's life and experience, even a weekend sailor, are marked out as stations by Conrad's great tales, by *Typhoon* and *Youth*, by *The Shadow Line, Lord Jim* and *The End of his Tether*. Present-day versions of the same thing would be a bit less florid than Conrad's, more inflected perhaps by Fleming's caustic humour, Robert Byron's irritability, but seasons of seafaring vacations confirm those stations with a directness and memorability hard to find in the more sedentary sequences of life. *Typhoon*, after all, is another bad-weather book, and a brush or two with bad weather is, like the trip to Nepal or to Spitzbergen, somewhere close to the heart of the matter. When Jonathan Raban[26] took a rattling little motor-boat with a pasteboard wheelhouse down the length of the Mississippi he wasn't just looking for the amiable middling Americans he found, but for the strong brown god of the river, its boiling traps, its running rages. When Conrad's dull hero-captain MacWhirr and his eager lad of a first mate Jukes brace themselves about their big old tub for the worst typhoon in the China Seas for a generation, the weekend sailors do more than lick their lips. Twenty years of beating down the Saturday channel from Southsea to Falmouth have taught them respect for the sea, as well as the intense pleasure of recollecting watery fearfulness in tranquillity and safe harbour.

There are moments of wilfulness in Paul Fussell's *Abroad*[27] where he simply takes for granted that arduous 'true' travel came to a dead stop in 1940. Thesiger to him, we might reply, and plenty more to come. But the sailor and the mountaineer are themselves a rebuttal of such simple-minded contemporaphobia. Jukes and MacWhirr are not vacationing, they're at work. But the vacation sailor can guess from his own smaller experience what a typhoon would be like; it was something he took up his sport to find out. The distinction Thesiger makes between an adventure and a stunt won't hold. The sailor could make the journey in a large and luxurious powerboat certainly, but doesn't do so. He and she arrange things to be more difficult and dangerous than that, because that way life is, to people of their tastes and experience, more interesting. But there was no particular necessity the other way. Conrad's combination of doing one's duty according to maritime tradition and being faithful to the work for the sake of the work has quite a short moral horizon. It will only keep you going if you don't lift your head up in order to see *where* you're going. If you do, the holiday sailor or mountaineer and the intrepid explorers of the world's oceans and desert places look much of a muchness, and the differences between them best measured as a slight change in moral climate and in the habits of cultural self-justification.

By this adjusted scale, there's not a lot to choose for high ideals and selfless courage as between Scott's expedition, Thesiger's long haul, Mallory's last climb and the comic canoer jaunts of Redmond O'Hanlon or Joe Simpson's return from death's doors in the Peruvian Andes.[28] The sons of the nineteenth century are characterised by what one of their more sharp-tongued critics, George Eliot, called their 'high, objectless yearning', although high-mindedness was not for her a subject for derision. The values which steered Scott to his death took a terrible beating in both wars, but worn with his kind of resigned intelligence or with Mallory's cheerful practicality, they hold up:

> Still, the conquest of the mountain is the great thing, and the whole plan is mine and my part will be a sufficiently interesting one and will give me, perhaps, the best chance of all of getting to the top… I want all four of us to get there, and I believe it can be done. We shall be starting by moonlight if the morning is calm and should have the mountain climbed if we're lucky before the wind is dangerous.[29]

Indeed, Mallory had said to a Harvard audience, to whom he had been lecturing about the disastrous 1922 expedition when seven Sherpas were killed, that climbing Everest was of no use 'other than to fulfil the desire of geologists for a stone from the summit and to show physiologists at just what altitude human life becomes impossible'.[30] What was more likely at stake for Mallory, when he set off (at 38) on his last, fatal expedition more or less against his own better judgement, was his sense of his duty to the tradition of mountaineering in general, and to his friendships in particular. As with sailing, mountaineering rediscovers the absoluteness of trust and solidarity – trust in other people's craftsmanship as well as courage – in circumstances of some physical extremity. That's part of the fun.

There is a common structure of feeling expressed in a common and class language which marks all these stories: Scott and Shackleton, Thesiger and Mallory, Ransome and Conrad, are all mutually recognisable. They sound pretty well alike and they feel the same. The difference from today is no doubt attributable to the imperial aura which surrounded feeling with such a glow no matter what ironic self-defences were called in play. For Scott or Mallory or even Arthur Ransome, it seemed simply natural that an Englishman would be first at the chosen goal (hence the stunned response to Amundsen's flag at the South Pole). In *Heart of Darkness*, Conrad's famous classic describing the human degeneration which may attend a passage to the distant centre of imperialism's evil, the narrator notes the expanses of red marked in the atlas, and says quite unironically, 'good to think there was decent work going on somewhere'.

After paying the imperial dues, however, the reasons the mighty heroes and ancestors of nineteenth-century exploration had for going where they went and the reasons people take their vacations in search of danger and various other extremities are wholly continuous. Feeling is not a primal surge of something inside ('gut-reaction'). Feelings are learned as a system of distinctions made by language, and the language comes to us, to be changed by our own, later uses, from the history of our society. This is what the transmission of culture means. It comes from the past, and we change it.

So to take a vacation in search of danger is to try out on oneself the feelings of the past. It is also, I would say, to find a little realm of autonomous and physical action – action from which social structure has been sufficiently abstracted, so that how one moves and where one sleeps have a novel independence and freedom to them. Of course, as it is the point of this chapter to contend, danger is only the name given to action made difficult, and those definitions come invented by culture. Exploring the desert is what the Englishman was doing; the nomads went along for the ride. Climbing deadly mountains or facing 40-foot waves are examples of fun invented and shaped by forebears for whom the life of the Edwardian gent seemed a little constricting. One might deepen the existential commitment to the mountain by seeing it as a restoration of vitality debilitated by the material comforts of modern domesticity, but setting aside the jargon, such reasons as given today would hardly have sounded ridiculous to the great Worthies.

Hard vacationing and looking for trouble will nearly do to describe Burton's and Speke's pioneer exploration. The difference between then and now is that it is in our leisure time that we look to renew certain key values residual in other areas of life. Courage, endeavour, endurance, stamina, the pleasures of bodily well-being come alive on the mountain and in the sea's jaws as they cannot in front of the computer at the office. At the same time, the great satisfactions of safety and familiarity are restored by our being away from them for a while, sharing a sleepless sleeping-bag with several gallons of icy sea-water. The inclusiveness of the old enemy 'consumerism' looks even less adequate when we discover that filling our leisure with our vacation restores life to such a very wide range of necessary values, feelings and experiences.

V

Our leisure is, as they say, 'free' time, for us to spend as we wish; it is where we can do as we wish, free from the orders of the boss or the necessity of wage-earning. When Joe Simpson arrives in view of the stupendous beauty of the Peruvian Andes, he has come to revive old feelings and follow an antique drum. The same drum was sounded by Whymper's Alpinists, and Simpson's small clichés echo their larger ones.

> [W]e headed north towards a high col above an area of broken rock buttresses. The camp disappeared from view and immediately I became aware of the silence and solitude of our position. For the first time in my life I knew what it meant to be isolated from people and society. It was wonderfully calming and tranquil to be here. I became aware of a feeling of complete freedom – to do whatever I wanted to, and in whatever manner. Suddenly the

whole day had changed. All lethargy was swept away by an invigorating inde-pendence. We had responsibilities to no-one but ourselves now, and there would be no-one to intrude or come to our rescue ...[31]

Set aside the informal rhythms and a touch or two of self-centredness ('responsibilities to no-one') and this is something of what all climbers say they climb for. Include the slight narcissism and this is what every holidaymaker hopes to find on the solitary side of the sojourn.

As it happened, Simpson also finds terror, fearful injury and the edge of his own death. Mountaineering, like sailing, is for that purpose also, never more so than for those who come back from the edge and may then confer the gift of their escape on those who did not go, who listen to and maybe love them. The return to luxury is itself a luxury. Our passions, like our ethics, constitute a system of differences, and we only know what we feel and whether we approve it by tensing the feeling against its nega-tion. I luxuriate in comfort by contrasting it with the lack of it. My recollection of the dangerous moments, of the frightening and hateful events, is made pleasurable by their absence, by my audience's efforts to imagine them. The immediacy of my plea-sure in the swift, onward passage of my boat, lifting and falling to the rush and shrug of the waves, is given by its unlikeness to my dreary rail journey across the stagnant marshes towards the quotidian town.

Figure 5.2   Snowdonia, North Wales
Source: John Cleare/Mountain Camera

These contrastives are at the heart of storytelling and are the ground of that imagining of a different life and world upon which holidays are built. Every story, including the story of one's own life, has its narrative thread, to lose which is to lose hold on that life. Every story also possesses a form of self-envisioning. We cast it as best we can in a certain light. We behold it. The thread of holiday life describes a circle. We return to the place at which we began. The envisioning of it is comic.

This latter really is a change in the structure of feeling. The structure taught by the ancestors is, as we have seen, high-minded and idealising. It had either strongly transcendental or spiritual-national components. This is equally true on either side of the Atlantic. Thoreau was an eco-nationalist Emersonian. So was John Muir, even if he was born in Scotland in 1838. By the time his first great book was published,[32] he was 56 and knew the magnificence of the Sierra and the gorgeous flower life of its valleys like no-one before or since. He found in these and in 'the summery melody' of the little water-ouzel ample 'varied expressions of God's eternal love'.[33] Like Wordsworth he too had 'bounded' from rock to rock and, what was more, gone on doing so into old age, but he joins decisively in the twentieth-century's long, meandering march towards democracy by his zealous championing of the cause of National Parks, becoming effectually the founder of Yosemite as a result of his book and his lobbying of President Harrison. In Britain, any such development, much more urgently needed by a much smaller country, had a long time to wait and the dull, selfish obduracy of the land-owning classes to overcome. In the United States, Muir brought together Charles Darwin, the love of God and progressive environmentalism, thereby adding an important new room to the capacious architecture of holiday feeling.

The comic coloration, however, came later. After warfare, no doubt, but also after the loss of a global mission. Fleming had put off mission, Shackleton hadn't. The victorious 1953 Everest expedition led by Vivian Fuchs still had it, Gwen Moffat and Joe Brown, greater climbers both, absolutely refused it (Moffat climbed in a bikini).

Comedy belongs to holidaymaking. The missionary journey is over. A holiday is funny because it is fun. It is funny when it all goes horribly wrong (particularly so when it goes wrong). A holiday is cast as comedy because it is a sally in the pursuit of happiness and as such a cheerfully individual affair. Tragedy is collective, whether the tragedy of collective belief, of nations, of racial groups or of social classes. Comedy is singular and happily so, but it is no less a vision for that.

So the dangerous summer is a joke. If it goes really wrong, as it did for Simpson, it's either a thriller or a bit of pathos. Paul Theroux starts where many holiday dreamers start, with the romance of the railroad[34] and, travelling alone, makes his an episodic tale of comic incompetences on his own part, and comic encounters with adhesive, unwanted but unfailingly lively other people. I mention his agreeable book to bring out the force of the new trope, that danger and discomfort are all very well for their revitalising of sluggish bloodstreams and restoration of dulled reflexes, but that once framed as individual and freely chosen, disburdened of both nature and empire, their dramatisation must be comic and as comic, filled with hope, 'lips parted, the new ships'.

Redmond O'Hanlon is our last hero in this and coda to our chapter. He is funny, studiedly and remorselessly funny, and so confirms a deep holiday trope. It is one borne out by countless snapshots in family albums depicting Father making a mess of things. Father mustn't mind about this and the family must laugh at him then and his photograph now; but fondly. The maxim is that the good holiday embodies a comic view of the world. O'Hanlon isn't exactly on vacation and his daunting trips are hardly stunts. He goes where only botanists and anthropologists have gone before, but goes in the guise of extremely cultivated buffoon, making friends with those who take him in, seeing the sights (natural historical ones in his case) and managing always to meet remote peoples he has gone to find with his magical geniality and gregariousness.

In all this he is, honourably, our ideal tourist. He respects, even loves, the wilderness and the oddities of human nature which he encounters; he is astonishingly and unassumingly brave, even reckless, just as he ought to be; and the very heart of his fable is its fabulous and scatological discomfort. He follows in the footsteps of great explorers and botanists, and carries the portly works of Alfred Russel Wallace in his bergen. But instead of the manners of George Mallory he wears those of Billy Connolly in his anecdotes.

> I changed fast out of my dry clothes, made a brief tick check by torchlight, pulled on my wet clothes and steeled myself for the first personal trauma of the day. In my own utopia I would elect to shit only in a lead-lined chamber half-a-mile underground, safe from enemy radar. Shitting two yards from Simon and five yards from Chimo was, I found, difficult. I hung on to a sapling with one hand, switched off my torch, took down my trousers and squatted over the black, swirling water.
>
> 'Don't look,' I said.
>
> 'Who's interested?' said Simon, leaning out of his hammock and pointing his torch straight at me.
>
> 'Push!' yelled Chimo.
>
> 'Bit runny today,' said Simon.[35]

Unfailingly good-humoured, O'Hanlon tries his friends pretty hard. He took James Fenton to Borneo[36] but when invited to the Amazon halfway down a bottle of Glenmorangie in Oxford, Fenton took his time and then, 'shutting his eyes and pressing his palms up over his face and the top of his bald head', said '*Redmond, I would not come with you to High Wycombe*'.

There is plenty in this for Peter Fleming and Graham Greene to recognise – the same friendships confirmed in the same sort of jokes and insults. When O'Hanlon is finally abandoned by his chum Simon, who can't stick the dirt, the awful grub, the bugs, the endless jungle, he goes on with his Spanish Indians until he meets the legendary pygmies, the Yanomani. As a token of esteem and hospitality, they take a long wooden tube and blow the household hallucinogenic powder yoppo high into his sinuses.

> It was, I realised, with the kind of panic that shrivels the penis, my turn.
>
> Jarivanau blew the dust into my left nostril. Someone at once seemed to hit me just above the bridge of the nose with a small log. I put my hands to the back of my head, to stop it detaching itself. Someone else eased a burning stick down my throat. My lungs filled with hot ash. There was no water, anywhere. Jarivanau offered me his reloaded tube. Bang. My ear, nose and throat system went into shock. I sat, unable, it seemed, to breathe, my hands

pressed to the back of my head, my head between my knees. And then suddenly I was gulping oxygen through a clogging goo of ejaculating sinuses; I mouthed for air as yoppo-stained snot and mucus from nasal recesses whose existence I had never suspected poured out of my nostrils and on down my chin and chest.

The pain went. I realised that I was still alive; that it was all over; that I was taking the best breaths I could remember.[37]

It makes a cracking good traveller's tale. It took courage. It is exactly the sort of damn silly thing to do which is much done on the dangerous vacation. There will be others down this trail, and O'Hanlon's fine regardlessness, his strong feeling for natural beauty and even stronger love for the sheer wanton plenitude of these infernal rivers, his absolute determination to see the birds his great ornithological predecessors saw and described so precisely and in such excellent prose take their honourable place in the long making of the travel narrative. His journeys having been completed only so recently, he feels much closer to us than the earlier names of the tradition invoked in this chapter. He feels, if I must put it like that, as much a tourist as a traveller. He is very vivid about the discomfort of it all, the dreadful, inescapable insistence of small flies packed up your nose, bigger ones biting your neck, and monster hornets diving on your head to sting it. He is endlessly kind to the deprivations he finds amongst the indigenes, and comes to them in a quite new spirit, I would say, compared to the one we find in Thesiger as he tries to become a Bedu, or in Fleming, *The Times* correspondent on his novel version of the Grand Tour. O'Hanlon is a charmer. He strolls straight through the prohibitions of anthropology, and makes people like him. He *befriends* the local Yanomani as he does, just as infallibly, the people of the inner Congo, and as he would, no doubt, the Tuscan peasants near his country cottage. He comes to the strange peoples simply as himself, cheerful, shaggy, wide open, shapeless, a hobby botanist with a passion for discomfort and about as free from the taints of colonialism as it is possible for a present-day universalist with a nice house in Oxford to be. He is, I would risk saying, a perfect gentleman, just like Patrick Leigh Fermor and Norman Lewis, and thereby shows us how still to sustain the story of what it is to go adventuring one fine morning, and to do so keeping your nerve, your good manners and a strong sense of the ridiculous. Doing so, he is a splendid example of what it is to modernise the tradition. Conduct yourself as he does towards those who live wherever you go and as a stranger and a tourist, and you won't be far wrong.

6

THE INDUSTRIALISATION OF MOBILITY

I

A general history of the passions in the twentieth century might be framed by the story of three systems of technology and the symbolisms which inevitably accompany them. The first only darkens by derivation the happy little corner of human endeavour celebrated here. It is the technology of death, beginning with the heavy machine gun perfected a little time before the demonstrations of its triumphant efficiency between 1914 and 1918. It was followed promptly by the tank and, in the second war, by the heavy bomber and the freight aircraft capable of delivering tons of explosives, equipment or human bodies anywhere within three or four thousand miles. In no time at all, of course, those same aircraft were delivering millions of tourist passengers, and the political economy of war had, as usual, done its bit for the continued thriving of capitalism.

After bombers, the death dealers spent their genius on devising ways of killing such enormous multitudes without the intervention of any but a tiny number of human agents that they disappear from this record and make their contribution to easy vacationing only by way of electronic gadgetry and the part played by technology in the second symbol system of the century, money.

Over this hundred years, money changes from gold to official paper to handwritten and spontaneous currency (cheques) to electronic digitation. The solid solemnities of banks almost fade from view, and money transactions all take place on a screen, whether as between oneself and one's overdraft or between the colossal debt and credit accounts of world speculation.[1]

These swift, invisible exchanges are decidedly part of our vacationing history, particularly so if we link them to the third of our giant systems wherewith one may frame a global story. Modern communication begins with the train and the telegraph; is enhanced by the bicycle and the telephone; pours out of the tidy grid of the railways into the dense, antique pattern of roads quite unprepared for such a flood with the coming of the automobile; is consummated across the same decades by the invasion of the skies by passenger aircraft.

In this vast extension of historical mobility the seas barely play a part. Liners came and went, no doubt, and freight carriers became bigger and bigger, but inasmuch as our history is so readily grasped as books of sheer numbers, then automobiles and aircraft and the imaginary bankrolls flickering down the wires are the mightiest makers of us and our emotions.

Putting things that way is momentarily to recast the history of the holiday as part of the history of globalisation. The term is much in vogue. It was Karl Marx who said in 1848 that 'all history is now world history', meaning that the vicissitudes of the Indian cotton crop bore directly on the well-being of south Lancashire. But globalisation has been hailed as the unstoppable tendency of world economics rather more recently; its dominant features are said to be the internationalisation of capital flows, the new, freebooting independence of transnational companies, the helplessness of labour in the face of these freedoms, the reluctance of governments to do anything about anything. This is 'turbo-capitalism'[2] on the rampage, and it is praised or blamed by Left and Right for what it does to rich and poor.

More cautious critics have doubted whether globalisation is quite so new let alone quite so clear-cut a phenomenon after all.[3] They have suggested that such features have been internationally discernible since the 1860s, that very few companies are genuinely transnational, and that most companies with a claim to the title do their international trading from a solid national base; that direct investment in other nations misses out the Third World and what there is concentrates in Europe, Japan and North America.

Hirst and Thompson agree that what *has* changed in the past twenty-five years has been the return of a substantial population of long-term and structurally unemployed, the creation of a high degree of currency instability caused by the deregulation of the money markets, and the emergence of the famously resourceful but, as everybody learned with a shock in 1997, veering economy of the south-east Asian nations. In particular they and other theorists[4] propose a change in human nature consequent upon changes in the technology of production. Instead of mass production according to the brutal but (at least) reliable procedures of the assembly line, the design and quantity variations made possible by computers have allowed employers to match their hiring exactly to their requirements, and therefore make casual, part-time and irregularly paid labour central to their profits. What work does to workers is changed, some say, as a result. The new worker is less settled in the job, less tied by solidarity to other workers, readier to move, much less well equipped with skill and craft. Where once upon a time the labour force was known to itself and its politicians as the masses, and poured massively out of factory gates to take its vacations *en masse* at the seaside, the funfair, the sports stadium, now the new kind of worker, so long as he or she has kept the job, takes a family car and a chartered aircraft in search, by and large, of something more differentiated, of the niche in the market represented less by the throngs on the promenade and more by the shot of an empty, silver beach on the Seychelles or in the Caribbean.

Too much is built upon the power of advertising imagery. Weston-super-Mare and Miami Beach are still packed at the right time of year. Global economies are not so omnipotent or ruthless but that a people cannot still put their cultural stamp on what they spend and where they go. Indeed, as it is a main argument of this book to contend, vacationing is a way of keeping up cultural continuity, of reassuring yourself of the familiarity of things, the safety of places, the friendliness of sun and sea. The industrialisation of mobility is one of the principal narratives of the last quarter of the millennium, but it makes for a reassuringly complicated moral, whether in Britain or the USA.

There is, in other words, no simple victory won by technology or economics over the localism of culture by the coming of global mobility. The crowded skies and roads are brimming with people whose holidaying is directed very specifically to purposes and aspirations which comprise an unpredictable compound of safety and daring, novelty and tradition. Those well placed in the world to take advantage of railways went wherever the train took them and sometimes the sheer joy of mobility was far more the point of the trip than the destination.

The railway companies grasped this idea very promptly and Pullman from its earliest days combined the imagery of old stage coaches (the panelling, the lamps), old inns (candle-lit dinners *à deux*) and the new, ostentatious luxury of the grand hotels (elaborate service, pile carpets, deep upholstery) all caught up in the delirious magic of the speed and the dark and the placeless landscape whirling by the window on the way to what the railwaymen called the long connections. No wonder then that the overnight rail journey became a lovers' rendezvous in the novels and movies.

By the same token, the cruise liners rapidly developed into mobile grand hotels on which, as the advertisements in Fodor guides still say, getting there is half the fun and the suspended nature of the journey, not here, not there, quickened that strong ingredient of the vacation which urges upon people the attractions of doing things they would never do elsewhere. You give yourself up to the irresistible directedness of the train or the ship and let it take you where it will ... The big labels[5] on hide suitcases spoke of the allure, the glamour (new word) of effortless mobility – Venice, Cairo, Tangier, Constantinople – and the bold railway posters did the same.

II

It wasn't just the bigness and power of the new travel technology which gave a quite new dimension to holidaying. It was the break to a new kind of freedom. This is the more evident if beside the brief and earlier allusions to the amazing expansion of the railways we set the winningly humble history of the bicycle, and give that harmless instrument the credit due it for its sterling contributions to health, freedom, happiness and a well-tempered environment.

The bicycle precedes the train, of course, but only in the rather comic prototype of the 1840s on which young blades whizzed themselves down a slope with the aid of their bootsoles. Cogs and a pedal drive only appeared in a popular model from the Michaux Brothers in the 1860s,[6] so slowly the attractions of the vehicle – its cheapness, its portability, its genderlessness, its unchaperoned freedom – turned it in Europe into the toy of the working and clerical classes. It suited best those fit enough to use it, no doubt, and those without young children. It was admirable for courtship, but it was also gregarious: the Cyclists' Touring Club was founded in 1878,[7] and had 60,000 members by the turn of the century. The National Cyclists' Union, acting precisely as a union, lobbied on behalf of road repairs, rights for cyclists, and fair deals at boarding houses. By the time Dunlop started to produce bicycles with pneumatic tyres in 1888, the campaign for smoother roads was launched and then confirmed by the coming of the automobile during the next decade. Indeed, the automobile itself started life in America as a quadricycle, built by Henry Ford in 1896, with four bicycle wheels and a two-cylinder engine (Louis Renault built his first car in 1898[8]).

The bicycle, Pimlott says, 'reopened the countryside to the people from the towns',[9] 'it accustomed us all to the idea of our highways being used by other than local residents'.[10] In Europe, at least, the bicycle introduced its users to the quite new experience of door-to-door travelling without the inconvenience and crowdedness of rail travel. It provided the chance not only to get well clear of the close grip of your neighbours and their observation, but to do so by yourself. It was the first instrument of what has been called 'mobile privatisation',[11] and it added to its instrumentality the agreeable pleasures of letting a bike *go*, down a long hill, the sheer exhilaration of wind and speed and weather on your face. Moreover, it wasn't so hard to cycle long distances – the French inaugurated a Paris–Brest–Paris race in 1891[12] and won with Michelin's new wind-inflated tyres in seventy-one hours *non-stop* – and the easiness and domestic accessibility of bicycles prepared people for the magical properties of the automobile, a tale which can best be told from the other side of the Atlantic.

For simple topographical reasons, bicycles occupy a smaller place in American history. Playing Butch Cassidy in a lovely scene from the great movie, Paul Newman apostrophises his new bicycle as 'the future' and chucks it away as he rides regardlessly back into the past. But the sheer size of the country as well as its awful roads kept bicycles for local, largely Eastern purposes. There had been cycle battalions set up during the First World War, but their attractions never stood a chance in the USA against the Model T.

By 1904 Ford had built a motor car which could travel at a new land speed record of 91 mph. The Model T was launched four years later, assembled from prefabricated parts on a hand-hauled trolley dragged along the line of workers each of whom fitted his little unit so that a vehicle could be built in 90 minutes instead of fifteen hours.[13] He sold 20,000 in 1910 and 200,000 three years later. Fordism had started, and the still-familiar Model T with its big, spoked wheels, its high-stepping running board, its railroad coach lantern headlights, its leather club chair driver's seat, is its metonym.

With a Model T one could easily go away to those short stretches of the east coast not annexed by the rich during the nineteenth century. The struggle of class and value in the United States, between the fresh breezes and freedoms of the shore and Constitutional reverence for private property was won hands down by the Constitution. Every spare bit of beach has been colonised by little summer chalets with an automobile parked at the side all the way from Maine to the edge of the Everglades. The only stretches of open dune and sand belong to the big houses planted confidently in front of the splendid ocean prospect. The metropolitan corridor[14] created by the railroad has now closed; the mobile privatisation of the motor car has been effected for the length of the eastern American seaboard.

There is one indicative break in this minatory history. Henry Phipps, Carnegie's partner in steel, built himself a mansion on New Jersey's Barnegat peninsula, reckoning to sell off in good time the great tracts of beach he acquired. Bad times and ill winds blew in 1929, and some good, as usual, blew in with them. Cleaned out by the Wall Street crash, Phipps let the beach lie empty except for its birds and its flora until the state bought it very cheaply and, Thoreau's second classic *Cape Cod* in hand, kept it for the people. Nowadays the said people turn up in their automobiles until Island Beach State Park is thought to have absorbed enough carbon monoxide for the day, and the entrances are closed for the better enjoyment and the conservation of space and sea.[15]

The triumph of the automobile was clinched in the USA by Alfred Sloan. In the 1920s, when he reorganised General Motors into the five constituent companies,

Cadillac, Oldsmobile, Buick, Pontiac and Chevrolet (the last named after his French engineer stolen from Peugeot), each company was assigned a price bracket and, by implication, a stratum in the class market. While Ford stuck too stubbornly to his single, successful design, General Motors, by covering the spectrum of class taste, choice and cheque book captured and held to this day 60 per cent of home-produced sales. The United States became the first society to travel everywhere by car, even from New Hampshire to Los Angeles.

It wasn't just the size of the country which gave the automobile its head, it was also its happiness of fit with American values and politics. 'The private car accounts for more than ... 75% of all tourist travel in North America',[16] and it does so because it matches the uniquely American ease of movement, nonchalance of displacement, restlessness of disposition, mobility of work.

This marks the very blurred distinction between the American vacation and the European holiday. The Americans have always travelled so much lighter than the Europeans. That was the kind of life they went out there, having left Europe, to make. The omnipresence of the road movie in the American imagination betokens that different envisioning of movement, the readiness to get on the move, be on the road, to be going somewhere, anywhere, so long as it's a long way away. The postwar boom, the ready accessibility of casual employment fell in exactly with this happy breed of traveller-tourist-pilgrim-odd-jobber-easygoer. It was never like this in rooted old Europe, even after the devastation of continental warfare. Making a journey was a move from known to unknown. Taking a vacation marked the boundary between work and leisure. In the USA work and not-work move in and out of the other's time and space.

American politics match this porousness exactly. The colossal road-building programmes of the 1930s were a part of New Deal relief policies. Its continuation in the 1940s and 1950s was a consequence of Cold War and the Defense Highway Act of 1944 intended to provide a national road network along which, as the story went, armies and refugees from nuclear war could be moved at speed.[17]

Ordinary economic growth impelled by cold warfare pressed things forward and during the 1950s the United States invented on behalf of all nations the modern road-and-landscape, in which traffic is functionally separated into such categories as fast and slow, long-distance and local, heavy and light, and the roadscapes planned accordingly, with long curves and big vistas for those travelling for hours at high speeds on expressways, with efforts at visual variety to keep tired truckers awake, and little horticultural oases around the gas stations for a break. Of course, things came out more or less messily when transplanted to Britain (Hitler's Germany was the European pioneer with the Autobahn stylishly designed also for military purposes), but in every country a tight knot was tied between economic growth, the production of cars and roads, and the pleasures of leisure. The automobile turned every weekend into a chance for an afternoon in the country.

The consequences for vacationing cannot be distinguished from the everyday life of the society. But the lavish size, the trowelled-on kitsch of American design, the enormous trunks and bed-sized seating fixed these monsters as *rooms*, as thoroughly lived in as the rooms of the sprawling one-storey houses-with-stoops to which they belong. When the owners detach them from the immobile home, he and she can live, sleep, cook and love in the car with that easy resourcefulness in setting up and striking camps which is so clearly inscribed among the peculiarities of the Americans. It is then no surprise to discover that General Motors also invented the last words in kitsch, the well-named mobile home and the camper, nor to learn that a million of these latter now patrol the holiday reaches of the USA in summertime.

The early history of the automobile is eloquent of its magic appeal. It started life, like all the luxuries of capitalism, as the toy of the rich and sportive. Racing was what gave the horseless carriage its visibility – Paris to Bordeaux, London to Brighton also, but the French made the better roads so Renault easily won the 1901 Paris to Berlin marathon.

It was, however, Ford and Sloan who saw what this creature would mean to people, above all to *the* people, long before Herbert Austin and William Morris had grasped the quite new principles of production involved. Looking at Fordism the British feared for labour relations. Looking at the pattern of holidays in Britain and the intensely local feeling which tied excursions to custom, they kept to Britain's cautious industrial habits and sold their cars to the middle classes. Ford and General Motors, in bitter competition, conceived a vast society of universal automobility and all to their profit. They created one. Hitler, much struck by their success, instructed the brilliant Dr Porsche to design a people's car or Volkswagen but at a third the price of the Model T. After the local unpleasantnesses, the Beetle came to change the life of European working-class families for ever. Mobile; private; leisurely; free as air; your own to go anywhere; the motor car held out more intensely than any other material commodity the beautiful, giddy ideals of personal escape into spontaneous action.

In doing so, its industry positioned itself as the fibrillating heart of national economies. The automobile industry, with all its crazy vagaries, its booms and depressions, symbolises well enough in the long curves and steep falls of its graphs of production the pattern of holidaymaking over the inter-war years and even, it may be, the satisfactions and retrenchments of consumer feeling as well. Plenty of production equals decently paid holidays and the bottled-up happiness it is hoped they will bring. The two leading social historians of our whole epoch, Alan Taylor and Eric Hobsbawm, agree on the central place of the automobile in the significance and momentum of the period. Taylor sees it as the weapon of class liberation, at least for the prosperous members of the working class.[18] In 1920 there were 200,000 private cars; in 1939, Morris's caution and under-capitalisation notwithstanding, there were two million, one to every 24 persons, and, Taylor drily adds, more people killed by cars in 1934 than in 1961. The thing could do no wrong; between 1930, when the 20 mph limit was abolished, and 1935 there was no speed limit in Britain at all, and the plentiful, dusty country lanes and the wide seaside promenades could easily accommodate everybody without anyone having to pretend that the others weren't there. Sunday became a day not for church but for countryside.

Hobsbawm[19] sounds a grimmer note with which to darken our sunny picture of the graph superimposed upon one of those old tourist posters featuring the girl, the motor car, the bay and the name of the resort. Quoting W.W. Rostow, he writes:

> unlike railroads or more efficient ships or the introduction of steel and machine tools – which cut costs – the new products and way of life required high and expanding levels of income and a high degree of confidence in the future, to be rapidly diffused.

Hobsbawm goes on, 'But that is exactly what was collapsing'.

Collapse, however, was too strong a word to characterise the toughness with which people, only recently come into the inheritance of holidays, would hang on to the best they could make of things. Incomes went up and down, confidence in the future might have to reduce its horizons but not many people would give up, when the going got rough, the hope that if not this year then next year would see them out of trouble far enough to go back to the Costa Brava if possible, and Perranporth if not.

The new products Hobsbawm refers to and the way of life they prefigure came to include not only motor cars but air travel and the full panoply of tourism and holidays. They flourish, no doubt, when pay and hopes are high. But as holidays moved a part of their meaning from luxury to custom (rather than necessity), and as two-thirds of the population of the wealthy economies came to count upon a holiday away from home as their due, such expenditure was gathered into the ordinary reckoning of the domestic ledger. The zest to spend is intertwined with a caution of feeling and (sometimes grudging) thriftiness of disposition learned over a couple of hundred years of the struggle for free time and not, even now, entirely eroded by the exhilarating debauchery enjoined by debt facilities now so mysteriously transmuted into the name of credit. The quondam consumer draws on an inheritance of mistrust-of-the-morrow and providence-for-the-day-after both absolutely necessary to sanity if his or her bank account is not to be so much froth on the seas of inflation. When the economic cycle turns down and rates of consumption contract, what is called confidence collapses correspondingly. The heading conflates many passions and they take in human steadiness and foresight, timidity and carefulness, as well as the usual ruthlessness in making money, the gambler's readiness to press the drive for profits over the edge of what can be paid for, the cheeriness of a decent wage packet, the calculation of what can be put aside for holiday spending, as well as the awful daring of a moment's surrender, never likely to be cheap. These feelings constitute a *structure*. According to the numbers and spending powers of those involved, economic cycles go up and down.

The history of consumerism as recorded by the industrialisation of tourist mobility is nonetheless a rather weightier business than this scanty algebra betokens. The mobility industry built itself into four layers with four economic geographies. Bicycle, railway, automobile, aircraft stood to time and space in a simple relation of scale, ambition and convenience. Bicycles and cars lived in the garage, aircraft and trains at the terminal. As they did so, sediments of expectation were laid down, symbolisms of expression devised, frames of feeling carefully balanced between excitement and resignation. Each vehicle at its advent promised (and kept the promise) of excitement, liberation, expeditions to new places, safe returns home. As each vehicle solidified into social practice and institutions, people struck a rather more settled attitude towards it. It became, in a strong sense, familiarised.

Thus the train, flashy, powerful, vastly over-capitalised, gradually turned into a stalwart icon of the industrial family: it became Thomas the Tank Engine and Gordon the Express Train. It entered the iconography of the children's box of toys, and by way of Dinky and Matchbox miniatures, the motor car quickly did the same.

By this feelingful and imaginative process, the mighty and magical innovations of consumer mobility are kept within emotional bounds. The system of production holds out *such* enticements they might become intolerable in anticipation, disappointment might explode the social order. In order to live tolerably within the system of consumption, however, each of us banks up a credit in scepticism and suspiciousness. (Only the stars can *always* spend; that is why we have them.) A car is just a tin box for useful travel. A holiday would be nice, but there again, if you can't afford it, you can repair the greenhouse instead.

It is a queasy settlement, this treaty between production and consumption. For a long season, it is the best we can do. It holds open the promise of happiness; it mitigates disappointment when the promise is broken.

Let us picture its sequences by way of the making of the aircraft industry.

III

The industry has, of course it has, a picturesque and glamorous history which lends itself vividly to the icons of tourist advertisement. Famously, Orville and Wilbur Wright got their fragile contraption off the ground in 1903, hardly more than a decade after internal combustion began. The wheel, the chain, the cog and the dynamo were industrially inseparable at that date, and the industrial corporations agog for development invested boldly in bikes, autos and aircraft without a clear sense of which would win.

Winning, to begin with, was for each form of transportation a literal race: bicycles to Brest, automobiles to Bordeaux, aircraft (with the gallant Monsieur Blériot) across the Channel in 1909. Michelin and Renault did the designs for another Frenchman, M. Paulhan, when he flew in a series of small hops across twenty-four hours from London to Manchester in 1910 and the *Daily Mail* did its bit for Britain and the thrills of the new toy first by sponsoring the competition to the (enormous) tune of £10,000 and then providing another big prize in 1911 for a thousand mile race round Britain in which four out of nineteen fliers finished the course.[20]

These sports quickly gathered to themselves a jaunty iconography of stage and dress: a bumpy meadow with a little wooden shack of a pavilion, the close-fitting leather helmet, goggles, and gauntlets borrowed from motorcycling, the capacious new garages built for the flying machines, the little throngs of wildly applauding spectators, their big, clumsy autos parked in the road beside the field.

It was of course the biggest contribution of the unprecedented kind of warfare devised between 1914 and 1918 to have launched the aircraft industry. France led the innovations up to 1914 but at the level of a rich playboy sport, in which the USA took scarcely any interest (in 1914 only 49 American aircraft were constructed).[21] Once the strategic importance of the aircraft was grasped, production and design combined with such vitality that by 1918 (and after the creation of a separate Air Ministry in 1917) Britain was producing 4,000 aircraft a month and the Royal Flying Corps had already created the ornate and playfully reckless culture for which the RAF became world-famous after 1940. The same culture, more relevantly, shaped the experience of flying for fun between the wars.

After 1919, the Northcliffe Committee in Britain sketched out a scheme for the development of civil aviation as jointly pursued by state and private capital, and offered the first outline of a system of international control and navigation. The year after the war ended, the two military hero-pioneers, John Alcock and Arthur Whitten-Brown, made their legendary first flight across the Atlantic, and all those with a taste for dangerous excursions conducted by other people had their imaginations caught by a vision of the frail aircraft battling through the dark over the tumultuous 30-foot waves, the wind tearing through the struts holding the biplane's wings together, rain and spray driving into the pilots' faces, the roar of gale and engine together tearing the few words one could shout over his shoulder to his comrade into rags scattered in the slipstream.

Such a picture of flying dominated the traveller-tourist's expectations. When he and she came down, they found the little airline stations as distinctive, as lovable and as strange as railway halts had been at Colorado Springs or Hereford seventy years before.

> He knew the airports of Europe as well as he had once known the stations on the Brighton line – shabby Le Bourget; the great scarlet rectangle of the Tempelhof as one came in from London in the dark ...; the white sand blowing up round the shed at Tallinn; Riga, where the Berlin to Leningrad plane came down and bright pink mineral waters were sold in a tin-roofed shed.[22]

Graham Greene, tireless and intrepid traveller, is, before all English writers, the one who has fixed for us the details of air travel when it was so generally unreliable, inconvenient, oil-flecked and vomit-speckled, windswept and, supremely, *romantic*.

The tale of Amy Johnson catches this moment at its most glowing and turns it into tourist myth. Thus and thus the past is surpassed but mythologised. This is the deep mutation of culture in history; it is endlessly fascinating. Our present emerges from these past, heroic endeavours; progress grows from dangers inspiringly overcome. Indeed, only by such ingenuity and resourcefulness can the comforts we must not take too much for granted be justified. Recalling the tale of Amy Johnson is one way of paying that necessary tribute to our ancestors.

This marks the change from flying as adventure to flying as transport. It was 1930. She was 27, a pretty Yorkshirewoman with a degree from Sheffield, a wealthy fishmonger-father and a passion for flying.[23] He paid up £500 for half a Gypsy Moth and, with fifty hours' solo flying behind her, she set off for the furthest point she could think of where they would speak English when she arrived. She aimed her little aeroplane, the *Jason* for Darwin, Australia. Edging her way along the rim of the globe, flying eastward into one dawn after another, she flew and refuelled, refuelled and flew for not quite twenty days. Scarcely sleeping, a few thousand feet up, she traversed the map of the world with a twirl of compass legs: to Paris, Marseilles, Rome, Brindisi, Athens, Alexandria, Basra, Dubai, Karachi, Raj Samand, Calcutta, Akyab, Bangkok, Penang, Singapore, Sourabaya, Koepang, Darwin. She came down untroubled in places with no airstrip, and waited sleeplessly until some antique truck brought her drums of fuel so that, before the pink dawn was up, she could draw on her gloves and fold her goggles over her eyes to wait for the clatter of the propeller and the coughing crash of ignition as the shadowy figures pulled away the chocks from *Jason*'s big spoked wheels.

She was in the headlines all the way and a world celebrity when she arrived in Australia. She marks the end of the first phase in the coming of a luxury. Like automobiles, haute cuisine, telephones and vacations themselves, the luxury begins by combining sport, wealth and fame. It fills the spare time of the leisure class; it both demands and conspicuously displays wealth; its possession attracts celebrity. This is the field of force of modern fame-making, itself indispensable to the maintenance of spending.

Meanwhile, industrial production, stimulated by war, takes off. Donald Douglas launched the aircraft company with a thousand bucks and an office behind a barber's shop (thereby making *his* contribution to certain tropes in the manufacture of fame). He designed the DT-1 which brought off the first round-the-world flight in 1924 and he had the foresight to start up in Santa Monica where the labour force and the climate conduced to building flying machines.[24]

Douglas gets the credit for launching the industry in the USA. William Boeing had been interested before the war, Major Reuben Fleet at the same time, but Douglas Aircraft supplied the US Air Force with most of its aeroplanes until 1930. As anti-trust legislation came into force as a result of the huge deals permitted after Roosevelt scrapped the Air Mails Act of 1934, aviation companies were dispersed into new formations. In 1933, the vice-president of the new airline TWA (Transcontinental and Western) himself flew the first production DC-2 (designed by Douglas) from Los Angeles to Newark in a record-breaking thirteen hours. The new craft indeed outclassed the aircraft it was designed to beat, Boeing's 247, and in the DC-3, which followed within two years, had a world-beater, cruising at 190 mph and carrying twenty-one passengers.

Modern airlines began here. They began to be domesticated; they appeared on cigarette cards and postcards, as toys for children. Air travel, however, remained a luxury until after the world had learned how to move its armies, their *Fallschirmjäger*, and their equipment for the purposes of war between 1939 and 1945. The development of the industry before hostilities broke out became sedimented with that agreeable mixture of luxury and danger which we have so frequently found to recur on holiday. In Britain the luxuriousness looked for a time suspiciously close to reckless extravagance. Imperial Airways, a union of Handley Page, Daimler and other diminu-tives, never broke even on their home runs, in the 1920s, even with a large government subsidy.[25] British caution and old class prevented large-scale investment; in 1929 there were only four municipal airports as compared with eighty in Germany.

Understandably, it was Imperial Airways' imperial routes which flourished, pretty well the same as the one followed by Amy Johnson. In Africa, of course, they turned south at Cairo and followed the Nile to Khartoum, then due south to Port Bell, east to Mombasa, south again down the coast to hospitality provided by the old Portuguese ally in Lourenço Marques, before taxiing up to the control tower at Durban and turning round.[26] Going east, they followed Johnson's path. By the mid-1930s, although there were still plenty of elderly-looking, newly-produced biplanes flying for Imperial – the Armstrong Whitworth Argosy of 1926, the Handley Page HP42 on the European run – it was the Douglas DC-2 and DC-3 and the Lockheed 10 and 14 which wore the convincing air of the future.

For cheerful tourists anticipating the sun, there were short hauls to le Touquet, Jersey, Paris, Dinard and, by way of Macon, to Nice and Montpellier. Even so, flying-as-transport remained a minority luxury. In 1925, airlines carried only 21,000 people in and out of Britain;[27] ten years later, Imperial Airways themselves, about to become the British Overseas Airways Corporation, only carried 66,000 people to all corners of the globe.

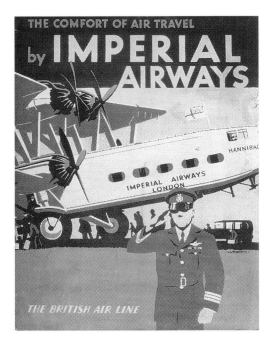

Figure 6.1 Imperial Airways advertisement, *circa* 1930
Source: The Robert Opie Collection, London

The Second World War was, of course, the occasion for launching mass air travel. After 1945 there were enormous numbers of unused and impressively safe aircraft standing in hangars and on runways. The sharp entrepreneurial eye of one Freddy Laker spotted them, after flying one of the spares during the Berlin airlift of 1948–49, itself a lesson in the inventive and life-enhancing deployment of aeroplanes. Two decades later, as everybody knows, he hugely undercut the complacent commissars of British Airways and, one might as well say, single-handedly initiated mass and cheap air travel. With Laker's day, the aircraft was fully familiarised.

The sluggish and uneven development of air travel in the 1920s and 1930s laid certain deposits in the social imagination. Glamour, let us say, is that nimbus which glows around a person electrified in roughly equal proportions by distance, recognition, desirability and money. It is a social category which only really emerges in its own right from post-1918 Eastern America as apotheosised by Hollywood, and then enacted beside the Mediterranean.

The glamour élite conferred its enchantment on air travel, as on so much else in the strictly pointless but still significant practices of holidaymaking. Its members board aircraft at a distance from us (behind the crash barriers), but wearing the unmistakable, instantly recognisable uniform of fame (brown and shining limbs and faces, nonchalantly perfect clothes – 'Who is she? I know I know his face'); they are desirable in themselves, in that careless air of being able to enjoy guiltless sex and inconsequential champagne at any moment, desirable in their situation because *they* need not stand in line to board, they will travel first class, disembark unseen, wait for no passport officer; finally, they gleam with the unmistakable, global dazzle of money, the energiser of glamour, the source (but not the embodiment) of power.

These vibrations glimmer on the runway or outside the Ritz-Carlton at the doors of the grand limousines, on the private beach at St Tropez. They burn like flares where travel and money and fame coincide. Some of the fuel they burn was laid down in the old airports of the Imperial, the Atlantic and the Paris–Berlin flights.

IV

One lesson to be learned from the history of mass mobility in relation to leisure is that transport systems are not easily superseded. In 1958, when the first jet crossed the Atlantic it looked as though the day of the railway was over. They were so convinced of this in the USA that they took up the track which carried the old-fashioned visitor from New York to Chicago, from Chicago to Denver, from Denver across the Rockies until the engine drew up in Oakland, California, on the very edge of the shining Pacific.

But as their many and devoted followers know, the railways fought back strongly, so that any minute now it will be possible to be whisked from the middle of Calais to the middle of Avignon in three hours while the aircraft lumber in and out of Charles de Gaulle airport and people check in ninety minutes early.

The railway's trail is far from ended, no more than the bicycle's. In Britain, as I insist, new technology grinds ahead in friction with social class. Between the wars aircraft remained the luxury toys of the rich and the powerful. Meanwhile, huge numbers of people bought bicycles and took to the railroads; fewer but still large numbers bought cars between 1919 and 1939, lots more took buses and open charabancs. But although in summer the call of the countryside began to drown out the bells of the Sunday church service, and every road became busy not with neighbours but with strangers travelling to somewhere else, no-one could go away very far or for very long until the battle, the class battle, for longer holiday hours was won.

Nearby seasides throve on the railway excursion from 1860 onwards. Bank holidays were enacted in 1871. In the big industrial cities of the north of England and in the coal valleys of Scotland and South Wales, substantial concessions were won by 'the Brigade of Guards of the Labour movement', which was to say the skilled artisans of the key heavy industries – coal, steel, railways, ships. In addition, the much older tradition of north country wakes weeks meant that substantial numbers of textile workers received of right some holiday with varying amounts of pay for almost all the nineteenth century. The lower clerical classes, as the novels of H.G. Wells and George Gissing testify, fared no better: three or four days off per year for most of them, their most daring venture a trip to Margate or even Brighton. The middle classes – senior clerks, managers, City workers, the new technocrats, could afford the transport and take a week. Plenty of employers saw the point of the argument which said that the labour force needed a break in order to maintain productivity. Labour relations came to birth in the great British class compromise which headed off the catastrophic social breakdown, prophesying revolution, reported from Russia, Germany, Italy, with even hints from the USA where the Wobblies went to gaol, between 1917 and 1929.

That compromise, still fractious on one side and downright mean-minded on the other, was consolidated when the survivors came back in a spirit of transclass egalitarianism to make a 'land fit for heroes to live in'. Once it was grasped even by the dimmer employers that paid holidays were simply another form of potentially benignant wage bargain, they began slowly to yield time. As R.H. Tawney wrote at about this date:

> The story of the struggle between humanitarian sentiment and the theory of property transmitted from the eighteenth century is familiar. No one has forgotten the opposition offered in the name of the rights of property to factory legislation, to housing reform, to interference with the adulteration of goods, even to the compulsory sanitation of private houses. 'May I not do what I like with my own?' was the answer to the proposal to require a minimum standard of safety and sanitation from the owners of mills and houses. Even to this day, while an English urban landlord can cramp or distort the development of a whole city by withholding land except at fancy prices, English municipalities are without adequate powers of compulsory purchase, and must either pay through the nose or see thousands of their members overcrowded. The whole body of procedure by which they may acquire land, or indeed new powers of any kind, has been carefully designed by lawyers to protect owners of property against the possibility that their private rights may be subordinated to the public interest, because their rights are thought to be primary and absolute and public interests secondary and contingent.[28]

Pimlott quotes a March 1925 figure from the Ministry of Labour[29] which put the number of British manual workers taking paid holidays at one and a half million. By 1937 four million out of 18.5 million workers earning less than £250 per year were taking paid holidays, with another million or so doing the same on higher income levels and different pay deals. As usual, the social democratic Scandinavians were the pioneers of this bit of welfare progress over these years, while assorted scrappy parliamentary Bills in Britain were fragmentarily blocked and enacted, until in 1937 the forgotten Lord Amulree chaired the Holidays with Pay Committee and recommended the phasing in of annual holidays with pay 'to be established, without undue delay, as part of the terms of the contract of employment'.[30] The Minister agreed, and although the terms of the Act were gutless (some farmworkers were actually worse off for leisure time than before), the case was official. During the blessedly co-operative war years, so many more and better agreements were struck that by 1945, ten million manual workers received holiday pay.[31] The Left declared (correctly) that more leisure made for a more fulfilled life; the Right said that paid holidays kept up productivity, and shortened hours without raising the wages bill. So another measure once the dream of luxury became a received commonplace, and all to the good.

The freedoms came unevenly, in both time and place. Slump stopped the growth in vacations on either side of the Atlantic for several years. Ernie Bevin, later Foreign Secretary and in 1933 General Secretary of the Transport and General Workers Union, proposed a national movement for paid holidays and in 1937 the Labour Party organised 150 seaside meetings with a million posters in support of the idea and in order to encourage the Amulree Committee.[32] They did so with the blessing of the most forward-looking of the new industrial conglomerates in the north-east, ICI.[33]

Social change being what it is, by 1983 the average number of hours worked every week by manual workers had fallen below forty for the first time and all but 5 per cent of the labour force enjoyed at least four weeks' paid holiday.[34]

Once the principle was fully established and once people really had enough money to spare, everyone poured into the same places at the same time. Between 1950 and 1980 average real wages in Britain doubled.[35] There was sporadic talk before and after the war of staggering the holidays, for in a little north-west island off the coast of northern Europe, such sunshine as there was occurred mostly in July and August, and there weren't enough hotel and boarding house beds to go round even in 1939. Globalisation wasn't due yet and the deep habituations of culture meant that holiday mobility kept quite a short horizon.

One Mr Billy Butlin was the first to recognise the possibilities of the shortage of accommodation. In 1936, the year before the Amulree Committee, he opened his first 'holiday camp' on Easter Saturday at Skegness ('It's so bracing' said the poster with the cheery and bewhiskeredly bouncing fisherman; he was right, it was snowing). It was followed in 1938 at Clacton-on-Sea in Essex, the nearest seaside for London's East-enders. A week's holiday cost between thirty shillings and three pounds; 10,000 people applied for places.

Butlin's provenance was mixed. The idea emerged from a strange mingling of assorted camping movements of the 1920s, including the Co-operative Holidays Association, a product of the more-or-less political but always neighbourly co-operative movement in the north of England, the Holiday Fellowship, the Youth Hostels Association (founded in 1929), various worthy church bodies, to say nothing of the vast annual excursion of the London poor into the fields of Kent to pick hops for the brewers in August and September, sleeping where they could, in tents, in the open, in any private house which charged little enough, in ancient automobiles and empty charabancs chartered for the occasion. In the Germany of the Third Reich, the people were vigorously encouraged by radio propaganda and folk music pumping out from street corner loudspeakers to join collective summer camps, boisterous, happy, communal affairs given just the slightest nudge towards the Führer by cheerful, good-looking young men and women in well-pressed shirts and shorts and the swastika on their upper arms.

Billy Butlin, a South African Canadian, built his fixed camps out of these predecessors. He left out the politics, of course, for this was England, but he kept in the communality, the throngs of people, the familiarity. Binding the whole new and terrific exodus together was the deep and reassuring conservatism which held and holds together the British working class. Butlin understood intuitively, as did Pontin's at the same moment, that this same gigantic, self-assured, not very reflective class wanted the pleasure of going away, but wanted to go away in order to take its holidays with its own kind – to meet strangers, certainly, but strangers from just round the corner, exactly as one could at Blackpool.

Indeed, it is hard to over-emphasise the influence of Blackpool and Scarborough, Ramsgate and Southend, on the topography and the social life of the holiday camp. The little, neat, slightly garish rows of chalets mimicked in small scale the unbroken lines of back-to-back terrace houses in Rochdale and Bolton, in Hull, Elland, Halifax. The big dining halls replicated the workers' canteens in which all the men and plenty of the women took their factory lunches. The swimming pool, generally indoors, was

Figure 6.2   A 'Quad-ro-bike' at a Butlin's Holiday Camp, 1950
Source: The Mary Evans Picture Library/The Barry Norman Collection

identical to the public baths at home, echoing tinnily to the shrieks of the kids, the air heavy with chlorine, the water unheated, clothes stowed in ranks of grim little metal lockers. The cinema, the pub, the dance floor, the music hall were powerfully familiar and familial, and everywhere the cheery redcoats in their flame-coloured blazers exhorted the people and their children to laughter, to connection with each other, to three square meals a day, to walks in the decidedly bracing air, to dance the Valeta and the old-fashioned waltz, to sing-songs and sandcastle competitions and the studious embarrassment of newly-weds. The life of the camps consolidated the best of Blackpool in a happy balance of greater freedom (no landladies, easy babysitting) *and* immediate solidarity (games, meals, singsongs).

It is easy, now the camps have largely moved to Torremolinos[36] or been replaced by Club Med, to sentimentalise a life one would not, speaking for the bourgeoisie, have turned up for after death. But I cannot easily conjure up a fuller or more perfect picture of the triumph of Britain's quiet revolution after the great Labour victory of 1945 than some such fresco of Butlin's at Filey or Bridlington or near the North Wales coast, while the legendary summer of 1947 shone on a happy island and Denis Compton moved effortlessly towards his eighteenth century of that glorious cricket season.[37] Billy Butlin was knighted in 1964. He earned it.

The fixed holiday camps mark an enormous qualitative as well as quantitative change in the history, and not only as it pertains to Britain. They came into their pride in the happy aftermath of war, when a satisfied pleasure at the defeat of Fascism and the coming of peace was strained by continued rationing, fuel shortages, the exhaustion of a people and an economy which together had been left bankrupted and at the end of their tether by the previous six years. Before the war, British and American holidays alike had been disfigured by dreadful food, extortionate and bullying hoteliers, contemptible snobbery and capricious house rules. After it – well, the war won no simple victories for co-operativeness and kindness, but people expected better of one another, and for two decades or so they got it.

The USA swept skyward on the mighty postwar boom and the beginnings of the Pax Americana. The automobile came into its own, eradicating the passenger railroad: by 1950 80 per cent of all long-distance journeys in the USA were by car. Thirteen years later almost half of all American families took a vacation trip – the drive as much part of the vacation as its destination – with an average length of 600 miles.[38] This was the fluorescence of that dowdy, necessary, all-American invention, the motel, and American vacationing was, for the working classes at least, inseparable from a society endlessly on the move, divine restlessness and the itinerant nature of so much work combining to transform sheer movement into a vacation. Road movement past the diners, the topless niteclubs, the vast parking and auto lots, the twenty-four-hour supermarkets, the towering signs 'ribs', 'subs', 'fries' and then the endless dark strips of road past the flat steppes, all this became its own vacationing adventure, and crossing the big country to stop in golden California its own rite of restoration.

In Britain the postwar holiday camp was the dazzling improvisation which caught the feeling of the moment. Billy Butlin knew his clients and believed also, though the phrase had hardly been coined, in consumer satisfaction. The dark side of the Blackpool landscape was the tyrant landlady. The holiday camp superannuated her, and provided instead not only the sometimes robotic cheeriness of cheerleaders but also a little city which did away with the boarding house's casual insolence and exclusion, whereby customers were shut out between 9 a.m. and high teatime. The camp was always open and much of it under cover; other people looked after the kids; you could dance until the lights went out at 11.45; the vagaries of north-west European weather suddenly mattered less.

Their day is now done. But it is worth adding that the holiday camp was the source of some of tourism's richest innovations. It implied the all-inclusive holiday, that freedom brought about by handing oneself and one's family over to the organisers in order not to suffer the intolerable freedom of organising everything oneself. In Britain, snobbery being an art-form in that country, non-camping vacationers turned up their noses at the regimen and timetables of Mr Butlin, not noticing of course that the same criticisms could be made of the high-status Swan's Mediterranean Cruises, with lectures by Sir Mortimer Wheeler on the Acropolis in the morning and a not-to-be-missed performance of *The Trojan Women* in the amphitheatre at 5 p.m.

The camps presaged and embodied the luxury of the day, and with it, the carnival-making and saturnalian festival in such *very* decorous versions (the dance, the bathing beauty competition) of the class and its history. They admit the consumer to his or her rights. They inaugurate mass-mobile holidays in packages. They make it possible to conceive of building whole new towns for transients (with horrible consequences in Greece, Turkey, Florida, Mexico). They are the true genesis of mass vacationing.

V

This has been so far a largely frictionless, even Whiggish history. The rich and privileged have been observed making and taking their vacations and their pleasures, and other classes, anxious to flatter, to mimic and to learn new pleasures have sought to do

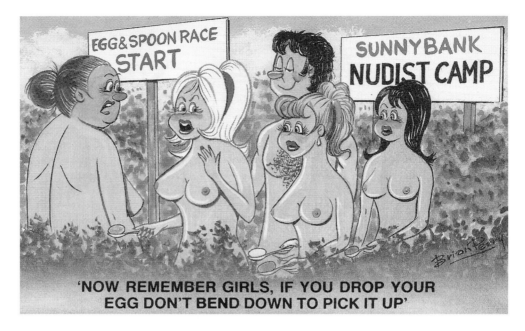

Figure 6.3   Brian Perry's Egg and Spoon Race postcard
Source: Bamforth & Co. Ltd/Dennis Print

the same. Where these pleasures have differed, social classes have drawn peacefully apart and enjoyed their differences in the places they have made their own, Blackpool here, Bournemouth there; Key West for the poets, Atlantic City for the gamblers, Disneyland for the people's kitsch. Sometimes it is a surprise that capitalism orders these divisions of labour, of pleasure and of pocket, so neatly.

Edward Thompson once defined culture itself as 'way of struggle',[39] and the industrialisation of mobility lies on that way. Technology and investment brought the bike, the auto and the passenger aircraft, and brought all three to war as well. The expansion of the power of each was settled, temporarily, by class and money; sales and status competed for dominance, as when General Motors invented a new automobile for every social fraction.

There is, however, only one world in which to walk, cycle, drive or fly and there is always a struggle about who may do which of these things, and where. As we shall hear, as indeed everybody knows, the numbers of people, millions of them on vacation, who want to fly in somewhere convenient at any time make parts of the globe uninhabitable. For twenty years, British governments have lied about the hellishness of living under the aircraft piling into London Heathrow all day, all night, forty-two aircraft per hour. They built a fourth terminal in 1979 promising that noise levels would be reduced, but of course they weren't, and since then one of the longest shows in town was the Official Inquiry into building a *fifth* terminal which would be, after Frankfurt and distinct from the first four terminals at Heathrow, the third largest airport in Europe.

These things are now protractedly disputed and opposed by the due procedures of law and hearings and ignorings. There was once something to be said for more direct forms of action taken on vacation. Long before the passenger aircraft came to dominate the argument about tourist access, a spirited little chronicle in the way of struggle was lived out in England.

It is still bracing news to read of resistance in the name of calling a countryside one's own, on behalf of one's people. The moment the motor car made the boundary between city and country so much more blurred, and encouraged romantic souls to build their bungalows along the roads that led into the meadows and lanes, movements and associations in queer old private-public England sprang up to oppose them, and to affirm contrary values on behalf of health, freedom, equality, nature and sunshine. The excellent orotundity of the Commons, Open Spaces and Footpaths Preservation Society is one key signature of the 1920s, and the same people, from a wide band of assorted middle-class fractions, recruited their sons and daughters to the Youth Hostels Association, whose members walked and biked in shorts, aertex shirts and knapsacks from one spartan house-in-the-country to the next, where they could kip down with the same sex for one shilling a night. The people, members as like as not of such loopy associations affirming a strictly local version of Englishness as the King Alfred Muster in south Dorset[40] or Arthur's yeomen in Somerset, as well as of the Labour or Communist parties, supporters of the League of Nations, came together to found such very varied bodies as the Ramblers' Association or the Council for the Preservation of Rural England. This latter counted, emblematically, among its leaders one Patrick Abercrombie, England's first Professor of Town Planning and among his allies was the wondrous architect-visionary Clough Williams-Ellis who conceived, paid for and built Portmeirion as forever a little corner of the Mediterranean in North Wales.[41]

Out of a contradictory formation, these movements stood up for healthy, free and mobile leisure (open air, picnics, walking, cycling). They stood up for rights and freedoms. They backed Old Tawney against property and profit. Their painters were their fellow-ramblers, the brothers Paul and John Nash and Eric Ravilious, their most powerful books the famous Batsford series, 'Face of England' and 'British Heritage' (an early sighting of the phase), now collectors' items.

Out of this surge of popular feeling, which could not help but increase the flow of numbers into the rural Britain the associations wanted to protect, came the government's National Parks Committee of 1929. Some forty years after John Muir's success with President Harrison over Yosemite and Sequoia, the Peak District, the English Lakes and Welsh Snowdonia slowly and inadequately became National Parks. The regimental battle honours of the movement went in all this to the Ramblers Association; its colours are marked eponymously with the great victory won after the Kinder Scout march, in Derbyshire in 1932.

This surge of popular self-assertion was not confined to Britain. Thoreau's admirers were deep into the wilderness at the turn of the century. The German *Wandervogel* set out in the 1890s and were shrewdly put to nationalist purposes in the 1930s. By the 1930s there were estimated to be half a million Ramblers in Britain, ten thousand of them out in the Derbyshire Peak District every summer weekend,[42] and 'the way of struggle' which is culture had a new battle on hand.

The Association's pungently militant journal, *Rambling*, under the editorship of

Edwin Royce, attacked those landowners who prevented legitimate access, by public footpath, to the rugged wilderness of the Peak where, it so happened, solitude also conduced to the breeding of the game the landowners themselves raised for slaughter by highly lucrative tenant shooting parties. The keepers hired by the landowner in question, the Duke of Devonshire, barred the way with gates, barbed wire and, ulti-mately, shotguns. The Labour-controlled Sheffield Corporation, which owned the adjacent land, supported the Duke and his men.

On Sunday 24 April 1932, led by the local (Communist) secretary of the British Workers Sports Federation, Benny Rothman, a large party of Ramblers numbering, says the legend, six hundred,[43] met in Hayfield village and warmed itself up with loud-speaker calls to action and the usual, admirable paraphernalia of self-righteous protest, including press photographers. They then trundled up to the top, scuffled with the keepers and came back singing. Five of them were gratifyingly gaoled by local magistrates for affray and became class martyrs. A series of similar actions including mild bouts of arson on the moors followed, gathering ever larger support such that 10,000 protesters turned out a year later, down the road at Castleton. In the end an Access Bill of sorts was passed in 1938.

The struggle of course continues. The history of the holiday had turned round a little and been made, by numbers, from below. The right-feeling reader, it needs hardly be said, can only be on the Ramblers' side.

7

THE MEDITERRANEAN

I

To take holidays as the focus for a short history of consumerism is to study, as I have suggested, the form of the correspondences the culture of capitalism has effected between the structure of our feelings, the definitions and orderings of our time, and the arrangements of our geography. The vacation predicates time and money to be spent finding the right place to have the best feelings. It is hardly a surprise that the place which best gave rise to the feelings in question was the Mediterranean littoral. Those seas, rocks, groves and sands gathered and intensified the images of leisure, luxury and freedom which started life, one could say, in the poems and architecture of the small city-states which, two and a half millennia ago, gave birth to some rough ideas of beauty, selfhood and human flourishing.

An affection for those origins lives on in the vacation carefully planned to take in sunshine, wine, cultivated idling, a little edification and a song in praise of that idleness. Without the Mediterranean origins, no way of conceiving the classical iconography of the grand hotel, let alone the seaside. Without Greek colonnades and porticos, no spas; without the Alhambra, no urban gardens; without Naples, no promenades; without the fountains of Rome, none of the pleasing municipal waterworks which, even on a squally day in North-western Europe, soothe and sparkle in the spirit of the harmless pedestrian on a constitutional.

The Mediterranean by way of Rhine and Rhône defined the actuality of the Grand Tour and, for the two centuries thereafter, filled to the brim the average vacationer's imagination. No wonder, therefore, that when mass leisure mobility burst open the doors of the air terminals, so many people were heading for the birthplace of their favourite pictures of paradise.

Vacations, holidays, tours are European inventions which spread, with Europeans, to North America. As that enormous half-continent came first to dominate and then to transform the nature of capitalism, then all that went under the name of vacationing was turned by capitalism's alchemy and its house magicians in the advertising agencies into an unprecedented world. It is a world in which fulfilment is always stretched a little too far, and aspiration tinged with disappointment; it is a world in which glamour, magnetic as it always is, attaches itself to those we can look at but cannot emulate, see but not be; it is a world of foreshortened experience, where pleasure is compressed into a workrate (one cathedral, one master fresco, one glass of

Figure 7.1   View of the Temple of Ceres
Source: Athenaion

Brunello is a good morning), and leisure required to pay a dividend (the hours spent lying in the sun pay for the shining golden tan).

It is the argument of this book that this complicated and hierarchical architecture of pleasure, with its many different rooms and contradictory principles of extension, was devised out of the history of the last two hundred and fifty years, in particular as that history so organised its production that the leisure and the increased longevity leisure brought with it provided fresh space and time for the exercise of undreamed-of freedoms formerly confined to the rich.

The rich we always have with us and the realm of their leisure expanded well ahead of everybody else's until they came up against the peculiar excesses of very late twentieth-century acquisitiveness, whereafter, for a time, power-hunger and stupefying wealth, taken together, will not let their owners rest. The strange new international élite who thus combine glamour and overwork, greed and asceticism, will figure as ominous omens of a post-millennial irresponsibility when, in Chapter 10, we come to the doors of the future. In the meantime, the creation of leisure and the competition to buy and sell it are best understood as a history of how to feel, how to imagine, how to yearn, and how to go places and do nothing.

As Braudel began by telling us, the people of northern Europe have a predilection to love the Mediterranean. It has always featured so very largely in the education contrived for European élites and then by extension for the less-than-élite children who have subsequently won an education for themselves. I have much insisted that present culture may be most easily grasped as an early nineteenth-century invention, and the history of our passions as starting out from the codes of feeling written down by the Romantics. Those codes, however, had to come from somewhere, and the whereabouts in question was the classical tradition.

In the 1760s Winckelmann reaffirmed antiquity as guide and tutor to the young blades and middle-aged scholar-sybarites of the Grand Tour, and taught them of the lavishness and grace of old Italy. Admiring the paintings of Claude and Poussin, they drank copiously from the Pierian springs. In visiting the excavations, at Pompeii and Herculaneum as well as in Rome, they rediscovered the power of the old poets whose lines they had learned by heart painfully to analyse and construe in the long drudgery of ruling class education in the eighteenth century. Behind them, in turn, stood the great fortresses of Renaissance learning built out of the materials of rediscovery, when the intellectual riches of Catholicism were first broken open by the Italians, the Germans and finally by the Dutch and English, and the new humanism was effected from the union of classicism and Christianity.

New culture grows out of old residues. Boswell and Lady Mary Wortley Montagu doubtless knew much of Virgil by heart, but plenty of those grandish tourists who solemnly visited Avernus just north of Naples, where Virgil was escorted by Aeneas down to the underworld in order to meet the shades, did not. Nonetheless, their little outing, presaging a large picnic, was tribute paid to those who *did* know the old poets by heart, and their brief moment of indifferent attention to the dark lake acknowledged the presence of the Mediterranean in their formation.

The Mediterranean meant, and means no doubt, much more than the imagery of the Latin authors. But the poets fixed up the first views of its geography. We owe to them, just as we do to Poussin, Claude and company, our familiarity with olive tree, cypress and vineyard, white marble and quiet water. We owe them the very idea of *belvedere*, of a view opening gradually beyond the slopes and coppices which frame it into the largeness of distance and the curves of the horizon. We even owe them the plans and poetics of the houses from which we shall see these views. It was the Augustan Romans who invented the country villa and its direct descendants, the holiday home, and the classier kind of seaside hotel with its courtyards, balconies and poolside greenery.

In 1840 the German architect, Karl Friedrich Schinkel painted an accurate reconstruction of one of the suburban villas built to his own design by a celebrated public servant of the Empire named Gaius Plinius Caecilius Secundus, known more briefly to the schoolchildren who used to translate him as Pliny. He is probably best known for his eye-witness descriptions of the obliteration of Pompeii by the eruption of Vesuvius, in which his uncle died, but his deep legacy to us is, first, the villas and, second, his letters about them.

One was built beside the sea south of Rome, near enough for him to be driven there after a day's work in the Forum. This was his winter home, the Laurentine villa, perhaps close to Castel Fusano. The other was in Tuscany, high enough in the Apennines to be cool in summer. Schinkel's restitution[1] shows a noble villa on a promenade immediately beside the sea, with a long colonnade at one end, a three-storey 'hotel' giving onto the cloister, and then a long, low castellated façade pierced only rarely by small windows (and therefore capable of being warm or cool by season), culminating in a deep courtyard sealed by a bold, round apse-like building with a dome and four high entrances on its hemispheric, sea-viewing side.

Much is rightly made of these days of more cultural differences which cause each of us, from our contrastive life-experiences, to see things utterly unlike the way someone else, from another society, sees things. Now is the time to insist also on some reassuring commonplaces about our common humanity and about the naturalness of human nature. For sure, the Romantic movement taught everybody to go looking for views of nature's wild and mountainous sublimity, so off everybody went with their Claude glasses to the English Lake District. Maybe it was true that, as Pevsner has told us,[2] when Vanburgh designed the splendid baroque of Seaton Delaval in Northumberland, the houses faced inland away from the sea because at that date (1720) a view of the sea had no great significance. All the same, Pliny's two villas enjoyed, on one hand, a view of the Apennines, and on the other, of the stretch of the Mediterranean he knew as the Tyrrhenian sea, and his repeated invitations to his friends play upon the loveliness of the views seventeen hundred years before Wordsworth (Pliny died in about 113 AD). In one letter, Pliny's description of the Tuscan landscape, intended to coax friends to stay, will serve as inventory of the beauties and refreshments of a month in the country for the next two, probably three millennia.

> The countryside is very beautiful. Picture to yourself a vast amphitheatre such as could only be a work of nature; the great spreading plain is ringed round by mountains, their summits crowned by ancient woods of tall trees... Below them the vineyards spreading down every slope weave their uniform pattern far and wide, their lower limit bordered by a planted coppice. Then come the meadows and cornfields... It is a great pleasure to look down on the countryside from the mountain, for the view seems to be a painted scene of unusual beauty rather than a real landscape, and the harmony to be found in this variety refreshes the eye wherever it turns.[3]

Just like a modern, Pliny thought that painting makes us see and feel about the beauties of nature in the way we do, and just like an eighteenth-century tourist, Pliny arranges for himself the best prospect of the landscape his villa may command. Pliny was, near enough, a contemporary of the great architectural theorist of Imperial Rome, Vitruvius, and between them and the silver poets of the same day, they sacralised the ideal forms of an Italian Mediterranean which thereafter shaped the imaginations and sensibilities of any European or North American seeking to bring together sun, stone, water and the most igneous greens of nature, in a single poetics. Some such coincidence is the search of the tourist-traveller on his or her days of solitude, whether the traveller-tourist comes from Japan or Chile or Scandinavia. Riga and Santiago alike have their deliberately Mediterranean effects, their leafy balconies, classical columns and tiled courtyards, and every culture is sedimented with deposits from the mighty imperial civilisations of the rivers Tigris, Euphrates, Nile and then of the Aegean and Tyrrhenian seas.[4]

II

Our Mediterranean associations take us rather nearer to the mysterious origins of civilisation than one would expect from the genial lubricity of Club Med. The sea's

116

power as a focus and magnet for tourist activity on such an incomparably massive scale as today's[5] is only explicable, I claim, in virtue of its peculiar position in the history of those of its social and political forms which, at least, won for the idea of democracy its present seniority. This victory was by no means inevitable and is far from complete; the mass and massive movements of Islam eastwards and westwards in the ninth and tenth centuries, of communism in the twentieth, are merely two instances of the tides that might have swept back the practical-minded, ruthless busyness of Greek democracy and Roman imperial trade, and then what was made of both by the egotistical modernisers and tyrants of Renaissance Tuscany, Umbria and the Veneto.

So one has to be a bit dry, of both eye and mouth, in figuring out the place of the Mediterranean in the fantastic hierarchy of holidays. Any such algebra, reductive in the extreme as these pages will have to be, adumbrates its alternatives: to understand the pull of the Caribbean or of Alaska, one would have to invoke – as Chapter 5 did – an old atavism of feeling and formation. And yet the point of this chapter is also that the Mediterranean really is special; it is *not* just an example with which to illustrate the direction of the argument.

No more was Blackpool, of course, nor the Empty Quarter. Each historical line goes back to an essential or a transient root in being and feeling: the ice, the desert, the English working class. But none, I think, goes back to anything more fundamental to social and moral feeling, to the promise of happiness and the feasibility of humanism, than the lines that tie the best of modernity, from whatever corner of the globe, to the lovely, blood-stained ratios of Mediterranean history and geography.

In his essay on the inland sea, Adrian Stokes suggested[6] that geography and history combined with special precision to permit a four-part counterpoint: first, of intelligible climate; second, of the opposition of liminals, of land and sea, Europe divided from Africa; third, the pellucid interplay of stone and water, the dependence of each on each; fourth, the striated, irregular topography which forced valley against ridge, rock against grove, sun against shade, and made for a new class of smallholder farmers and fishermen, bound in allegiance to one another, free of distant emperors, vigorously self-reliant, working the year round. From Athens to Rome to Renaissance Florence these strictly material forces worked their effects within the limits of the Mediterranean, compounding the inevitable egocentricity assured by the astonishing, two thousand year achievements of Greece and Rome and the House of Medici. Then their very own inventiveness spread abroad, the Spanish and the Portuguese quit their local lake for the Atlantic, and modernity began.

The memory of those perfect ratios remains, however, for the tourists to return to, and marvel at. They transpire in the art of the region, and it is that art, above all the art of landscape as loved by the artless, which so configures the meaning of the Mediterranean. The art idealises, as everybody knows it does and should. Actually *living* on the shores of the sea was, for most of the history for which there are records, a precarious and frequently tormented affair.

Braudel[7] defines the 'true' Mediterranean as lying below the northern limit of the olive tree, which runs across Spain below Catalonia, crosses into France under the foothills of the Pyrenees, threads through the Hérault and Provence, turns down to the foot of Tuscany and northwards to Trieste, down again beside the Aegean, always hugging the shore, the Riviera, a narrow ribbon never more than a thousand kilometres deep, often less, winding its way along the Turkish littoral and coming to a halt in Israel, where the desert begins again. The palmgrove line, which Braudel defines as marked by '*large*, compact groves' (his italics), cuts more or less across the north-western slice of Africa, taking in Morocco, Algeria and some of Tunisia. Palmgroves extend much further south, of course, providing, as we saw, a staple food for the Bedu, but it is a struggle for them to survive in the desert where they are husbanded beside the roads, marking the route, always threatened by suffocation from the sand. Single palmtrees, by contrast, become exotic signifiers, sedulously planted on seaside prome-nades wherever (in England and Wales) warm enough air brought by the Gulf Stream will keep them alive in Torquay, Llandudno, Prestatyn.

Dates along the southern coast, olives along the north and east, oranges, lemons, figs, pomegranates along both, fill the Mediterranean fruit-baskets and define its agri-culture. The vine reaches much further north but even then, it is the sunline along the Loire and down the Rhine which tells the whiteskinned Nordics when they can smell the scents of the Mediterranean, and the holiday traveller sits up keenly as soon as he or she passes the notice on the *Autoroute du Soleil* marking the watershed of France.

The vast plenty of grapes and olives was always hard-won. The Atlantic brings the cold winds and heavy rains, even the snows and frosts of winter, but at the equinox summer returns in a trice, the desert winds blow warmly and smoothly over the sea, the anticyclone off the Azores swells and blocks the depressions moving eastwards above the grey waves, the air and the ground begin to go dry and hard.

This climatic overlap recurs at about the same latitude, in both the northern and southern hemispheres, in California, Middle Chile, the South African Cape and South West Australia. It is an agreeable endorsement of the argument to note just how powerfully the land-and-townscapes, architecture, homesteads and everyday domestic culture of these other Mediterranean rivieras are influenced by their common origins. The classical pillars and entablatures, the bougainvillea, juniper and evergreen oak, the balconies and boardwalks, marble fountains and orange groves take their form and mystery straight enough from the agriculture and economy enforced by climate and geology on the medley of peoples and tongues under the Greek and Roman imperium a couple of thousand years ago.

The pentecost of Mediterranean tongues is made intelligible by a common agricul-ture, on land and sea. By the sixteenth century, a native of the Mediterranean, wherever he might come from, was at home in any port of the sea – hence the ease of migration. This winning gregariousness sorts well with historic pictures, recreated in films, of crowded and colourful quaysides, ship-thronged waterways, pyramids of brandy barrels, rakish adventurers; the same crowd scatters in the same yarns as the corsairs and brigands sail into town. The sometime thriving port of Amalfi, birthplace of the compass, assumed its weird topography of labyrinthine passages, alleys, stair-wells and tunnels exactly because these were unknowable to enemy pirates, endlessly defensible by the home guard.

But the real enemy, for the sixteenth as for the first century, was not the corsair but the desert. As Braudel says:

> The truth is that the Mediterranean has struggled against a fundamental poverty ... It affords a precarious living, in spite of its real or apparent advan-tages. It is easy to be deceived by its famous charm and beauty. Even as

experienced a geographer as Philippson was dazzled, like all visitors from the North, by the sun, the colours, the warmth, the winter roses, the early fruits. Goethe at Vicenza was captivated by the popular street life with its open stalls and dreamed of taking back home with him a little of the magic air of the South. Even when one is aware of the reality it is difficult to associate these scenes of brilliance and gaiety with images of misery and physical hardship. In fact Mediterranean man gains his daily bread by painful effort. Great tracts of land remain uncultivated and of little use … the … soil … is responsible for the poverty it inflicts on its people, with its infertile limestone, the great stretches blighted with salt … the desert lies in wait for arable land and never lets go.[8]

Snow on the mountains, fierce winter storms at sea, the harsh and arid mistral, the failure of the uncertain rains, all kept famine prowling only a little way outside the towns. Not until the amazing productivity advances of the mid-twentieth century in chemical agriculture and hydraulic support was such privation finally ended, and then largely for the subsidised farmers of the wealthy European Union.

Yet even after this detour into historical geography, it still seemed reasonable for Stokes to say 'I for one expect a Japanese to feel in Greece and Italy that here is the home of man.'[9] We may perhaps be correspondingly large with our similar claims because they are made on behalf of a class of visitors who already have enough to eat and whose interest in the labours of others, though always lively and protracted, is strictly that of a spectator. This being so, Stokes's panegyric, matching Pliny's, is the more persuasive. He is talking about the making of our moral imagination, a process with a long provenance.

He pays tribute to certain happy accidents of photosynthesis. The greens that belong to the Mediterranean are dark; they make for dark shade and groves; they set off the glare of the August sun. Likewise, the dry, stony ground permits water to run lucent and clear; no mud or opaque depths here, here are the dark clarities which serve as the mirror in which Narcissus saw himself and fell in love. Indeed, as Stokes says, limestone is the domain of water, rainwater which has seeped and soaked through the thin, pebbly soil until it finds a long, level shank of stone it can run along. So men dug for it and brought it back to the surface, fashioned their own channel for it, lined it with cut limestone ashlars, turned aside the stream so that it fell onto terraces waiting gratefully to receive it as it irrigated what it found there, the roots of olives, lemons, vines, wheat.

All this designing, engineering, making shift with and for water brought the Mediterranean peasant to a fine state of readiness and inventiveness. The intensely local nature of the life, the ground divided by short valleys and steep mountains, broken into little, local harbours, its unstopping cultivation, the unyielding *demand* by Nature that she will only give up subsistence if you work at her all year, all this made both for terrific application and stamina as well as for a high degree of pride and independence. Honouring these labours, and kneeling to a climate whose twin motions of Atlantic and deserts make it possible for crops and vegetation to grow for every one of the twelve months, Stokes can say:

> There is something 'reasonable' about the Mediterranean climate and about the varied and independent communities which that limestone geography harboured. In this smallness of scale, man gained the courage to manoeuvre natural forces, to be inventive … however vast [his control of those forces] has now become, we owe it in the first place to the smallness of the Mediterranean unit, to that climate and geography whose light and contour gave to man, whose cultivation demanded of him, a well-sustained courage and good sense … These methods, the outcome of Mediterranean conditions, will, at one time or another, breed self-dependent individuals who are yet not the broadest highlanders. There have been other free and independent men, but those of the Mediterranean loved dispute: they found even talking to be an art. To them, Europe owed the faint yet immortal democratic idea.[10]

Some version of this simple theory of genesis is, I believe, lurking in the collective consciousness of most of those who make their way to stand amazed at the azure sea off Capri and Cefalu or bake their backs brown on the shingle at Knossos. Many layers of hope and expectation cover them up, no doubt, some of them filthy and miserable ones as well, but the *Ur*-genesis of that pull southwards is surely tied to unvoiceable beliefs and feelings that beside the Mediterranean one will find the right order of things.

That spellbinding mixture of memory and imagination which gives plot and shape to our cultural history finds such an order everywhere, even after the dreadful coming of the film stars and the building contractors. We find it in the variety and piquancy of the fruit and flesh – tomatoes, figs, oranges, truffles, tuna – which so lend themselves to being eaten out-of-doors, and we reconstruct the same history from the *scale* of Mediterranean places, their propinquity to fresh and sea water, the bold drama of the climate. The severe alternation of the seasons even controls the expectations of those who live right outside its reach, so much so that everybody looks out for cold, wet winters and sunny summers on the coasts of Norway, Michigan or Bohemia.

Above all, the Mediterranean tourist finds this order of things in the limestone sculpture and architecture of Greece, Ancient Rome and Renaissance Italy. The gods of the world were local deities; Zeus and Jupiter were the names of the rain-god with his head up in the clouds on the top of Mount Olympus, Mount Parnes and in the grove of Dodona in Epirus, on the rainy side of the Pindus. Round his head gathered the chariots of wrath giving off flashes of lightning, and dark was his thunderous path on the wings of the storms. The storm was his anger, and the rain his mercy. When Antonio Allegri da Correggio painted his wonderful picture of Jupiter ravishing Io in 1532, the god appears to the mortal woman as a cloud, just discernible as the form of a huge biped, one enormous bear-like paw beginning to embrace and transport Io to rapture, the terrible, irresistible, cloudy head bent towards her closed eyes and opened lips.[11] The godhead of rain and the everyday excess of sex merge in an easy ecstasy. This dream lurks in the imagined Mediterranean.

The art embodies the dream, as it is supposed to do. The propitiatory temples of the gods stood on promontories or, as at Paestum, at the sea's edge, to summon the god's guidance to sailors that they avoid the shoals, and to announce to them the god's succour when they came to land. The heaviness and solidity of the carved limestone bring their own reassurance to the pilgrim, casual or devoted. The proportions of the temples were human proportions; the buildings were metaphors of the body, as all buildings ought to be[12] and as, perhaps, the tourist somewhere recognises as she takes a snapshot of the family sitting familiarly on the steps of the fountain, the temple, the forum, the baths.

When those abstract stone components – pillar, entablature, pediment, step – returned to bodily forms as head, torso, limbs, why then the perfect relation of humankind and the waters of life are reaffirmed. The limestone, sluiced for aeons by water, speaks in the flowing draperies and graceful gestures of the carvings and paintings[13] of the ease and *caritas*, the 'perfect reasonableness' of the Mediterranean settlement, so long as weather behaves itself and sun and rain keep their stations. On the quayside, the white stone stops the water, tolerantly; the water laps and, by and large, respects the limit of the stone. The Mediterranean is not a killer sea; it souses Venice from time to time but that's all. No tidal waves, no slow, monster rivers drowning an estuary, only the Nile fructifying the grateful fields with its reeking bounty.

Limestone contains both sunshine and water. It holds warmth and conducts water. As architecture, it puts the world to rights: foursquare, solid geometry, commemorating the covenant between humankind and nature. The Italian Renaissance is the peak of this expression. That is why all those people pour into Tuscany, Umbria, the Veneto, Rome and Sicily every summer. They wouldn't put it with quite such a flourish, but millions of souls sing every year because they gaze[14] upon the loveliest possible representation of human bodies at home in sun and rain.

To write like this of all those ill-distributed shoulders, bellies, bottoms and knees shuffling past the sculptures in the Bargello or lowering themselves gingerly into a millpond sea off Bandol is to invite the jeerers. Let us meet them head-on, at the harbour wall.

We have seen the people gathering down there already, and been alerted to the pleasures of the harbour by Alain Corbin, let alone Monet at Etretat, Winslow Homer at Alnmouth and all those Cornish painters, from Stanhope Forbes to Alfred Wallis, down at Newlyn and St Ives. But the receptive idleness of someone sea-gazing at the iron balustrade on the edge of the quay is close to beatitude. Freud speaks of the weaned child forever seeking the irrecoverably lost connection of 'oceanic bliss' felt by the infant at the breast, soothed, he speculated, by unconscious recollection of the soft and floating safety of the womb. It is an easy step to pursue this hint with similar musings about the pleasures of swimming as similarly being a brief return to the transport of amniotic fluid. (It is all the stranger, therefore, that swimming for serious pleasure only reappeared at the start of our present brief history.)

Beholding the dreamers on the quayside, one is surely safe in attributing to her and him some similar associations. One leans over the iron railing, eyes on the middle distance, watching the waves tranquilly gather, swell, curve and break with a thud on the stone below, wetting the spectator with a slight, pleasant spray. A little way along, on the inside wall, the other watcher sits amicably on the top of the short rise of steps going down into the water at high tide, and onto the mud at the ebb. The water slaps and sucks slightly at the white stone, the seaweed lower down splays and sways with the tide. The water is perfectly clear where a shoal of sprats nose a bulging plastic bag, and a boat at anchor, out of vision, creaks and rolls. The gulls cry. The kind old sun is hot.

Such interludes are the stuff of holidays; they are the sort of thing recollected in tranquillity as *being* the holiday. It is an old truism about modern life, versified by W.H. Davies to ask (in a poem called, indeed, 'Leisure'):

What is this life if full of care,
We have no time to stand and stare?

Truisms may be true, and standing-and-staring at the sea is best understood, I suggest, as an act of devotion to our common origins, as civilised human beings, alongside the Mediterranean. Ruminant paddling, leaning over the railings of the pier, sitting on the harbour steps watching the water pull the stone out of shape, are forms of contented idleness paid for by the farmers, fishermen and citizens of Greece, Rome and the Renaissance.

III

All history must have a prehistory, if one is not to be deceived into thinking that a short history of events is all that really happened. This making of the Mediterranean must serve, apart from being the preface to 'visible cities', as our prehistory. Certainly, the great colonialists of Spain and Portugal sailed to Latin America and tried desperately hard to recreate the Mediterranean when they arrived. They couldn't grow grapes or olives or figs, not in the north at least, but they could make courtyards, squares and balconies. Wherever imperialists found the right climate and its accompanying geography – Argentina, Chile, California, the Cape, Victoria and New South Wales, they built a colony which reproduced the antique relation of stone and water they recollected, however vaguely, from the Mediterranean. The lighthouse replaced the temple on the promontory, but the moles, the quays, the fountains and the piazzas were much of a muchness.

Modernity, however, swept in through the Straits of Gibraltar and on its irresistible tide was also carried the flotsam of meanings which make for the other side of tourism. So far, I have spoken (from the bottom of my heart) for the noble settlement and sediment of Mediterranean life in our feelings and values. But here come the others, the boisterous, the gluttonous, the lecherous, the sociable, the reckless and the free, come, as the slightly priggish narrator in *The Great Gatsby* himself put it, 'with a simplicity of heart which was its own ticket of admission', and 'after that conducted themselves according to the rules of behaviour associated with an amusement park'.[15]

Until, let us say, the 1890s, the male halves of the *haute bourgeoisie* on tour had made no distinction between those places in which they would be assiduous in scholarship and culture, and those places where they would misbehave themselves with women, wine and a general class propensity to throw things about and break them. Tintoretto and Cicero, swimming or riding and falling in love with married women, went together just fine for Byron and Boswell.

That strain in the complex interminglings of the tourist's values which pulls our heroes towards tasty licentiousness began, towards the end of the nineteenth century, to find for itself a separate zone of practice. The undoubted attractions of fun and games had been happily indulged when the Grand Tourists arrived in Florence and Naples, for they hadn't looked around much on their condescending way through

Provence. If they had, indeed, there was little enough for them to see: evil lodgings, wretched fishing villages, a mere glimpse of the Romans at Orange and St Remy, nothing of the magnificence with which they associated antiquity and its Renaissance restatement, and would find in the fountains of Rome. News got back home about their antics, of course, and angry fathers paid off betrayed mistresses, met the cost of breaches of promise, and closed down allowances to their prodigal sons. But misdemeanours of this sort went, as they say, with the territory, and the territory in question was the big city on the tourist trail; Paris first no doubt, but above all, Italy.

Capitalism in general, and railways in particular brought a new moral tone to tourism. The respectable middle classes were on the move south, and while self-improvement by judicious contact with uplifting masterpieces was very much the point of the trip, drunkenness and fornication were not. Though there is no doubt from all they wrote that the young men and, beside them, the young women of the travelling *bourgeoisie* found the whole adventure to be, when the moment was right, exhilaratingly free and reckless, they were easily and, so far as one can tell, non-sensually satisfied. The tougher eggs among the women – someone like Mary Kingsley for instance – had stomped off into the wilderness to see (and understand) what the natives were up to. But for her sisters, to whom such travel was new, the excitements of art were quite thrilling enough. Lucy Honeychurch in *A Room with a View*, in spite of her deep respectability and a temperament capable when things went wrong 'of joining the vast army of the benighted, who march to their destiny by catchwords',[16] is swept up by the appeal of young Mr Emerson to freedom, to spontaneity and the wise recklessness of the heart.

As this new middle class came into its mercantile inheritance, a new social group, born of revolutionary hopes and disappointments in France, began to define itself as being in all its actions and its semiotics only intelligible as *against* the bourgeoisie. Whatever would outrage them, pleased it. The new Bohemians, led by Baudelaire, the 'doomed poet' of the Parisian barricades, and his brother artist, the free, the dashing, the radical and utterly unrespectable Gustave Courbet, turned *outrance* into a way of life.[17] *Epatant les bourgeois* was its own justification.

This class fraction led the way in restoring an agreeable licentiousness to being away from home, and sex being what it was for respectable Victorians, its members made much of breaking the sexual rules. Being an artist and sleeping with people to whom one was not married went happily together. The scenery of *La Bohème*, of not having any money and living in a top-floor attic studio comes from the same moment of *fin-de-siècle* as does Gilbert's and Sullivan's sardonically named *Patience*.

There are always plenty of people, however, eager to join in a little self-indulgence and flouting of convention quite without the prior qualification of artistic talent. The enthusiasm of the appropriate segments of the ruling class for a high old time was hardly diminished by the arrival of the censorious bourgeois, and indeed may have been confirmed by it. The rich were becoming, in this unprecedentedly money-making and mobile society, not only enviable but emulable. Plenty of novels and moralising anecdotes of the 1880s warned of the debauchery of younger sons wasting their fathers' new-made fortunes.

So there was a mutual pull towards one another of raffish aristocracy and artists. The division of labour being what it is, artists sought out other artists to talk to. Now that the art-patron had disappeared and stately old genre painting gone down before this new impressionist stuff, artists needed dealers, buyers and markets just as they urgently needed good light and cheap lodgings. Paris was expensive and rainy. The place to go for the light and the colours as well as much cheaper rooms to rent was the south. Van Gogh wrote on his arrival in Arles to his brother Theo:

> One night I went for a walk by the sea along the empty shore. It was not gay, but neither was it sad – it was – beautiful. The deep blue sky was flecked with clouds of a blue deeper than the fundamental blue of intense cobalt, and others of a clearer blue, like the blue whiteness of the Milky Way.[18]

He painted the bright yellow lights of the café, and the amazing blues, at midnight and midday, of the Provençal sky. And he painted the sun and its flowers.

This was a new kind of painting, familiar, domestic, cherishing the small details of sunlit life in the south. Cezanne had been down here for ever, doing the same thing of course, and together they established a local subject-matter – pine-trees, fruit, chairs, unguarded, off-duty human bodies – which drew other painters, world-famous ones, after them, Bonnard, Matisse, Picasso. Quickly and involuntarily, the south of France became a place to play the quite new game of celebrity-spotting.

It wasn't the artists who invented the *Côte d'Azur*. (The phrase was coined by a guidebook in the literary manner published in 1887.) Money had to do it first. But as money did, it brought its different flush of colour to the Mediterranean passion.[19]

Until the coming of the railroad, the coastlines of Var and Vaucluse provided only the hard and stony road to the Alpes-Maritimes and the crossing to Italy. Behind them reared mountain ranges, Maures, Luberon, Esterel, craggy enough to pass, less dramatic than the Alps. In front there was only Nice, where Smollett bathed in the sea in 1763, and the much smaller Cannes. Half a century after Smollett, a handful of wealthy English people became hibernators in the two towns, in the case of Lord Chancellor Brougham (he of the Brougham conveyance), building in 1834 a grand enough villa in Cannes, with the pillared marble portico and stone balustrades already fashionable north of Naples. He so launched the place into an orgy of hotel-building that by the time the town did him the honour of a centenary commemoration in 1879, there were fifty such hotels and grand villas along its seafront.[20]

These were the years of the invention of the seaside. People with money and political power also took themselves away from the cold Parisian grey and, like Napoleon III's prime minister, Ollivier, built themselves Plinian villas in which to write and become leisured scholars and sages. For a long time Nice had been an anomaly, geographically in France but belonging to Italy (as not many people know, Garibaldi was born there). The chief ports of the coast had always been Genoa and Marseilles and it was not until 1860 that Cavour and Napoleon III struck a deal, the Niçois voted 'yes' in a referendum, and Nice, having always been either Provençal or Italian, became French.

More to our point, the railway arrived from Marseilles in Nice in 1864 and one François Blanc, a hugely successful casino-owner in the German spa of Bad Homburg, so oiled the wheels of railway development with cheap and enormous loans to the French exchequer that the trains from Nice began to arrive in Monte Carlo by 1868. Within two years, visitors to Monaco totalled 150,000 and in 1875 celebrity-spotters were gratified by the arrival of the then Prince of Wales, later and briefly

Edward VII, a presence certain to encourage all big spenders, stout parties and genteel adulterers.

The colossal success of the Casino at Monte Carlo and its lesser imitator down the railroad at Nice, meant that the money pouring into the south of France had an agreeably risky, raffish, chancey savour to it. It lent the *Côte d'Azur* more of that daring perfume which separated it from the classical itinerary of the Tour and made this a place not only for *outrance* but also for gay abandon, kicking over the traces, sowing wild oats, all those touchingly dated phrases to name the delightful risklessness of holiday impudences so easily deleted from one's experience when one gets back home to work.

The mixture is well brewed by 1880. Monte Carlo for the gambling and the celebrities; St Tropez and Cannes for the artists; Nice for the lavish hotels and the *promenade des Anglais* – the splendid palm-clad seafront, overlooked by all those priceless, bulbous, Palazzo-style hotels, dominated by the *Palais de la Mediterranée*; lastly, Menton for the hypochondriac, the convalescent and those dying of tuberculosis. All those hotels sprang into such solid and towering reality in the same two or three decades as everywhere else, but on the *Côte d'Azur*, of course, they were covered in dazzling, icing-sugar-white stucco, still the ultimate sign of Mediterranean and Victorian luxury. The *Promenade des Anglais* is one long line of opulent wedding cakes, this one with a timely touch of Moorishness, that one pure Victorian Gothic, here a little further east, the arcaded, pillared, stained-glass monster Casino, the Palais itself, completed in 1929 as it were from the picture-palace recipe books, Odeon, Regal, Granada, of the day. The casino at Monte Carlo, antedating it by half a century, is a different sort of monster, colonnaded, domed, crenellated, minaretted, every kind of sumptuous ornament in and out, and surrounded by elaborate tropical gardens, but still sedately of its day, the home of the *haut ton*, king, electors, princes, counts, taking the kind of time out they would have called 'naughty'.

The new class of high livers had a short enough day beside the sea, dressed in the new clothes of glamour. By the time the Second World War came and the Mediterranean closed for a season, glamour had become the key commodity of this weird new *Stand* (Max Weber's word) whose outline one can see in Nice, Monte Carlo, St Tropez and Bandol by the late 1930s, and which now occupies so much of our publicly imaginative life.

A *stand* is a sub-class and the members of this one were the smart set, the *demimondaines*, the Bright Young Things, the Idle Rich, the fashionable writers, artists, film-directors, aristocrats, quondam princelings, bankers, playboys, millionaire titans and their innumerable hangers-on and *vivandières* who flocked to the strip of beach, sea-front, main street and scrubby hillside which was the Riviera. Scott Fitzgerald apotheosised them in *Tender is the Night* and saw, with bitter regret, how the Beautiful People turned flabby and mad, the devastatingly good-looking *ingénue* boiled hard, and the brilliant pyrotechnics burned out. Maybe Fitzgerald himself was much too apt to flourish his own metaphors – ones like fireworks cascading and fading into darkness. It is a tonic instead to hear Martha Gellhorn tell Mary Blume roundly that when she hitchhiked there to stay with a college friend in 1930:

> I just knew it was no good – a bunch of crooks and loonies, low-class American expatriates and filmy people like the Dolly Sisters. We went one

night to the casino and I saw those claws coming out covered with rings and I thought thank God, I'm young and poor.[21]

Applause for that. When you look at the rich vacancy, the preposterous nothingness of the life led on the Riviera by the Duke and Duchess of Windsor in amongst all those other deposits of the belated end of absolutism and *anciens régimes*, then you think, serve them right.

Yet that pointless, self-celebrating way of life made something enduring – horrible, perhaps, but still with us. It assembled the culture of glamour, cut its uniform, wrote its schedules, planned its manufacturing procedures, weighed its profits. The *Côte d'Azur* was, with Hollywood, a showcase for advertising and what was soon well called show business. Indeed, Nice and Cannes and the rest, warm and splendid as their front-of-houses are, became the lens through which we could see really close up the stars who make fashion and turn the wheels of its industry. The celebrity mixture of the 1930s – out-of-work royalty, film directors, film stars, gamblers, artists and gangsters, the awful motley of the international rich – prepared the ground for the big shows of the postwar boom to be thoroughly institutionalised. The Venice Biennale for painters, the Cannes film festival, the countless minor self-displays of related industries fix the French Riviera in a crucial spot for the functioning of the cultural industries now, as everyone puts it, at the leading edge of capitalism.

The metaphors for such life lie ready to hand: 'frothy' maybe, 'scummy' even. One can only turn away in disgust at what all this parading and photographing and crowding-round-to-get-a-glimpse-of-the-star does to people on either end of the camera. When Roger Vadim made in 1957 his utterly harmless little movie about the prettiest girl he'd ever seen, *Et Dieu Créa la Femme*, Brigitte Bardot lost any chance of living a happy or even a sane life, and St Tropez finally lost any chance of remaining the neatest fishing village on the coast.

It won't do, however, just to wag one's elderly head over the deturpation of things. Movies are seriously judged at Cannes, paintings at Venice. Indeed, the Côte d'Azur is still a magnetic geography for painters joining the great, living tradition of impressionism and modernism. After all, Mont St Victoire stands exactly as Cézanne painted it so many times. Matisse settled down there for the second half of his life, paid little attention to the Germans, found his red room and his headland, painted the big pines overlooking the Cap d'Antibes and faded quietly away in the plain house with peeling shutters behind the closed iron gates. When Patrick Heron, fine English painter in his own right, came to pay homage in 1947 the old man was too infirm to see him, so Heron walked on down the road to the corner until he was suddenly certain he stood on exactly the spot from which Matisse had painted *Le Grand Pin*. Pressing up against the wall to fix the position for certain, his eye was caught by a smudge of colour on the dry stones. Scratching with his forefinger, Heron uncovered the oxidised smears of oilpaint left there by the artist as he wiped his palette knife during the composition of his masterpiece twenty years before.

And sure enough, there I found old palette scrapings of scarlet, ultramarine, violet, lemon and emerald, all oxidising deep in a small crevice. Thrilled, but not surprised, it was a discovery I still recall with intense emotion. To have the experience of standing precisely where the great painter once saw what I now also saw, but *through* his paint, *through* his brushstrokes, *through* his selected distortions of the visual data yielded at that exact point in the landscape … this was an experience it was essential to have.[22]

It's a marvellous tale, and it serves to remind us that great art retains its power, and so does a beautiful coastline, whatever the rich do to them. Moreover, people will always conceive new places for new self-conceptions. As vacations, holidays and tourism exploded into the vast new industry of the postwar Western world, the *Côte d'Azur* offered itself as the ideal spot to try out self-indulgence, excess, prohibitions, reckless-ness, all in the name of the hoped-for happiness and excitement this novel sort of excursion could bring.

IV

The coast had no history. It could have been made into anything. The contrast is with Italy. Italy started out, of course, with the rather striking advantages conferred by classical antiquity and the Renaissance. Then, as we saw, the Grand Tour marked out the stations of education-with-indulgences for the *haut ton*. The tourist trail then slowly mutated as the middle classes arrived from all over Europe and North America, finding that, as usual, the intellectuals, the artists, the titled heads and the robber barons had got there first. The meaning of Nice and Monte Carlo is more newly whipped, creamy and sugary, and that is one part of the tourist's Mediterranean. The meaning of Venice, in another corner of the sea, is older and stranger and more potent.

Perhaps one could still say that railway tourism rediscovered it, except that it had hardly disappeared from people's imagination. As a power in European trade Venice had shrunk to nothing compared with its heyday in the sixteenth century when it was the point of exchange between the wealth of Ottoman and of Christian Europe, and a synonym for fabulous wealth of its own. Those associations and at least some of that wealth remained in 1800. But the city had seen occupying forces of Italy and Austria come and go by the late eighteenth century, and its resident princelings and countesses mattered little in European politics; its fabric, as always, was dropping to bits, and in short it seemed an unlikely candidate for the great seaside charivari about to begin. Byron made something of it, what with sex and swimming, and so did Shelley; Boswell must be counted in as having been present at its rediscovery (in Pemble's phrase[23]) and he too rediscovered the concupiscent joys of Venetian masquerades as much as he did Tintoretto.

A substantial part of its resumed glory came from the 'orientalism'[24] of the new Romantics. Wortley Montagu was our first trendsetter to change into Muslim attire and Byron our second. But the renewed flow of visitors – traveller-tourists, let's say – in the earlyish nineteenth century saw the city as more oriental than the orientals. Painters like David Roberts and Ingres had, shrewdly enough, confected an Orient of massive architecture and doe-eyed ladies of the Seraglio; William Russell Flint and Frederick Leighton efficiently turned this latter sweetmeat into soft pornography. But the near Orient also stood for the exotic, the barbarous, the magnificently jewelled and, when William Beckford wrote in 1782[25] 'I cannot help thinking St. Mark's a mosque, and the neighbouring palace some vast seraglio, full of arabesque saloons, embroidered sofas and voluptuous Circassians', he caught with plangent vulgarity exactly what Anglophone visitors would hope for over the next century.

Ruskin changed all that; Ruskin, Turner and the railways. Byron and Shelley and company had to arrive by sea. Turner came by sea for both his visits. The viaduct from the mainland was opened in January 1846 and the railway ran to Vicenza. By 1857 it had been extended to Milan and after the tunnel through the Alps under Mont Cenis was opened in 1871, Venice became an easy enough ride. The Orient Express, with its walnut panelling and carriage lamps, its sumptuous sleepers and attentive servants started promptly out from Paris.

By then, Ruskin had found his great example of the Modern Painter and had his say about Venice. The Ducal Palace expressed the grand reconciliation of the three architectures of the inland sea and human civilisation: 'the Roman, the Lombard, the Arab'. With prophetic authority, Ruskin tied the health of a nation to the state of its supreme art, architecture, and saw both as the product of its religious inspiration. 'The decline of her political prosperity was exactly coincident with that of domestic and individual religion', he wrote, and that decline could be read as precisely as a thermometer in the stones of Venice. So long as a building was Gothic, it was good and, what was more, was the product of the artist-masons' own good lives. 'The majesty of [the Ducal Palace] was able to give pause to the Gothic imagination in its full career; stayed the restlessness of innovation in an instant.'[26] Its solitary splendour was inimitable:

> It is *impossible*, as impossible as to raise the dead, to restore anything that has ever been great and beautiful in architecture. That spirit which is given only by the hand and eye of the workman can never be recalled … *We have no right whatever to touch the buildings of past times*. They are not ours.[27]

Ruskin was not the sole teacher and arbiter of Victorian taste in these Mediterranean matters, but he was both the most influential and, for us, the most indicative. He taught as well as painted the minutest detail of Venetian stone, and then caught the temper of the age by giving aesthetic perception moral force. He founded thereby a doctrine of tourist perception and geography, of which these are the main, Mediterranean precepts (in my paraphrase).

> Venice is like nowhere else.
> Venetian architecture goes wrong when it changes from the Gothic to the Renaissance.
> This is a change from expressive and spontaneous genius to mechanical and repetitious production.
> Old architectures decay as the spirit which informed them dies.
> They must not be restored, but left as venerable monuments of human aspiration.
> Additions or changes to the original conception are damnable.

There is much more to which many modern tourist bosoms would return an echo. Nor is Ruskin mocked. He *is* mocked a little, by E.M. Forster, who admired him, in *A Room with a View* when Lucy Honeychurch, dutifully doing the sights in Florence, Ruskin's own *Mornings in Florence* in hand, is more caught by the people she sees than the nobility of the roof in Santa Croce. But there, she's only young and, having found Beethoven, has love to find next. Forster watches her leave anxiously, for she has a grisly scene to see played outside the Ospedale dei Innocenti. Ruskin escapes intact, for all he wanted is that tourists should *look and see*, rather than be instructed in what to glance at by the guidebooks of the good Mr Murray.

> Without looking about you at all, you may find, in your Murray, the useful information that it is a church [Santa Croce] which consists of a very wide nave and lateral aisles, separated by seven fine pointed arches. And as you will be – under ordinary conditions of tourist hurry – glad to learn so much, *without looking*, it is little likely to occur to you that this nave and two rich aisles required also, for your complete present comfort, walls at both ends, and a roof on the top. The chances are a thousand to one that, after being pulled from tomb to tomb round the aisles and chapels, you should take so extraordinary an additional amount of pains as to look up at the roof.[28]
>
> (Ruskin's italics)

Ruskin sustains the line from the grandest of Grand Tourists – not Boswell, out for the good times as well as the educative ones, nor Byron the adventurer who, rather like Thesiger, set out to *become* the strange peoples he stayed with. Ruskin takes up the cause from Winckelmann, Lessing and Goethe, and at home, from Wordsworth and Coleridge. That is to say, Ruskin picks up the torch from all those writers for whom tourist travel had a moral purpose, and never more so than when the tourist encountered art.

Ruskin was, in spite of himself, a teacher and, like Mr Murray, must perforce teach through his textbooks. He won the day. Millions of Murrays, worthy as they were, are long unavailable but *Mornings in Florence* may be bought tomorrow from Penguin. Ruskin extends and deepens the maxim that a holiday should do something to improve the spirit and enlarge the mind. Nobody was going to forget about Florence and Venice, but without him people would not have learned to see and feel how close indeed lies the artist's determination only to accomplish his best, most truthful work next to the techniques he has to hand with which to tell the truth; next also to the moral climate of culture and society. In Ruskin's view (and for what it's worth, mine), the great work of art is such that those who come to look at the work carefully enough and in a spirit of goodwill, will be able to see for themselves whether what has been made is any good, is good anyway, and therefore is good for the soul.

V

On our simple map of meanings, Mediterranean France means one set of things (gregarious, hedonistic, liberated, unhistoric, transgressive) and Mediterranean Italy another (educative, aesthetic, solitary, formal). Greece partakes of both, each sternly allocated its own space. Other countries do as they do, investing more or less in history or hedonism, the show of art or show business. Spain, the great unmentioned lacuna in this tale, in part effected its own ruin at least along its coastline, as we shall see in the next chapter.

No sooner have we a nice, simple cartography than the only thing to do is scribble on it with improvements and corrections. This dashing history of the sea has not mentioned the sheer weight of numbers which are wearing out its coastline and filling its barely moving waters with their droppings. It has hardly mentioned, especially on behalf of Italy, the desperate struggle to live of those millions of poorish inhabitants which the tour companies have to be at such pains to keep invisible. The history of the Mediterranean and its visitors includes them; it is only fifty-odd years since, for example, Norman Lewis was a young intelligence officer in a Naples recently freed from German occupation and Fascist government, and sentenced thereby to starvation, typhoid, and a corruption shared equally by Mafiosi and their gallant liberators.

A little patchwork of anecdotes may serve to suggest a more structural history. Lewis noted in his diary, 'A year among the Italians has converted me to such an admiration for their humanity and culture that were I to be given the chance to be born again, Italy would be the country of my choice.'[29] Lewis was an involuntary tourist, learning the ways of local life randomly. He sees with horror what his fellow transients will do to the people who live in the foreign land becoming to him a home time will force him to leave. But Lewis is helpless to help, as tourists are. All he can do is bear witness by writing it down. In one terrible epiphany, dining in a grubby restaurant off sticky, unadorned pasta, he and a Neapolitan friend are interrupted by the arrival of 'five or six little girls between the ages of nine and twelve [who] appeared in the doorway'.

> They wore hideous straight black uniforms buttoned under their chins, and black boots and stockings, and their hair had been shorn short, prison-style. They were all weeping, and as they clung to each other and groped their way towards us, bumping into chairs and tables, I realised they were all blind. Tragedy and despair had been thrust upon us, and would not be shut out. I expected the indifferent diners to push back their plates, to get up and hold out their arms, but nobody moved. Forkfuls of food were thrust into open mouths, the rattle of conversation continued, nobody saw the tears ...
>
> The experience changed my outlook. Until now I had clung to the comforting belief that human beings eventually come to terms with pain and sorrow. Now I understood I was wrong, and like Paul I suffered a conversion – but to pessimism. These little girls, any one of whom could be my daughter, came into the restaurant weeping, and they were weeping when they were led away. I knew that, condemned to everlasting darkness, hunger and loss, they would weep on incessantly. They would never recover from their pain, and I would never recover from the memory of it.[30]

One cannot afford too many such experiences as that; or one can if one has to but, as people say, '*that's* a nice thing to tell me when I'm on my holidays'. Lewis says at one point, 'to all intents and purposes we were living in the Middle Ages' and the point still stands for all passers-by like ourselves in the wrong quarters of Naples, Erzerum, Cairo, Rabat, Kaduna.

It is a grim chord to play but here in the Mediterranean and on the shores of old humanism, it must be struck. One *cannot*, in the very name of humanism's humanity as embodied by Greek, Roman, Catholic, Muslim, Renaissance, Enlightenment, Risorgimento Italy, blind oneself to the anguish of the blind little girls. They stand for the shocking actuality of the human misery just the other side of the view of the sea and its lovely sands. To go to strange and historic places for a good time is, the history of tourism teaches, to change one's sensibility and educate one's sentiments. No doubt it is natural enough to try to arrange for the sentiments in question to be nice ones, but such an arrangement can only be guaranteed by keeping oneself half-dead on holiday, which is not at all the idea we start out with. The stations of the Tour are marked out by unignorably vivid reminders of traditional suffering. Crucifixions, flayings, battles, raped or massacred innocents and utter beggary line the gallery walls, and whatever dues old masters might also have been paying they didn't intend that those who gazed upon the terrible scenes should fail to convert them to the facts of life outside the picture frame.

A virtuous social conscience will not go amiably to sleep on vacation. The tourist gaze, in Urry's phrase, cannot edit out suffering any more than squalor. Indeed, the very meaning of the vacation, slowly accumulated over the two and a half centuries of its making, requires that since it is the edenic paradise we seek, the place put up for such a candidature not only should have as little misery as possible on show, but as little exploitation and the filth it scatters about it also. As I have often said in these pages, close to the heart of the modern identity of the well-off, decent-spirited consumer is a picture of the new good place, harmonious, serene, unoppressive, free from toil, beautiful, *clean*.

Age, it is to be feared, accumulates dirt, and the Mediterranean is an *old* civilisation and an even older sea. It was only in 1972 that Peter Ritchie-Calder reported that the sheer weight of numbers of people around the sea was going to kill it off without drastic emergency action. 'The Mediterranean Sea is sick. It needs intensive care, day and night nursing.'[31] To everyone's surprise, that action was taken. This flouts conventional cynicism. In spite of enlightenment lessons about the inevitability of progress, most people are prepared for the worst. When the doom-heavy reports came out in a cluster in the early 1970s – Club of Rome, Ritchie-Calder, *The Ecologist* – vacationers had long been used to avoiding the sewage in the Bay of Naples, mistrusting the seafood, stopping their noses to Venetian canals, clearing away the broken glass before lying down in Alicante, wiping oil off their feet in the *Golfe des Lions*.

> Over a quarter of the world's people live in coastal areas, up to 90% of the world's currently exploitable living marine resources are to be found in coastal waters, and contamination of the marine environment is generally most severe in semi-enclosed seas and along the world's coasts.[32]

The recognition of this state of affairs, together with the legendary significance of the sea it has been the concern of this chapter to invoke, led in 1985 to the drawing up of the Med Plan under the auspices of the United Nations Environmental Programme (UNEP).

The programme was dispassionately co-ordinated according to certain critical-theoretic approaches. The first ('neorealism') held that co-operation would be brief and led by the most powerful state. The second ('historical materialism', no less) considered possibilities in the harsh light of the poverty and powerlessness of the smaller countries involved in the face of the ruthlessness of capitalism at large and the attempt of large countries to manipulate small ones for the benefit of the wealthy. The final approach studied the role of experts and 'epistemic communities' as they sought to get urgent new knowledge across to the individual leaders of states.

The Mediterranean came out looking grim under all three analyses. There were endemic mutual hatreds; the rich Northerners ran the sea; heavy industry dominated it; science would stick to national interests and states attend only to acute security threats; you can't compel 'hegemons' (i.e. the dominant) to pay up.

What happened was, so far as it went, a triumph of patient reasonableness and the disciplined application of theory to experience, and vice versa. The immediate security threat to their health, their tourist takings, and their amenities was clear to France, Italy and Spain. They each, but France above all, wanted, in Habermas' distinction,[33] policies to achieve instrumental control not the protection of ultimate values. But France was losing economic dominance in the area and wanted to restore it by way of being on better terms with the partly Francophone Southern littoral states of Tunisia, Algeria, Morocco. She had far and away the greatest scientific prowess. Moreover, UN contributions by way of scientific discussion and access helped weaken the loyalty of French scientists to their nation-state and turn them towards the universalist values for which international science traditionally stands. Algeria and Tunisia followed. France led, but behaved well. Even as her political domination wavered, she stuck to the plan, quite against the theory of *Realpolitik*. France conceded leadership and (some) control to her sometime subordinates. She agreed to clean things up off Marseille quicker and more expensively than their economies allowed poorer nations to do. Governments of the less developed nations like Turkey and (then) Yugoslavia got access to new, relevant scientific knowledge. Egypt in particular among the Arab countries showed a readiness to redefine her national interests in the light of both new and unexpected scientific knowledge about pollutant dumping, for example, and because the Egyptians spotted the chance of new commercial openings consequent upon pollution control.[34] Ultimate values trumped instrumentality.

The heroes of the tale are undoubtedly the scientists and the international officials from UNEP. Social and scientific theory, so often maligned for its removal from real life, conspicuously changed real life by slowly climbing an arduous ladder from laboratory to seminar to committees to advisers until, finally, to persuading different governments on behalf of millions of different people, divided by language, religion, geography and power, to take the filth, the oil, the algae and the shit out of the ancient sea. So the sun rose again and shone upon the blue water which is, for a season, clean.

Such stories are needed with which to counter some of the grislier anecdotes told in the next chapter. It is only twenty-five years since the imminent death of the old ocean was so confidently announced. It has been postponed by reason, will and money. But poverty and filth will remain part of what there is in front of them which people try not to see on their holidays. Insofar as they fail, they remain human. No amount of prating about other cultures and their way of life can save us from feeling the anguish Norman Lewis felt at the sight of the blind children. Lewis's noble diary is a document in self-education; you could read it for its lessons in how to be a sensitive, loving, even happy tourist. Lewis, of course, was also an Army officer, on active service and with absolute duties to observe. The holidaymaker has human duties larger than a soldier's. Each one of us is, after all, a citizen-democrat, even in shorts or a bathing costume. In virtue of being there at all, the tourist is an internationalist, a soldier of UNEP. Sitting staring at the blue of the Mediterranean is hardly an occasion to forget the roles which were born there in the first place.

8

FOREIGN BODIES

I

As Corbin told us, the beach was always a place where anything goes. Henry James's actress gave a *frisson* to the promenaders by turning a somersault off the diving board, and long before that women let their hair down and men took their trousers off in public. A certain respectability reasserted itself when those well-established males of all respect-worthy classes decided what was what in the way of bathing attire and that lasted until the fast set turned up on Bandol beach and its members were observed glistening as they sunbathed, almost naked, 'the men in nothing more than bathing shorts'.[1]

There was more to this than outraging the always outrageable and respectable classes. Foucault has taught us[2] that of all the codifying discourses of society the discourse of sexuality goes deepest and orders most, most of all when its utterers are professing spontaneity and sincerity in their desire for another. The code, says Foucault, dictates what shall count as expressive and permissible, and what shall count as inexpressible and forbidden. It orders that sex itself shall be placed at the fount of human being, that it is a matter of ponderous solemnity and that it will not tolerate, on pain of a loss of one's full humanity, playfulness, abuse or anomaly.

On Foucault's argument, the discourse of sexuality is one unbroken code whether spoken in the Blackpool boarding house of 1890 or in the sumptuous suites of the Niçois hotels in 1960. D.H. Lawrence wrote in 1922, 'I labour always to make the relation between men and women valid and precious' and for Lawrence, for Freud and for everyday experience, that relation was sexual. For Foucault, the sexual licence of the beach at St. Tropez is of a piece with the supposed repressions of the Victorian bedroom. Each is just another version of the tyranny of sexual discourse, a tyranny which came into being with the formation of the modern industrial state and its drive to legislate as normal and normative every corner of human being, so that transgression became only a legal name for how things were instructed not to be, and playtime as much a work-schedule as labour.

One sees his point, and yet still one insists in taking pleasure in not-work, for the *change* it is. There was undoubtedly a change in those Riviera beaches, however soon it might be regimented. It wasn't just that the clothes changed, became looser, less formalised, less distinguishable as between men and women. It was that these sartorial changes coincided with similar values beginning to emerge about other freedoms in relations between men and women. The ready explanation, plausible as far as it goes, is that the First World War had shown for what they were the killing conventions of patriotism, sexual abstinence, uniformed obedience, manly courage. E.M. Forster wrote a few years after the end of hostilities, 'If I had to choose between betraying my friends and betraying my country, I hope I would have the courage to betray my country.'[3] His remark, made on behalf of that little group of artists and intellectuals now known as the Bloomsburyans, is one which inaugurates an era which in Britain and the USA was to exalt personal relationships into a supreme value, counterposed in itself against the monolithic value-systems of Fascism and Communism which began to offer their account of a radically social and collective redemption at about the same time.

A life lived for personal relationships may obviously turn into something with such short moral horizons that it becomes madly egocentric. If the criterion of success in such a relationship is that the individuals concerned live with a serene and laughter-filled reciprocity and regard, then no-one will make it, and for the value of the relationship will be substituted the ultimate value of a self forever striving to free itself from all social structures.

Let us say that it all started on the beaches of the Riviera in the 1920s. According to the simple model of cultural transmission deployed earlier, certain values were selected and concentrated in the lives of the privileged and wealthy as proper to the meaning of leisure. They are to be signs of enjoyment and the fulfilment of desire which may be displayed in periods of time consecrated to not-work. Because they belong to the privileged these values glow with an aura of distinction. As leisure increases, the values in question become available to other social classes, but remain tinged with recklessness and abandon, because not fully possessed by the new owners, only borrowed for that time in which they can temporarily afford to live like the wealthy. The vacation is a time when one may try out on oneself the selves one might have been. It is free time indeed, when the demands of the self one habitually is may be put off. One pleasurable risk being taken – the one so popularly taken in the movie *Shirley Valentine* – is that the self one finds one can be on vacation feels so good, so fresh and restorative, that it is taken to be the true self one has to be. This is why vacations include love affairs and the end of marriages.

For over two centuries, the central value of the polity has been work. As Christianity relaxed its hold as an explanation of why we are here and where we are going, the missing answer came to be supplied by work, but work placed in a particular relation to advancement. The point of one's life was the work one did, certainly, especially if one were a man; it provided the point of a woman's life also, in the working and middle classes during peacetime, with the difference that her work was housework and unpaid; it subtended male work. Together, within a family the definition of which was that it had a second generation to come, that work paced the parents through lives expected to end pretty well as soon as work ended, but a life's work which would be commemorated in the lives of more prosperous children. The point of the work, synonymous with the life, was that it provide the children with better because better-off lives.

A feature of such better-off lives would be greater leisure. Since 1950 or so, soothsayers in the op-ed columns of the newspapers and the parallel shelves in the bookshops have been forecasting a leisure society in which work, much of the heavier parts of which would be done by electronic machinery, would matter increasingly less, individual livelihoods would be assembled in some much more flexible and temporary way, and selves would be a product of free choice and happy experimentation. Things haven't happened quite like that, of course, as the casualisation of labour, the return of large-scale unemployment, the deregulation of capital flow and the deliberate destruction of trade unions have combined in the new leviathan of 'turbo-capitalism'[4] which has, since its monster parturition after 1973 or so, been little restrained in its progress through ordinary lives.

But the reduction in working hours goes on. The steelworkers are all redundant, but there is more steel made in Sheffield today than there was when, in 1968, the industry employed 100,000 men. Understanding these changes has hardly been a matter of arranging for everybody to occupy their increased leisure in life-enhancing ways, but whatever the changes signify, there can be no doubt that experimentation about life-changes takes place on holiday *at the self-same time* that holidays are also used to conserve and restore old trusts, lifelong bonds, the known, loved and familial.

It is a lot to ask of two weeks in the Caribbean or down the Costa Brava, especially when desire meets actuality. But the inarticulate demands made on the time and space marked out for experiment must find their means of expression from somewhere. For those for whom the recovery of life-significance is a matter of physical exertion, geographical venturing and testing for courage in dangerous places, then, as Chapter 5 illustrated, your experiments will take place by following the models of other people doing the same thing at the sea jaws or the world's end. If freedom to experiment turns out to mean old-fashioned floutings of convention, a search for new selves down forbidden paths in paradise gardens, a giving of oneself to strangers and to suddenly discovered friendships, a stripping-off of old attire, both literal and metaphoric, in a strictly conventional assertion of unconventional naturalness, then the conduct of the glamorous rich and the excitingly artistic on beaches in southern France and northern Italy between 1920 and 1939 will have a very strong influence on what happens next.

Nakedness, sunshine, sexuality, drunkenness, gluttony, speed, new machinery – these were the contents of the timetable of glamour. The benefits of naturism and nudism fitted the post-war rediscovery of the unconstrained physicality of self. Taking one's clothes off and treating the beach like the bedroom, where anybody could create, by an act of will corroborated by the conventions, a pool of intimacy, soporific or sexual, was an extension easily conceded on its tolerant strand. In any case, naturism taught that the sun will do you good, and the sign that it has, is to allow it to cook you as brown as you can get. You will then exude natural health.

You will also exude glamour. Northerners can only bake themselves that brown by going south. For well over half a century, until the healthfulness of a suntan was qualified by the decided unhealthiness of a melanoma, the wearing of a glistening orange suntan was a sign of the wearer's health, wealth and glamorous enviability. The most glamorously expensive suit one could acquire, set off by the tiniest adornments – a gold fillet, diamond earrings, the bottom half of a bikini – was a birthday suit. Even then, the Riviera kept its historical licence. A woman may tan her breasts in July on a Provençal or a Tuscan beach, but not on a New England one.

Candid nudity connotes easy sexuality, and back in the 1920s there was indeed a doctrine, to match naturism, of 'free love'. Certainly, the friendly licence of nakedness, especially as dressed in the perfect tan, conduces to sex. It is meant to. And, as we have seen, tourism also conduces to sex; sex is written in its bill of expectations. On tour, you may abandon yourself to pleasure. But also on tour, your misdemeanours may be nicely calculated not to rebound to your discredit at home. One complication for the European is that the increased presence of the new Union in everybody's life means that people have to commit serious misdemeanours much further away from home. If freedom on holiday turns out to require seriously transgressive sex or hard drug-taking then better to go outside the Union, which is adequately policed, and try the international capitals of such commerce in the Far East or Latin America.

There are tough and soft ways of conducting vacations, the point of which is to glory in the body, where 'glorying in' may also mean liberating excesses of constriction or punishment. The doctrines of naturism emphasised the liberations brought to a body devised, concealed, bound in by clothing and policed by the stares of Mrs. Grundy's respectability, by throwing off clothes and conventions and restoring one's skin to the fresh air and kindly sun. One has only to watch the chortling satisfaction of a 2-year-old with nothing on pottering along the sea shallows to be reassured that this is a natural pleasure, whatever Foucault says. Sea breezes and hot sunshine on bare skin do much for a body, and bodies are nothing if not inextricably part of our selves.

D.H. Lawrence was a, perhaps the, key figure in the advance of naturism in the 1920s, and of the undoubtedly liberating belief that sex may certainly take place between people who are not married to each other (and may well be married to someone else) as well as passionate advocate, no doubt to be found in previous genera-tions, of the value of sex and the fulfilment it should bring if your passions are in healthily passionate order. His splendid short story *Sun*[5] is the best example of the movement one could find, accurately situated in Sicily at the beginning of the decade. The heroine is nervous, ill-feeling, out of sorts. She takes her little boy and, leaving her husband (grey-faced, grey-suited) behind, goes to Sicily for a holiday. She becomes a sun-worshipper, lying naked daily in the sun, feeling the sun's saturating heat burn out the 'cold dark clots' of bad feeling and living which her body harboured as a result of the thwartedness and nullity of English middle-class life. The sun comes to her as a lover, ravishing her in an ecstasy of heat and cleanliness (she never sweats, let alone sunburns) and it is the same for her sunny little boy.

Her husband comes to visit her and finds her not just restored but engorged by sun, a proud bronzed Artemis whom he follows down the lemon groves of the garden, 'watching the rosy fleet-looking lifting and sinking of her quick hips as she swayed a little in the socket of her waist'. She doesn't desire him, desires instead the dark-eyed, dark-skinned portly young peasant who gazes lustfully at her, as well he might, from across the olive terraces. But she amiably resigns herself to her grey-faced man and 'the fatal chain of continuity'.

It is a magnificent piece of sensual realisation by Lawrence, however open in its sillier turns of phrase to Stella Gibbons's wicked satire in *Cold Comfort Farm*. It would serve as liturgy to the theological end of the naturists when they (like everyone else at the time) organised themselves into a movement, arranged the inevitable summer camps around the perimeter of which inevitable peepers were arrested, and launched a genteelly absurd magazine called *Health and Efficiency*, which advocated nudism, cycling, communal aerobics, vegetarianism, and what it even-handedly discerned as the nicer sides of Fascist and Communist health camps.

Sexual union in all this remained pretty straight. Homosexuality was a crime in Britain until 1967 and although it was frequent in all-male institutions like the armed forces, prisons and ruling-class boarding schools, only the upper classes got away with seriously homosexual liaisons uninterfered with by the police, and even they had their scandals. In several southern states of America, sodomy is still a serious offence. When leisured homosexuals on either side of the Atlantic went looking for sex without fear of policemen, they went to the tolerant old Mediterranean where homosexuality had always been normal and rarely been illegal, even under Catholicism. When Norman Douglas published in 1911, at the age of 43, his extraordinary medley of classical reminiscence, idiosyncratic scholarship and sardonic folklore *Siren Land*,[6] (his own subtitle is perfectly accurate), he openly commemorated his conquests among Sorrentine boys:

> Compared with that of northerners, the mental outlook of these boys is restricted, and a narrow frame will hold the picture of their hopes and fears. But this picture has all the directness, the *naïveté*, of what is called the youth of the world; a very ancient youth, since it already bears the impress of uncounted generations of anti-lawlessness. It is not praising them unduly to say that their minds, like their limbs, grow straight without schooling, and that they possess an inborn sobriety which would be sought in vain among the corresponding class in the North. Inured to patriarchal discipline from earliest childhood and familiar with every phenomenon of life from birth to death, they view their surroundings objectively and glide through adolescence without any of the periodical convulsions and catastrophes of more intro-spective races. Their entire vocabulary consists, I should think, of scarce three hundred words, many of which would bring a blush to the cheek of Rabelais; yet their conversation among themselves is refreshingly healthy, and many subjects, popular enough elsewhere, are tacitly ignored or tabooed. Not Puritans, by any means, nor yet the reverse; they will bend either way, but, the strain relaxed, they forthwith straighten like a willow wand: if this be not virtue, according to Aristotle's definition, what is? Emigration is unfortu-nately producing a very different crop of youths; gamblers, wine-bibbers, and flashily dressed *mezzo-signori*.

Even in 1911 things were going to the dogs, according to the vacationer's law that all holiday spots gravitate that way. More important, however, is that Norman Douglas, speaking for many men of his preference and private means, went to the Bay of Naples for plentiful sex, just as his touring predecessors of any sexual persuasion and sufficient social elevation had always done.

There again, there was plenty of impromptu and unofficial sex in early twentieth-century Blackpool, and elaborate courting and seduction rituals to conceal their consummations also.[7] What happened after *Sun* and *Tender is the Night*, after the making of the *Côte d'Azur*, was simply an extension and an intensification of these antique holiday delights.

Naturally, there is a limit to the alterations effected in feeling and conduct by a bit more travel, a bit more leisure and some extra disposable income. Lawrence's teaching may have cleared the way for sexual desire to become rather more respectable, but it was the experience of the people's war, when the line between combatants and civilians became so very permeable, which persuaded unprecedentedly large numbers of people that things were much too precarious to make it worth while putting it all off. In wartime, the women had jobs as never before, and the men had been places as never before, places – Italy, the Philippines, Japan – where there was a lot more sex than at home.

These commonplaces are by way of indicating that the 'brilliant breaking of the bank, the quite unlosable game', as Philip Larkin put it in a sour poem on the subject, wasn't just caused by a brace of novels and the 'fast set' from Evelyn Waugh's *Vile Bodies*. World war is a bigger force for change than an increase in holidaying. What these coupled forces – of total war and freer time – may be said to have done is clear a way through to sexual holidays in sexy places.

II

Not that there is anything new about men travelling long distances for the kind of sex they were forbidden at home. One of the facilities of empire for young British administrators and soldiers – severe though the Army and Navy were on such matters – was sexual opportunity. As so many stories by writers like Somerset Maugham[8] and 'Saki' illustrate, the boundary between courtesan and respectability was blurred in different social settings and different geographies. Roughly speaking, European permissiveness became easier the further east one was from the nearest garrison. In the hundred years up to the Japanese invasion of Singapore in 1942, prostitution was central to the local economy – 2,000 women were legally registered as prostitutes in an indigenous population of only 140,000 – but there is no suggestion that, whatever Singapore's mythical status in the imperial imagination as gateway to the East, many people made the three- to four-week sea journey from Tilbury just for the sex.[9]

The brothels were run almost exclusively by the Chinese (with some Japanese competitors) for the Chinese and for the enormous numbers of sailors of all nationalities passing through the port. The women were almost all Chinese, many refugees from famine in China, a handful on the run from Russia, others sold by their Chinese parents as chattels into prostitution in order to feed the rest of the family. The British authorities acknowledged that there was no question of trying to eradicate prostitution; all their efforts went into the attempt to control epidemics of gonorrhoea by compulsory medical inspection and treatment. After varying the more or less liberally intended policies of enforced medical treatment and recognition of a notional free agency on the part of women in thrall to their pimps, the Protectorate barely held the line between open panic and repression until in 1927 it was decided to pursue a doomed policy of official closures which, as serious civil servants immediately pointed out, made things worse.[10]

The local history, horribly gripping as it is, is important for our purposes only in its contribution to mythology. In 1912 a best-selling mythmaker was published called *The White Slave Market*, written by a man and a woman (Mrs MacKirdy and Mr Willis), in which Singapore, at that date much more important strategically and economically than Hong Kong, featured largely as the destination of abducted white women, as the centre of the opium den[11] trade of Empire, and as the origin of a coming plague of venereal disease. Along with lurid stuff about 'innocent girls decoyed to the East'[12] a lot of the figures in the book for sexual disease were accurate. The book caused a storm; the phrase 'white slave trade' entered tourist mythology and Singapore became the fixed type of the Oriental sin city, headquarters of sexual possibilities at once prurient, alluring and dangerous.

This same intoxicating mixture served to characterise Manila in the imaginations of the US Navy once the Philippines assumed such strategic importance before and after the second war. It is a redolent image with deep roots in Western culture, varying only in the capital city which captures it for each imperial power: Saigon for the French, Jakarta for the Dutch, Manila, Honolulu and Seoul for the Americans, Singapore for the British. Nothing much changed in the stereotype over this century. Oriental sex was dangerous for medical reasons and because it took those looking for it out of well-lit and crowded thoroughfares into the dark, mean streets where they didn't speak the language and might easily disappear for ever. Oriental sex was alluring because the women who made up its labour force had in truth certain dependably arousing and desirable attributes: they had their wonderful cataracts of black hair; they displayed that intense and submissive femininity strenuously taught by their traditions; they rarely ran to fat, their skin was a pearly, unbroken brown in colour, they had refined manners. The contrast with the heavier, paler, ageing harlots at home, often ravaged with bad skin and worse teeth also remained stark.

Above all, sex in the Orient would take place in an imaginary world of gleeful irresponsibility and recklessness, given its edge by the dangers of a chancre on the penis and a knife in the kidneys. The red lights glowed from east of Suez for half-a-dozen generations of servicemen, and when the sexual revolution began in 1963 then, as is usually the case, the myth of Oriental sex enclosed and dissolved into its time-honoured forms the experience.

There have long been sexual tourists, Boswell and Byron among them. For half a century or so they have been allowed to be more or less explicit about it. A geographic folklore is attached to a narrative line and an emerging frame of feeling. Imperial and military travels led young men on adventures of all kinds including sexual ones out of the corner of the Mediterranean by way of the Suez Canal, to Aden, India, Singapore, Hong Kong. The long distances permitted a loosening of the conventions; the dangers of war and empire encouraged a few risks. The variety of sexual rules, the dramatic changes in physiognomy and physique turned the ordinary womenfolk of the Indian Ocean and China Seas into the mysterious, liberated, sagaciously sexy creatures of a Western imagination fed on fragments picked up from Rider Haggard's *She*, Conrad's *Lord Jim*, Malinowski's *The Sexual Life of Savages* and Gauguin's Tahiti paintings.

This rough cartoon serves to suggest how feelings and the conduct they cause find their form: in this case, as the narratives of empire and of warfare attached the thrilling fuse of exotic experience to the explosive force of sex. One could sketch, in a similar outline, a diagram of transatlantic desire fastened to military expedition, as the Americans went west, by Hawaii and Guam, to find the East. They found the same mythic East as Lieutenant Pinkerton found in *Madam Butterfly*, and inscribed at its climax was the act of betrayal. Pinkerton abandoned *Butterfly* and so did thousands of GIs the women they cared for and cared about while they were there, fighting the Korean war, the Vietnamese war, and settling the Japanese down into such a formidable version of capitalism after Hiroshima in 1946. Countless young Americans learned the joy of sex from local women supplying the sexual economy of warfare. This was part of the rhythm which has made sexual tourism into such a lucrative market niche.

The magnificent luxuriousness of American consumerism meant that the 'rest and rehabilitation' breaks for its troops were of unprecedented magnificence in warrior history. The troops in Korea and Vietnam were largely conscripts and had to be kept at a high level of morale. They were increasingly unconvinced by official propaganda about the wars, and lavish 'R and R', though hardly a way to keep soldiers keenly battle-ready, was certainly a solace and an anticipation. Since the soldiers were all men between the ages of 19 and 40, it is no surprise that what they most eagerly anticipated was sex, and the solace by which they were most comforted when they returned from combat was the attention of women, and the regional wars between 1950 and 1975 established Seoul and Bangkok as their sexual capitals.

There is some dispute about just how prodigal Bangkok really is[13] in its investment in the sex industry. Enloe says there are over a thousand premises catering for the sex trade in Bangkok alone, and Brock and Thistlethwaite quote a traveloguist who has counted 450 advertisements for 'the skin trade' in the Yellow Pages alone. They offer breathtaking (and unreferenced) estimates that 'one third to one fourth of all young Thai women work in the sex industry',[14] and that a million prostitutes are waiting to satisfy that '60% of all the country's visitors [who] came only for the cheap sex. The Public Health Ministry bid 77,000 in 1993, but everybody scoffs at that'.

The work is illegal and much better paid than any other job available to all but well-to-do young women (twelve times the average wage of a country girl) and it may have attractive perquisites – gifts, access to the accommodation of wealthy tourist clients, more stylish clothes and the like. (Under business law prostitution is listed as 'personal services'.) Nor is the good name of the young Thai woman too much damaged by work as a prostitute. The social and the sexual attentions required by her clients may not be so very different from marriage, and if she's lucky and has saved a decent amount, she can still make, as they used to say, an honest woman of herself.

At any rate, it cannot be doubted that Bangkok now features in the mythology as one of the two capitals of sexual tourism (the other is Rio de Janeiro). It has made the transition, in Enloe's phrase, from bases to beaches. Its clientele for its sexual hospitality is now all-tourist. The myth is that Bangkok is fairly throbbing with sexual activity and that every sexual tendency will find its opportunity there. With Rio, it is believed to be the city where cross-dressing transsexuals are even better-looking than the women, where sex-change 'lady-boys' are found in any sex bar, while Bangkok is where in the district of Patpong men and women may go to strip shows the ads for which, handed out by street touts, list among the attractions 'girl and snake sex dance, long-eggplant push into her, boy and girl fuckingshow, pussy shoot banana' and where an almost naked girl, lying back on the floor propped on her elbows and her high heels will expel darts at a balloon from her vagina.[15] The long evening wears on while fourteen young women, perfectly naked apart from their high heels, grip fiery sparklers in their vaginas while suspended upside down on trapezes. The anthropologist watches, caught between revulsion and fascination; her male escort, utterly drunk, is bored. Indeed, what there is to see, mostly along these same lines – anybody could jot down the performance list in a few minutes – is lowering and squalid, and that's all. Everybody seems to agree on its anti-erotic nature. It is as if the men who own the clubs and pay the girls, young men some of them, with their own pretty boy faces and swept-up hair, gold lamé wide-lapelled suits, high shoes, fix the nature of the gyrations the women must perform with obviously humiliating overtones. Then the women keep humiliation at bay by their blank eyes and empty faces, their hard stylised movements, their contemptuous turns of hip and heel, both assumed and real. Then they come off duty, and are warm and cheerful and funny.

So there is a glimpse of heaven even at the gates of hell. Cleo Odzer and the excellent Jeremy Seabrook[16] both report the kindness, cheerfulness, youthful tenderness of Thai prostitutes and strippers towards their clients once they are off-stage. They provide businesslike sex at once, but their real purpose is to turn the contract into a relationship, and sex, as they put it, into love.

Some of them brought this off. Seabrook met a middle-aged English truck driver, ditched by his wife out of the blue after seventeen years, who went to Thailand for sexual solace, but then rescued a young woman twenty-five years his junior in a boating accident and discovered for himself an unexpectedly high class of escort. He had turned blue with pulmonary distension the day after his bit of heroism, and after she'd sat by his bed for seventy-two hours, fetched (and paid for) the medication, he married her.

> I'm very happy. They are good people. Loy can't do enough for me; as a matter of fact, it gets too much sometimes, but if I say anything, she is hurt. She does things for me which I can actually do quite well for myself ... yet this woman is very intelligent. She has two degrees.[17]

Cleo Odzer meets an Australian who buys a young woman out of her hostess work in a sex bar because he's sorry for her, overpays her for sex anyway, and then, persuaded to bring her to Bangkok, pays for their board and lodging together as well as giving her 500 *baht* (about $20 in 1988) pocket money a day.

Figure 8.1   Thai massage parlour
Source: The Hutchinson Library/R. Ian Lloyd

> Actually, I'd like to get rid of her but I don't want to hurt her feelings. I get bored with just the two of us. I don't speak Thai and Sow speaks little English. But she has a good heart. She buys me things like fruit, or 10 *baht* worth of something or other.[18]

It breaks one's heart to hear it, and see the violence of disparity in money values, thrust up against each other like this, finding a kind of pacific settlement, what's more; what more could the boy do?

One can't come away from the official business of Patpong, however, in a sentimental haze, although one can from talking to the girls (Odzer's noun) themselves. One girl she thinks of as 'the sex goddess' because of a photograph Odzer sees of her, artlessly dressed in nothing but a tellingly tight bikini bottom, her thick hair loose around an extremely pretty Thai face, rosebud mouth, broad nose, high cheekbones. But the sex goddess, ravishing a little later in a tight strapless top and miniskirt is stricken that Odzer has the snapshot, since it can only have been given her by the man for whom it was supposed to be a keepsake.

Beside this touching tale, one tries to get rid of the picture of a man seated at a bar while a hostess vigorously sucked his penis, her head pumping up and down without interruption or straightening her back for seventeen minutes. The man watches her, occasionally looking casually around. Finally he ejaculates. The woman mops up with toilet paper.

The desolation of such a scene, its monotonous dreariness, goes on forever. It has no horizon. It is continuous with the emptiness of vista which brings the more helpless, slow-witted peasant girls to Bangkok in the first place, abject with fear of their masters, faithful to their village, their families and to their past, stupefied in response to anything that may happen to them, better paid than by anything they could ever find in the north.[19]

Seabrook, in his little casebook, treats the women as he treats everything except irresponsible wealth and cruel power, tenderly. He points out that for all the visibility of the sex industry, not many people work in it, and that tens of thousands of young women in the Bangkok garments industries work a 15-hour day in airless, windowless sheds, occupy dormitory beds twenty-five to a room, endure extortionate pay. He points out (in the unlikely company of the Fodor guide) how *safe* Bangkok is; even in Patpong the solitary tourist is safer than in the Bronx. This is a monstrously unequal, peaceable country in which the government is never called to account and is openly ineffective and incompetent. Contracts are bought and sold across and under the counters of everyday business.[20] A complete absence of public services complements the corruption as well as the fabulous money speculation in private capital. The symptom of both is the stench of sewage in the city, the undrinkable water in the taps. The top floors illegally added to one of the city's new hotels, designed luxuriously for tourists, collapsed in 1995, killing British visitors trapped in the lift.

These are details of an economy, only recently crashed from its rails, in which the home banks have hugely overbid themselves in unsecured loans to construction speculators inspired by the legends of Manhattan, and in which the vast, temporary surplus of capital found investment in the profitable triad of airlines, hotels and tour packages. Given the truths and myths about sexual freedom in Bangkok, the link between Patpong and the value of the *baht* is pretty direct, especially when one sees how plainly the sexual market in Bangkok is adjusted to the single male visitor. When the tourist replaced the American soldier, nothing had to change in the logistics. The appalling monologue Bishop and Robinson quote[21] juxtaposes Seabrook's decent truck-driver, leaving us to do some fairly commonplace ethical reflection about what it is to act well as a tourist when you are not rich at home, but here so much richer than the company you keep and sleep with.

> OK. Pick one. Any one! We're talking short-time here buddy. Who knows, maybe you get lucky and want to keep her on, but check her out first. There's plenty more where she comes from, so don't sweat it ... Take the edge off, bro, so you're not drooling later and do something foolish like spend too much or get shackled to a scuz ... Now you're moving into Big Mango mode. You're getting down and dirty, and you're loving it. Admit it. You can't do this at home ...

Must the tourist always be an imperialist and an exploiter? The severe voices of the academics mostly tell us yes. If we are to get closer to the enormous significance of sex in the imaginings and the industry of vacations, maybe we should consider those people for whom the next sexual encounter is the next piece of life, and find, if we can, social circumstances where such encounters are more or less equal.

Such a private place would be our sexual laboratory, notionally free of exploitation, suspended in pure vacation time with no thought for tomorrow except where tomorrow's sex will come from. But to set such conditions for an experiment in thought is to see its impossibility. Sexual tourism a long way from home has exploitation inscribed in it. It is part of what is looked for, and the only way to mitigate its cruelty is to bear the business with occasional insouciance, like the Bangkok girls.

III

Everybody has a sexual tourist hidden in some corner of their nature. There must be thousands of tourists who come to Patpong simply as spectators, much as the crowds stroll down along the canalside shop windows in the red light street in Amsterdam, gazing at once pruriently, longingly, sympathetically, *interestedly* at the plump, well-looking Moluccan women sitting domestically in their skimpy dresses on neat beds with gingham bedspreads. But mere pedestrians are drawn into the action and then into feeling and so in up to their necks, and nobody who prefers human beings to robots would have it otherwise. The omnivorous consumer goes to buy sex; buys the transaction, feels the sensation, finishes. Consumption, apart from a slight tremor at its ingestatory semantics, is a precise enough word to describe the exchange. The hard male likes it that way, and if he wants to pay the additional room services then those too may be finished off with the same finality as the courses of a meal.

The no-nonsense bully of a male consumer could say that his purchase discharges him from reflection. He buys sex from her. It's over. The Thai prostitutes, however, serve to remind us of the softenings and entanglements which attend and complicate the starkest market exchange. Bonds, mutualities and trusts, as the commercial use of these very terms indicate, are made involuntarily by making love, and while plenty of customers are able to refuse such obligations, plenty more are not.

This is, I suppose, another lesson on the reciprocal intertwinings and corrections which take place as desire and actuality, hope and experience try to match up to each other. The holiday matching of these quantities is, as I have contended, a rare opportunity to give desire and hopefulness a longer run than actuality and experience can usually permit. No doubt this is why sexual tourism, like other forms of tourism, trades so heavily on the gap between fantasy and fact. The photographs outside the sex shops of Bangkok or Rio de Janeiro deal with two radically opposing female physiques in such a way as keep the dream of women firmly beyond verification. In Bangkok the hard, youthful skin, the small, neat, compact bodies, the excellent white teeth, in Rio the tumbling masses of black curls, the copper skin, the long legs and full bosoms alike declare the complete undamageability of the sexual surfaces, their utter freedom from the rankness of the body's juices, its creases, its random hairiness, its sheer weight and fatigue.

That is the fantasy and a huge industry of image confection, advertising and more or less official pornography in the lifestyle magazines works busily to keep it believable; desirable; even accessible. In the fantasy physical satisfaction never fails; pure sensation never lets anyone down; what Stephen Marcus once called 'pornotopia'[22] where sex is inexhaustible, pain pleasurable, boredom inadmissible and embarrassment unspellable hovers at the edges of most holiday supplements and vacation television. Insofar as *any* man or woman goes on holiday with one eye cocked on the passers-by of the opposite sex, then there will be a gleam of pornotopia on the headland of the bay. The very clothes worn in Perranporth, Sorrento, Fremantle and Phuket reflect the gleam. The shiny black lycra bodystockings of the boy surfers are designed, like the gorgeous sun tans, to imply a nakedness honed to an alert, statuesque classicality, the bulge of the genitals is as prominent and discreet as those in the *Piazza dei Signori*.

Sexual tourism is one big wave in the huge holiday-going tide which began to sweep over the world's beaches and sunspots on such an unprecedentedly larger scale in the 1960s. More money, more leisure and more fantasies of fulfilment and happiness crowded the screens of consumption, and it would take a curmudgeon – whatever one's pangs and doubts – to say it all should never have happened.

This book is very far from being curmudgeonly and I am pleased as anyone else by the evidence of quite so much sexual happiness as one can see in the staidest promenades of Majorca or Waikiki. It takes a stony heart and a cold eye to insist that there is a reckoning even after fantasy time. But a cold eye is something called for, most of all when we are too much addled by the sweetness of things, and sex being so obviously and on its day an occasion for the exchange of tenderness and intimacy, then sexual tourism, inaugurated on the Riviera in the 1920s but tumultuous since the 1960s, merits a cold eye right now.

In the second volume of his autobiography *The Kindness of Women*,[23] J.G. Ballard pits himself against those who make all noncommittal sexual encounters into exploitation by men of women, and particularly those chosen by single men on vacation in countries the travel brochures would list as exotic. He disconcerts the reader by making one such encounter of his own into a grimly objective object lesson.

His beautiful wife has been killed by a fall onto stone steps at the beach. Ballard brings up his three small children alone, leaving them with friends from time to time to pursue writing work in films and to look for kindness. He goes to a film festival in Rio de Janeiro, not a kind city, one in which the striking good looks of so many men and women, set off by their rich colour, the profusion of dark and coppery hair, and the inheritance of prominent dark eyes enhanced by very expensive artifice, lend the people in the streets and open automobiles their confident stride, their inviolability, their brilliant smiles and quickness of temper. These are the clichés of the guidebooks but these are what the tourist actually sees, especially when the film-makers and their stars are in town.

Ballard and his close friend, a presenter of television science programmes, push past a crowd of arms waving, pleading for their custom to come and watch voodoo, chicken-fucking, 10-year-old sex, to go out to dinner with the leading film critic of the city. He has brought with him two of the festival's camp-followers who 'filled with such character, elegance and hot beauty' survey their new prizes 'with the eyes of empresses'.[24]

They go back to the room rented by the women. It is, inevitably, in a grim, dim, jammed tenement. The two men are offered sex next to a doorless room where three middle-aged women and a child are packing tawdry mementoes of the film festival for street sale. They buy some minutes' privacy and the workers move out into the corridor. The bedroom is deeply squalid, the sheets on the bed sweaty and lipstick-covered, the pillows soiled with mascara and vaginal jelly, underclothes everywhere, crumpled tissues all over the floor where the women dropped them after mopping themselves up. Discouragingly, a cine camera surveys the scene. Ballard notes everything coolly, all the way. This is an unnerving tourist. He is detached from the actions he is making by the sense of its all being there to watch. He treats this bit of his own life as a spectacle made for him on film. He cannot break out of the protection afforded by being a spectator. This is the real difficulty of the tourist in a strange place. Only familiarity or shock will set him running again in his own time.

In his essay on photography,[25] Roland Barthes distinguishes between two kinds of effective news photograph. The first is the *studium*, well-made, recognisable, clear; it informs the reader plainly and quickly; it does not draw him into that already past present of which it is a representation. The second is the *punctum*, where the singular handling of the picture punctures the epidermis of our attention, makes us bleed sympathy upon the picture, causes the past event to become present to us.

These perhaps are also two ways of being there, in a strange land and sorting the strangeness of the people. Ballard perforce seems to stay with the *studium* but it is his business as a writer to make us feel the *punctum*.

> She noticed me lying beside her and returned to work, shaking her head over my feeble erection. She took her left breast and teased out the nipple, tapping it with her sharp nails until it grew erect. Raising it to my mouth, she pressed the warm body of the breast against my nose and chin, placed my hand against her buttocks and steered my fingers down to her anus, pushing the tip of my ring-finger into the soft pad. She reached down to the root of my penis, searching for my prostate. When my penis came to life she nodded encouragingly, made sure that my eyes stayed on her breasts and my fingers on her anus. With her strong arms she turned me onto my back and squatted across my hips, sitting on her haunches so that the only part of her body to touch me was her vulva.

> Like a fisherwoman at an angling hole, patiently waiting for a bite, she moved about on her heels, the tip of my penis between her labia. At last, when the rake of both penis and pubis had matched to her satisfaction, she settled down and let my penis enter her vagina. She bobbed away energetically, glancing briefly at herself in the dressing-table mirror, and now and then blowing the hair from her eyes.[26]

There is a glassy calm to the writing, but there again, the sex as described is hardly sensational. Ballard seemed to have no great expectations of it, either, but to take it, not unkindly, as it came along, aware that she was working as hard as the older women next door. Like her, he has his matter-of-factness, and this is his salvation. Even the sexual vacationer has a code of conduct; he can't behave like this at home, but there's no reason why he shouldn't do as he would be done by.

IV

Ballard was symptomatic in his exotic, matter-of-fact, disappointing-but-what-the-hell escapade in 1970. The changes in sexual optimism summarily chronicled and illustrated here coincided with that larger tide in the popular feeling of the 1960s which made for the great crowds of new tourist-travellers, for sure, but also made for the more broadcast kinds of defiance, radical new self-conceptions, personal experimentation and social revolution by which the decade is now so completely defined.

World-reported and world-visible upheaval made for something thrilling and rippling in the air. Sexual defiance was easier and more immediate an act of self-definition than rioting. There were chiliasm and millenarianism walking abroad as they hadn't done since before the Second World War. And as always, capitalism, unburdened by any moral commitment except to its own enlargement, took its chances and played back to delighted youth the images and equipment of its own self-entrancement. This also was the opportunity for its other economy, the one forbidden by law but driven by desire, to expand into the extraordinary realm of pharmaceutic aids to momentary self-enlargement and the glories of abandon. This was the moment which launched Colombia out of its handfuls of marijuana leaves into the 50 tons of cocaine which were entering the USA[27] by 1987.

Across these ten years but continuing up to and beyond the present, a quite new sort of tourist cavalcade began to roar away into the distance, beating a new tourist track south, through France or down the Rhine and the Danube, leapfrogging across the Greek islands leaving riotously cheerful beach parties behind, and then striking unexpectedly across the bleak grey wastes of Afghanistan, whose main crop is heroin and which had been unvisited by travellers since Robert Byron was there. At the end of the Khyber, the troop met up with a similar pilgrimage which had come the other way, west from California or up from Victoria and New South Wales, all heading for the mind-and-body altering and uplifting experiences which Nepal would provide in the form of snowcapped peaks and the other lines of snow lying ridged on tinfoil.

Not that this new, cheerful multitude can be caught in its act by the tired old fulminations of the *Daily Mail* about the feckless, reckless, drug-taking, sex-happy, shaggy and unwashed young. This sudden extension of a tourist route was, one might say, the first drastic redrawing of the vacationer's map of the world since the Grand Tour. It was also, no doubt, the product of a new rite of passage invented by the liberated children of the old middle class, a rite which still situated them as not-quite-adults-yet and permitted them, after taking their degree and working non-committally outside the career structure for some savings, to take off round the world for their year out, carrying nothing but a backpack and a credit card, breezily dedicated to a few scores, a lot of interesting discomfort and a view of the world from the *Hitchhiker's Guide*.

The trail was marked out in the first place by the new chiliasts and millenarians, who offered a highly Westernised and weirdly eclectic version of Eastern transcendentalism, a heretical mixture of Buddhism, Hinduism, Sufism, with which to counter the deadly rationalities of science, the even deadlier acquisitiveness of capitalism. Amen to that, but this wasn't exactly a surge of political expression, though there were frenzied political messengers to be found on the way. It was more like a new category of livelihood of which the practitioners went to work for a while in this place and then that one, working often only for their keep and by the light of a small flame of idealism which lit them across the Indian subcontinent and beyond, until their time and money ran out. They interspersed this generosity with themselves, with their lives and mostly trusting hearts, by natural breaks on the beach[28] or in the foothills of the Himalaya.

Between 1960 and 1966 the bus services across Turkey multiplied by ten. The first charter flights flew into Goa after Portugal's bloodless revolution in 1974. The Holiday Inn opened in Corfu in 1967 and in Lourenço Marques in 1979. The number of tourist visas stamped in Nepal (most applicants were admitted at the frontier) rose tenfold between 1959 and 1971. Between 1965 and 1980 Bangkok built 276 new hotels with more than 200 bedrooms each.[29] The rise of visitors to Greece and its islands between 1985 and 1995 was eleven million; to Namibia, four; to Venezuela, nine.

This little jumble of statistics not very dependably provided by tourist offices does no more than tell us, as we knew, of the astounding rise in the numbers of visitors to what became a new index of sacred places. Of course, the raw figures cannot differentiate between dropouts, gap years and people on their annual fortnight off, but for the purposes of this argument I shall claim that it was, so to say, the Woodstock and Glastonbury generation which led the way. Dropping out meant refusing to step on the treadmill of work, productivity, ambition, money-making, all that, the moment one was deemed ready. It meant a brief refusal of those murderous sobrieties, and in that, it sorted well and expressed itself well with the mood of the holiday. I would also risk saying that the building of the hippie trail was a response to globalisation; it still is; Australians, Americans, Britishers are still trooping to Katmandu and taking the buses south. Young Americans may have gone south to find the blissful powder cheaper than in Brooklyn, but plenty more found in Colombia and Bolivia, among the shocking poverty and frightening criminality, something worth finding about the steadiness of poorer lives, their quietness, their reassuring immunity to what bad men are doing.[30]

As always, a new generation taught itself to feel differently from the old. The Woodstock and Glastonbury groups went to places the rich had never been. They exemplify, in some much more casual, easy-going spirit that view of the holiday which embraces the luxury of discomfort, of sleeping rough, of local food eaten with your fingers, of recovering the ease and happiness of a carelessness one can call natural. In the long aftermath of what came to be called the hippie trail,[31] this generation acquired and wore an attractive and smiling indifference to bad luck and acute discomfort in order not to allow inconvenience to obstruct access to the foreign land and its inhabitants they had come to see but not to stare at, to live among without difference and, above all, without exploitation, status, privilege, all they'd left behind.

Transcendentalists, flower-power hitchhikers with the milder drugs in their jeans, amateur Buddhists, world revolutionaries, Weathermen, Panthers out on the loose, incipient mercenaries, Rambos, buccaneer sexualists, and the regiments of the crazies taking their name from the wildest sponsors, rap artists, drug allegiances, the beach fashions of California, all this kaleidoscope of groupies is still patterned over the international trails, looking for something other than life on Main Street or in the market-place.

There are some very wild characters among them, and some bad hats as well. The excitement of violence hardly needs explanation; they are almost synonymous. Violence in the air puts a glitter in some people's eyes (mostly men's). They savour the knot of fear and anticipation which gathers in their entrails. The waiting is all part of the excitement, the overture to action.

There are tours for these people also. They are looking for something different to those following in the tracks of Wilfred Thesiger, Robert Scott or Eric Shipton. These men (and a few women) aren't explorers and mountaineers, though they also have their own social groups with a code of honour, an idiom, some myths and heroes.[32] Fielding's famous guide has become, it claims, a 'rallying point for a new type of traveller'. Its authors are men who have deliberately gone looking for the roughest journeys, the most abominable of local wars, the most precarious balancings of risk, whether in geographical, political or climatological extremity. Like mountaineers, they play down and clip off the dangers. Their favourite trope is understatement but they are very funny with it. They would, I think, despise the sexual tourist, but they are chipped off the same block. '*Soldier of Fortune*,' they say in their usual idiom, 'adds a little too much macho gun-love salsa to what are typically skanky, sweaty low budget guerrilla tours with complicated political backgrounds.'[33]

Yet the guide bears its witness to the reality of the fantasies it feeds, as does its substantial list of travel agents who will make the necessary arrangements for those who want to go and see the action and, perhaps, get enough mixed up in it to say they'd been there. At the edges of the busy, beaten tracks of holiday-making travel are these groups of people with a slightly fixed gaze and not many friends. They are the ones who answer flight calls to Kashmir, Phnom Penh, Mamburao, Tirana, Grozny. They travel, many of them, alone but they go in sizeable numbers to the places where that part of the tourist economy which will cater for their fantasy intersects with surprise and spontaneity. At this crossing, they hope to be caught by the accident of a collision which will turn fantasy into action just long enough to ward off present boredom and provide memories for the future to live on and off.

Happiness, I suggested, is a perfect fit between the feelings you have and the space-time of the experience in front of you. Sexual and venturesome action are alike in making it imaginable that space-time will so contract that you forget who and where you are in a transport of momentous fulfilment. If this is right, no wonder people try to wrap it up and sell it as a vacation. It is an acute case of looking for life before death.

9

CITY STATES

Fortunately for ordinary life, most people can make this match between desire and experience, spontaneity and expectation, in quieter ways. Wherever travel takes the tourists, it leads them always towards the city and, after the big words, industrialisation, capitalism, empire, democracy, have done their mammoth work, nobody can deny the power of the city to change and reorder all of life. In his study of the relations between the two, *The Country and the City*,[1] Raymond Williams says:

> H.G. Wells once said, coming out of a political meeting where they had been discussing social change, that this great towering city was a measure of the obstacle, of how much must be moved if there was to be any change. I have known this feeling, looking up at great buildings that are the centres of power, but I find I do not say 'There is your city, your great bourgeois monument, your towering structure of this still precarious civilisation' or I do not only say that; I say also 'This is what men have built, so often magnificently, and is not everything then possible?'

This is surely right. At the astounding, commonplace epiphanies, as we see the eponymous city, perhaps for the first time – the stupendous mass of Manhattan; the wonderful spidery line of Venice on the horizon; the instantaneity of the magic Orient on coming out of the station and meeting the heat at Cairo – all these bring home to us the simple grandeur of Williams's response: 'are not then all things possible?'

If we do know the city, we are immediately afraid as well as thrilled. There are so many stories about the young (or the elderly) innocent being fleeced or worse the moment after arrival in the strange city where one doesn't speak the language or know where to go. Surely a taxi will be safe? (but watch the clock). Then one will be at one's hotel, part of a rhythm one understands and enjoys, even loves. The hotel is central and small, the woman at the desk friendly, the room just as one had hoped, simple, a bath closet partitioned off in the corner, high, heavy cornices for this was once a larger room in the days when bathrooms were down the corridor with vast, curved, cast-iron baths and huge gurgling drains stopped with a heavy standpipe. Almost the whole of one wall is taken up by big french windows giving onto a little balcony. The noise of the city is muted to a steady drone by the small street below, with its large-screened windows opposite.

This is what it takes for the tourist to open her visit to the splendid city. She threads familiarity in little beads of safety along an unfamiliar line of travel into its heart.

Taxi, hotel, a quick visit to the café, a walk along busy streets lined with shops, and there's the river only a few minutes' walk away. Rivers reassure; so do bridges. She has leaned over many railings, just as we all have, and watched, staringly, a bit distrait, as the strong current boils around the blunt piers. In a little time, she and the friends she is with will thread another, lovably safe bead on the line; they will go down another street, daring a tricky little route in the dark perhaps, to a restaurant for dinner. The restaurant will be through a high archway in a flagged courtyard; it will have lights in all its high windows. Tomorrow she will go to see some of the sights and walk the boulevards for which this city is famous, and she will begin to say to herself excitedly that she is getting to know it – Paris, Prague, Lisbon, Melbourne, Quebec, Montevideo, Capetown, Hong Kong, whichever it may be.

Getting to know a city is a matter of interleaving the strange and the recognisable. We carry with us a partly inherited, partly intuitive poetics of place. In his marvellous book of that name, Gaston Bachelard[2] sketches such a poetics, where he takes the term to mean some kind of epistemic structure. An episteme, let us say, is a fundamental unit of the knowable world. For Bachelard, the fundamental units of our being in space include drawers, chests, wardrobes, *nests*, shells, 'intimate immensity', and these he orders into an intuitively pleasing structure, which is to say a poetics. Thus, we make ourselves snug, pleased with its shape, at home in the world by devising a sufficiently safe, sufficiently beautiful alternation of openness and enclosure, where receptacles (wardrobes, chests) fit neatly into recesses, and keep space under their lids and within their doors; where the lovely *surroundingness* of a room of one's own marks off a clear little kingdom; and where windows and doors open surprisingly on a sudden expanse of space without terror, agora with no phobia. This is his 'intimate immensity' and the great originary landscape gardeners, like the architects of seaside piers and promenades, knew exactly how to create it.

Bachelard goes on:

> the images I want to examine are the quite simple images of *felicitous space*... They seek to determine the human value of the sorts of space that may be grasped, that may be defended against adverse forces, the space we love. For diverse reasons, and with the differences entailed by poetic shadings, this is eulogized space ... Space that has been seized upon by the imagination cannot remain indifferent space subject to the measures and estimates of the surveyor. It has been lived in, not in its positivity, but with all the partiality of the imagination ... it concentrates being within limits that protect. In the realm of images, the play between the exterior and intimacy is not a balanced one. On the other hand, hostile space is hardly mentioned in these pages ... For the present, we shall consider the images that *attract*... The imagination is ceaselessly imagining and enriching itself with new images. It is this wealth of imagined being that I should like to explore.[3]

In a book more specific to our purposes, Kevin Lynch[4] started out from a small research exercise in perception and, prompted by the theories of the Gestalt psychologists, actually quizzed a sample of citizens on how they composed an intelligible image of the city they each lived in, for their everyday use in getting about.

The three cities concerned were Boston, Jersey City and Los Angeles and from his own predilections as a historically well-educated architectural critic and a town-planner of vision, together with what his obliging little research sample said and drew by way of diagrams, Lynch came up with a not dissimilar series of epistemic units which he contrived into a framework.

Lynch's five basic units are: paths, edges, districts, nodes, landmarks, and each of these, as is plain, has a greater conceptual force than Bachelard's order of the spatial sentiments. But they share a common and fourfold orientation towards, first, *shapeliness of ambit*; second, *distinctness of direction*; third, *the invitation to surprise*; fourth, *the systole and diastole* (the pulse) *of passage*; finally, *the parental monument*. These formulae are, I should add, my extensions and enlargements of Lynch's straightforward scheme. For the sake of the city-visitor and this book they suggest the criteria of an everyday poetics we carry with us in order to get the feel of, and in order to judge the new, exciting city we have come to admire.

Lynch, working doggedly from his empirics, rightly applauds his collaborators for wanting clear, safe pathways, whether on foot or in a car. He understands the satisfaction provided by a clear edge; it satisfies us as making it easy to know where one is, but it satisfies also in its finality and definition. No edge is more finished, as we see all over the Mediterranean, than a waterfront, and the Bostonians were all just as satisfied with the edges made by the magnificent expanse of their harbour and the clarity of the quick-running Charles River. Jersey City people, on the other hand, could only look mournfully on the missed opportunity of their two waterfronts, Newark Bay and Hudson River, where in each case the edge was (in 1960) either messy and unmarked or else brutally exclusive, what with the burning dumps then on the edge of the Hackensack and the barbed wire and spiked railings of the docklands. In Jersey City it is still easy for the stranger to become completely lost, especially in an automobile, and few contemporary experiences can make one more anxious.

It's a bit hard on Jersey City to use it as the type of dystopia, but it might help to bring out what it lacks by way of suggesting what it is about the great world capitals which so brings the tourists teeming in. Lynch says flatly:

> What might have been its natural shopping center was stifled by the artificial creation of Journal Square on the upper land so that the city has no natural center, but rather four or five. To the usual formlessness and space and heterogeneity of structure that mark the blighted area of any American city is added the complete confusion of an uncoordinated street system. The drabness, dirt and smell of the town are at first overpowering.[5]

This outsider's first impression is then painfully borne out by Lynch's interlocutors. The only good thing about Jersey City was that you could see the Manhattan skyline. It was trapped by its own traffic barriers; a sensational site had been destroyed by wasted edges, directionlessness, dreariness and repetition, blankness of passage, an absence of any lovable monumentality. Poor old Jersey City still lacks each of Lynch's epistemic features: it has no node, no landmarks, harsh edges, pointless paths, indistinguishable districts. Los Angeles, by contrast, has mighty landmarks, significant spaces (Pershing Square), bold paths (Broadway) even if those who lived there went on (and Lynch agrees with them) to criticise the city as 'too spread-out', dispersed, formless once one tried to reduce the grand scale of the preliminary image to a legible topography. This is after all the city that invented urban sprawl.

Jersey City is destination for few tourists, Los Angeles, with all its faults, for many. But wherever we visit on our holidays we are looking, I suggest, for Piero's Ideal City, Michael Frayn's celestial one, our own imagining of the Good Place. In his splendid book about Los Angeles, Mike Davis quotes Walter Benjamin on writing about cities:[6]

> The superficial inducement, the exotic, the picturesque has an effect only on the foreigner. To portray a city, a native must have other, deeper motives – motives of one who travels into the past instead of into the distance. A native's book about his city will always be related to memoirs; the writer has not spent his childhood there in vain.

Benjamin implies a distinction between the city-dweller and the renegade hero of this book, the tourist. As usual, the tourist comes off worst, universally despised and condescended to. The tourists arrive on vacation; they have come to gaze. But the tourist gaze has more than two lenses to its spectacles,[7] and in any case is always a gaze along the perspectives of the past. For Benjamin, with the habitual snobbery of these polemics, 'the exotic and the picturesque' are 'superficial inducements' catching the eye only of the mere 'foreigner', almost certainly a tourist. Sure, the tourist comes to gaze at exoticisms and picturesqueries in the city one hears so much about, but then the only way to see even these elementary features is to travel into the distance of history. 'No percepts without concepts' was Kant's slogan for the intelligent eye, and the vacationer cannot even see the Pyramids, the Taj Mahal or the Hanging Gardens without at least a few sentences from the guidebook.

II

There are places which, as we say, captivate or enchant us. They pull us back to them, perhaps by way of their very exoticisms or picturesquerie, perhaps for innumerable other reasons. 'I fell in love with Venice,' people say; I would, for one. What is it to be in love? It is presumably to long for the company of another because that other captivatingly combines strangeness and familiarity. The perfect stranger is so perfect because she recognises in us something potential and unnamed, something we remembered was there but had never managed to find, something which, now acknowledged, may unfold at our centre into happiness. And we see in her the creature with the power to bind this spell.

There is a glimpse here of those 'correspondences' writing of which I quoted Richard Wollheim in Chapter 2. We find in a cityscape reflections of the feelings we bring to it; we *project*. Conversely, bringing to the prospect quite different, it may be alien feelings, its special character *instructs* us in an unexpected range of feelings; it *tells* us what to feel. Wordsworth's wonderful sonnet on the city of London is a lesson in the making of such a sentiment from both ends:

Earth hath not anything to show more fair:
Dull would he be of soul who could pass by
A sight so touching in its majesty:

> This city now doth, like a garment, wear
> The beauty of the morning; silent, bare,
> Ships, towers, domes, theatres and temples lie
> Open unto the fields, and to the sky;
> All bright and glittering in the smokeless air.

But as we learn from *The Prelude*, Wordsworth himself felt constantly lost and afraid in London, when the fixed social ties of his homely Lake District were disregarded or broken. Only London as a panoramic horizon – as Canaletto painted it – matches the kinds of feeling which Wordsworth is capable of bringing to this affirmation.

André Aciman marks some kind of middle point between the raw tourist with the always-to-be-commended Baedeker and the city-dweller who knew it and loves it and, so often, quit it anyway. The literature and the demography of modernity is full of strangers for whom the city is the place of exile, the place to which they came for refuge, for freedom, for work, for peace, but which was, inevitably, crowded, scary, noisy, uncomfortable, filthy, *not like home*. They stayed anyway; it was, for now, the only place to be. Gradually they learned it and found time to care for it.

The tourist has bought such time, has spent so much money on it that the time is free. Aciman is an immigrant in New York, has lived there fifteen years or so, but his experience is, I'm sure, something like that of the tourist who, by dint of repeated visits, comes to know the beloved city, much as one might know a person's life, or the life of a work of art.

Aciman was one day walking along Broadway towards his favourite little park, Straus Park on Broadway and West End Avenue at W106th Street.[8] It looked as though the Park were being demolished; the statue of a reclining Mnemosyne (the goddess of memory, mother of the Muses) had gone, there were hardhatted workmen, a generator, a portaloo, piles of torn-up tarmac and strips of orange ribbon fencing. It had always been a rather grubby, scruffy sort of park, its fountain long arid and dead, its population the awful derelicts of the modern city, but Aciman was attached to it because 'I wanted everything to remain the same' and he goes on:

> It is precisely because you have no roots that you don't budge, that you fear change, that you'll build on anything rather than look for land. An exile is not just someone who has lost his home; it is someone who can't find another, who can't think of another. Some no longer even know what home means. They reinvent the concept with what they've got, the way we reinvent love with what's left of it each time.

A visitor to a new city, you might say, one taking a vacation there, has come deliberately to try out some of these feelings; not so much as someone who has lost a home but as someone who has come to assemble certain selected spots and landmarks as the ideal city, specifically not the city the holidaymaker has come away from, but the perfect city reinvented out of the bits one most wants not to change, or wants to find *improved*, strange and fresh perhaps but fixed for future visits as well.

Aciman, like many other people, several of them immigrants like himself, used to pause for restoration in Straus Park and invent it for himself as a home from home. His trouble was that he had no home, though quite at home in New York, and he made out of Straus Park the sort of loved, unchanging city corner which children make from favourite picnic spots.

This was possible, he suddenly realised, exactly because the park could be, as the poet said, both a little room and an everywhere. It was at a centre of Manhattan, W106th, Riverside Park one side, Central Park the other. It had, he realised, *four* addresses for him, could be used to prefigure four troops of memories, summoned by the goddess to inspire her progeny.

> West End, decidedly Londonish; 107th, very quiet, very narrow, tucked away around the corner, reminded me of those deceptively humble alleys where one finds stately homes along the canals of Amsterdam. And 106th, as it descended towards Central Park, looked like the main alley of small towns on the Italian Riviera where, after much trundling in the blinding light at noon and the stagnant odor of fuel from the train station where you just got off, you finally approach a sort of core, which you can't make out yet but which you know is there, hidden behind a thick row of Mediterranean pines, over which, if you really strain your eyes, you'll catch the tops of striped beach umbrellas jutting beyond the trees, and beyond these, if you could just take a few steps closer, the sudden, spectacular blue of the sea.

Looking westward towards Riverside he glimpses Paris, where the Hudson will turn into the Seine and the sixth *arrondissement* would coil its alluring streets before him. Beyond all these pleasurable projectings and correspondences, so dear to his feelings and to his objectless yearnings, there may be 'the beginnings of another unknown city, the real city, the one that always beckons, the one we invent each time and may never see and fear we've begun to forget'.

All this, however, is no meditation upon nostalgia in a plangent key. We play delighted *arpeggios* on our memories but the times don't necessarily make us want to be there, wherever it is. Our composite city may be our best home when we are *not* there, but when its special coincidence marks our recollection with its keen edge and clarity, when Paris, for example, becomes compacted into four remembered spots – so typical, as we rightly think – the *rue Buci*, the *Pont Neuf* over the swift, dark river, the wide, crunching gravel and the peeled plane trees of the *Tuileries* gardens, the boiling torrent of traffic below as one crosses the *Periphérique*.

Making a topography is a matter of generalising our comparisons. As we heard Charles Taylor say earlier, without comparisons we can learn neither to understand nor to sympathise. Great cities, which is to say, cities varied, overlapping, complex, manifold enough to provide imaginative fulfilment to millions of different visitors, owe their magic to exactly this, their *unsubsumeability*.

In a famous paper, a town planner[9] once applied two kinds of mathematical set theory to the conceptualisations of the planners. In set theory, 'tree-diagrams' designate single-feature sets, each mutually exclusive. British new towns, the well-intentioned products of post-war social reconstruction, fitted tree diagrams. Each zone of the city was separate to its function: shopping, production, dormitory, all joined along their mutually exclusive boundaries by a grid system of roads, for the essential unit of transport in this kind of planning was the automobile.

That of course remains the case. Whatever punishments are contrived to keep car owners out of cities, and however heavy taxation becomes with which to plug the holes in the ozone layer, short of cataclysm the automobile will continue to dominate the cityscape. It is this which makes difficult for planners the application of another, obviously preferable kind of set-theory to the understanding of cities old and new.

The 'semi-lattice set' accommodates those combinations and overlappings it is the purpose of the tree set to exclude. The semi-lattice prefigures as its function the manifold and interpenetrative relations tree diagrams hold apart.

> The semi-lattice axiom goes like this: *A collection of sets forms a semi-lattice if and only if, when two overlapping sets belong to the collection, then the set of elements common to both also belongs to the collection* ... We are concerned with the difference between structures in which no overlap occurs, and those structures in which overlap does occur.[10]

Alexander's pleasure in the topological axiom is caused by its compression of distinct sets into a single collection while still keeping them identifiably distinct. The subtlety and complexity of the semi-lattice is that one such, based on only twenty elements, could contain a million subsets. A planner who could so combine twenty elements would have a wonderfully rich and absorbing city on his drawing board.

Transferred from cyphers to the solidities of buildings and people, the semi-lattice pictures for us those spatial organisations in which we bump into ourselves and others in all our multiplicity of social being. Planning with the semi-lattice in hand allows for the individual to be customer, client, consumer, citizen; pedestrian, passenger; spectator, participant; active, passive; in motion or at rest, garrulous or taciturn, all within a few paces and as the creative mood takes her and him.

It's a fixed fight of course: the tree diagram represents the blank hellishness of bureaucratic efficiency, the semi-lattice the busy delights of civic intercourse. Everybody wants the latter, nobody the former – or at least not until they are trying to drive to the airport in Naples, or find the hospital in a hurry in Cairo, or simply discover the fountains in order to sit by them in Rome.

Then it won't quite do to say that the great, successful city – the city, as I put it earlier, as a work of art for the artless – will happily blend the order and efficiency of the bureaucratic diagram with the beautiful jostle and messy vitality of actual markets. We want both, of course, but their achievement will be accidental as much as reasonable, historical as much as aesthetic.

III

It was Kevin Lynch's admirable contribution to our understanding of cities to insist that planners and people must be mutually intelligible, and to throw into relief the everyday necessity for a topographical theory of the city one lives in. The whole point about the holiday city, however, is that one does *not* live in it, and that it is as much visited for its exhilarating strangeness and in order to test its reputation against one's ignorance of it, as to find in it some fulfilment of the universal dream of the ideal city so revealingly pictured in Piero's version as a city with no inhabitants.

Nonetheless, I believe, Lynch's little framework fits the way we thread our beads of familiarity on the narrative topography of the city, and those cities are best and most

Figure 9.1   View of an Ideal City, or the City of God, probably painted by Piero della Francesca
(panel), attributed to Luciano Laurana (*c*.1420–79)

Source: Galleria Nazionale delle Marche, Urbino, Italy/Bridgeman Art Library

beautiful which allow the visitor to have things both ways: that is, cities which make
possible an intelligible and satisfying image reasonably quickly, and which also allow
for reiterative surprise and unexpected conjuncture. One might take, among famous
cities of the world and regular holiday targets, Singapore as the last word in clearly
planned efficiency, and Cairo as our much-latticed, densely intertwined and vividly
crowded picture of the city as market.

Of the two, Singapore commits itself, under the genial authoritarianism of its
government, most wholly to the idea of a city where people come to spend money. The
old Singapore was pretty well swept away after the velvet divorce from Malaysia; in
ten years it put off its ancient, redolent reputation as imperial gateway to the Far East,
its structural position on the hinge of British naval strategy, its enormous docklands
and its biological urgency for millions of sailors as the haven on the horizon after
thousands of womanless sea-miles. The Raffles Hotel, famous in song and story,
where British expatriates could return to cool, high, dim interiors with dark mahogany
floors and white colonnaded courtyards, was turned into a Disneyland shrine whose
sacred objects are customised versions of the imperial past: chestnut leather suitcases,
diamond watches, long foaming cylinders of iced gin-and-tonic.

The docks are now long, paved walkways beside wide, empty water; the Indian quarter,
shrunk to a tiny simulacrum of itself, a dozen narrow streets sprinkled with high-speed
curry cafés grouped around a tiny, darkened square where the men meet after dark in this
hygienic little ghetto, and remind themselves amiably of their minor ethnic grievances.

The rest of the city centre is a hardly differentiated shopping mall. The horticultural imagery is sustained – tall palms, evergreens, small grassy parks, but the long
thoroughfare of Orchard Road is a repetitious sequence of glass-and-gold malls, true
cathedrals of consumption, where the shopper wanders through sedulously undefined
space, the glass walls which separate shop from shop, and shop from walkway, serving
to set off the models in their skimpy clothes blazoned with the irresistible Italian
names – Versace, Armani, Gucci – as well as to allure and to check the mesmerised
gaze of the pedestrians. The glass permits gaze but not access; you have to walk inside.
The silver and gold promises the glamour of the wealth you would symbolise if you
put on these clothes. The women who serve are dressed in them and are chosen, one

guesses, for their passing likeness, got up with a lot of blusher and a little eyelash elongator, to the fabulous supermodels who first wore the prototypes.

And that's about it. There is still the splendid cricket ground, an adequate art gallery, the governmental and university buildings in Lutyens white. History is packed away onto Sentosa Island to which one is carried on a sort of funfair funicular, and where the magnificent aquarium is adjacent to the ghastly waxworks. There, in the first room, waxy ghosts of the British command of 1942 surrender to the Japanese, and in the next, waxy ghosts of the Japanese surrender in their turn three years later, each indiscriminately caught on their camcorders by the thousands of contemporary Japanese tourists who troop round the island and consent to eat the dreadful sweet pancakes in the fastfood outlet.

Around this centre and the endless peeping of the credit card machines stand the new hotels, each towering by twenty-five storeys over the diminutive, white Raffles; each echoing, according to its nicely judged place on the hierarchy of expensiveness, the kitsch imagery of the mall, gold, glass, silver, polished wood; the traffic of each, in a saccharine imitation of Frank Lloyd Wright's Fallingwater, revolving around a cascade of water pouring through an indoor glimpse of the Malayan rainforest on which the island has firmly turned its political back.

Beyond the ring of hotels spread the rings of high-rise apartment buildings packed with the two-and-a-half million Chinese who have so calmly brought into being this model of the ultimate fantasy of capitalism. They, the Chinese, the overwhelming majority in a tiny state, manufacture nothing but judiciously effect a little value-adding to many commodities and run to their enormous profit the biggest independent market at the meeting place of the two economic worlds, Western and Pacific. In the age of heedless and directionless air travel, Singapore owes its origins to geography but its wealth strictly to enterprise. To bring off this victory and make itself, on behalf of the Pacific future, into the showcase of conspicuous consumption, the centre from which, if things go well for that kind of capitalism, the Indonesians and Chinese will learn luxury, glamour and the joy of shopping, Singapore transformed itself into this clean, well-lit, brochure city.

It is an experiment the unheeded failure of which ought to be as significant as that of Brasilia. Each fails in virtue of its boringness; Singapore as the shopper's city, Brasilia as the visionary architect's. If both are awful, what shall we do with the way our beloved cities truly are? When Le Corbusier declared war on the urban street then, as Marshall Berman shows us:

> the old modern street, with its volatile mixture of people and traffic, businesses and homes, rich and poor, is sorted out and split up into separate compartments with entrances and exits strictly monitored and controlled, loading and unloading behind the scenes, parking lots and underground garages the only mediation.[11]

Berman is very funny about the excitable Le Corbusier ('We must kill the street') and knows the polemical literature well, particularly Jane Jacobs's reply to Corb and all who thought like him. For Jacobs 'a lively city scene is lively largely by virtue of its enormous collection of small elements'[12] – an observation turned into a geometry by our friend the semi-lattice – 'the stretch of Hudson Street where I live is each day the scene of an intricate sidewalk ballet'. For Jacobs as for Dickens the life of the city *is* its street, particularly its sidewalk life. Berman feels the force of this; he was brought up in the Bronx and remembers the unbelievable day in 1953 when the omnipotent Robert Moses, City Parks Commissioner, City Planning Commissioner, Chairman of the State Power Authority, and Lord High Everything Else as well, announced that the homes of about 60,000 people would be bulldozed to build the truly dreadful Cross-Bronx Expressway.

And they were. As Berman says, 'the vistas of devastation stretched for miles to the east and west as far as the eye could see',[13] as he goes on powerfully to contend, such destructive absoluteness in the massive construction of industrial molochs – freeways, bridges, dams, nuclear power stations, even shopping malls and leisure centres as well – is for many people what the modern city *means*. The heavenly, motorless quiet of the Renaissance hearts of Florence and Venice are treasured exactly for their not being modern. When the traffic stops, time stops with it; a breathless, ancient history may then, if we are respectful enough, slowly fill the silent space left open for it.

Yet this is not how we find our favourites – Florence or Venice say – to be. One is keenly grateful, of course, that the traffic is turned aside at the end of Via Cavour when it comes to the edge of the Duomo, but as one wanders into the huge crowd eddying before the West Front and Giotto's Campanile, pink and fresh and decidedly postmodern, exactly as if it were finished yesterday, the orange buses and ritually irritable taxis tootle by a few paces away from the reverent faces gazing at Ghiberti's bronze doors; and history, as usual, is being made in this entirely commonplace process. Part of the memorability of those two lovely and amazing buildings is that they dominate so effortlessly our complex experience of the living city. They do so by their sheer *visibility* as well as by their beauty. Everybody knows them. There is no more famous metonymy of tourism than this pair. Kevin Lynch, emphasising the simple significance of landmarks in our imaging of a city,[14] points out how the Duomo and Campanile together serve to orient the tourist and the city-dweller alike, wherever they may be about the city, glimpsable at the end of so many streets, commanding the panorama of the city either from the north or the south, clearly oriented to the river, triumphantly distinctive, affirmatively Florentine.

Not many cities can boast such landmarks, though it is worth adding that most of the cities we think of as *great* cities have something to enter into the competition: Eiffel Tower, Big Ben, St Peter's, San Giorgio Maggiore, Sphinx (if you allow the ride), Sugar Loaf Mountain, Sydney Opera House, Golden Gate, Charles Bridge, Bronze Horseman ... but you can make up your own, perhaps less European, less conventional list anyway. What matters is that a landmark of this kind is, like all good totems, capacious, accommodating to change, stable, reassuring, beckoning. It can only be so if it remains within the city's true and everyday living.

All this is, you might say, a roundabout way to agree with Berman's horror at Robert Moses's destructive will-to-power, while also agreeing that part of the thrill of the modern city drives through the hurtling traffic. The point, however, is not traffic, but *movement*. Life moves; itself and us. So New York would not *be* New York without the crazy medley of yellow cabs, its calm mastodon buses, its jammed sequence of high trucks, pick-ups, armoured security vehicles, U-Hauls, obsidian-windows stretch limos, and vast old clattering Buicks all lurching to a stop at the lights, as the Walk-Don't Walk signs neatly despatch the obedient crowds to the four points of the compass.

Figure 9.2 Brooklyn Bridge
Source: Kathy Williams

The particular life of New York is certainly prefigured in its ceaseless traffic. But the life of all great, visitable cities balances on some undiscoverable fulcrum between its present, vital busyness and the many signs of its times. Even New York, where the demolishers have done such unforgivable things over the years, has come over the period of modernity to realise, like all our great, wounded capitals of tourism, that (as they should have known) to demolish the signs of the past is to demolish memory, and give a city amnesia, like Singapore.

IV

Traffic therefore serves in this argument as no more than a token of the flow of a city's lifeblood. There is a difference to be felt immediately between a dead and a living city. As Lynch's interlocutors agree, Jersey City, while hardly dead, is maimed and blocked in its daily functioning; Pompeii, on the other hand, is still alive. You can see how it works; learn its paths, nodes and landmarks quickly and interestedly; its history flows through you. Singapore, I am claiming, for all its busy exchange and sedate street manners, is blank. It has the lifelessness of the robot. This robotic nature is a consequence of its rooting-up of its own memory. Lynch's first premise is that a city, in order to *be* a city, must have structure and identity, and his 'epistemic units' are intended not only to provide a syntax for the analysis of these essentials, but like Bachelard, to suggest that when each of us is presented with the rules of this syntax, we will realise how naturally it comes to us. We have been speaking this language all our lives.

Singapore has structure, but no identity. Cairo, we might say, comes close to having identity but very little structure. Having that identity, it is unmistakably alive, but as is the way with the 'exotic' (which is to say 'out of one's ken'), it is easy to be lost there.

On the map, or seen from the circular panoramic chamber at the top of Cairo Tower, itself a magnificent combination of modern and traditional forms, a slender central pillar housed in an Islamic lattice, Cairo makes ready sense. The ancient city is spread evenly on either side of the Nile. The colossal, calm breadth of the river, blue from up here, brown from the bridges, provides the universal edge we crave from a place. Along the riverside range the enormous modern buildings, the vast rotunda and the mad administrative Mugamma with its thousand-and-one guichet windows and spiral staircase, gross in scale as compared with the exquisite mosques, but confidently meeting the modernist's demand for sheer size and assertiveness, for the rugged development view that massive construction is the same thing as progress.

No-one can roundly say such a judgement is wrong.[15] If on a clear day you look along the Thames Embankment towards the Houses of Parliament, upriver from where Wordsworth stood on Westminster Bridge in 1814, you see the colossal scale of the post-1960 buildings dwarfing the official monuments of British imperial and democratic history, let alone, further east, the almost-invisibility in this crowd of the exquisite churches, Gibbs', Hawksmoor's, Wren's, which are so much part of the city's secular identity. Yet you could hardly wish, at this date, that there were *no* such buildings, that the brutalism of modern architecture, along with its audacity, philistinism and blind will, had passed the city completely by. Lewis Mumford, for all his strictures on modernity's bullying ignorance, claims for great cities that they can take it;[16] that to be great cities at all they must change and accommodate themselves. They can't take *anything*, of course; many cities, Hong Kong say, Bucharest perhaps, both victims of the totalitarianism implicit in modernity, have been destroyed in both structure and identity. Others, Venice, Vienna and Paris among them, have only been saved by an exceptional compactness and immutability of the heart.

A city is like a work of art in that its meanings change as one sees it from different angles; it expresses a culture in its capaciousness towards novelty and its power to discard the past; it is like a person in its growth and decay, its ageing and in its distinctive characteristics and features: it may be aloof, mysterious, welcoming, charming, harsh, indifferent, courteous, munificent.

It is important that I mean these qualities literally. These are not 'subjective' attributions. Cairo may show any of these qualities to the visiting tourist, and getting to know her is equally a matter of understanding her experience, learning to love her art, becoming familiar with her culture. No doubt, as with a person or a work of art, we may fail to be captivated, may even dislike what we find. Inasmuch, however, as the tourist, for his or her part, comes with good will, comes openly and trustingly to find the judgement of countless others that this is indeed a wonderful city vindicated, then you and I should be able to find the charm and the character of El Qahira.

Everybody loves a panorama,[17] just as they turn familiarly towards a landmark. The view from Cairo Tower is marvellously complete. Like God, one can hold the city in one's mind during a single stroll round the chamber (this was the grip of the *camera obscura* for its eighteenth-century inventors).

THE DELICIOUS HISTORY OF THE HOLIDAY

Back on the ground, structure dissolves into teeming identity. We recover ourselves by looking for what is typical. Why not? Much of a sanctimonious kind is written these days about the awfulness of stereotypical thinking, but without some stereotypes to fix our categories, we cannot think at all. Similarly, one is reproached for treating individuals as objects. But as encountered in the street, they *are* objects, though nonetheless deserving the respectful treatment we would accord objects which are not our possessions, which may be damaged, and which cannot offend us.

Consequently, when I see this Egyptian woman walking towards me in loose, brilliant turquoise silk trousers and old gold headgear, I see her as at once typical and exceptional, and a pleasure to the eye and heart.

I walk downtown, towards Wust el-Balad, fairly sure of my whereabouts, bounded by the river, the Garden City and (a bit vague and worrying, this part) the citadel and el Khalifa going a couple of kilometres east. A mile or so behind me, overwhelmed by a crazily improvised and horrible system of overpasses, is the beautiful façade of the Ramses railway station, its pediments and entablatures set with blue mosaics, its pillars dressed in lovely, soft, sand-coloured marble. Over on my right (westward) is the Gezira, an island in the middle of the Nile, bisected by the October bridge, site of Cairo Tower and the just-as-dazzling, Arab-and-European opera house, built in 1988 with a gift from Japan to replace the old one, destroyed by fire.

This is an easyish part of Cairo for a European, largely because Khedive Ismail, the ruler of the 1860s and vastly impressed by the megalomaniac success of Baron Haussmann in Paris at the time, hired European architects to devise a system of Parisian boulevards for downtown Cairo. The wide sidewalks, the avenues of palms, the dusty gardens large and small, which provide shade and pallid greens in the terrific, heavy heat of Cairo's interminable summer, recall for us that this is another Mediterranean city, holding the desert at bay on the sufferance of the Nile, and preceding the white colonnades of Greece and Rome, their public, conversational forums and piazzas with something much more Egyptian, Islamic now, once Fatimid, always different.

By the time the walker has turned towards the citadel, called on the gilded nineteenth-century excesses of domes and doorways in the Muhammed Ali Mosque, and bent back north, up the road called Sharia el-Muizz, he or she is deep in Islamic Cairo and difference, the name of our new moral order, is everywhere. There are glimpses of home. The trees lining the Sharia are big palms, slightly too high for forgiving shade. The traffic is tumultuous and unstoppable, but quite without the sudden obedience of the Manhattan barndance or the cortège advance of London traffic. The people – well, the people, whom one notices so piercingly because, on holiday, one is here to notice and memorise things, they summon up all the same adjectives, so unavoidably close to indiscriminate cliché, which their city does. Their attire sets them apart, but less so than was once the case. There are plenty of galibayas in London today. Their manners are better than those on the streets of London. The invocation of the deity is as courtly as the American's 'you're welcome'; this is the politics of politeness, one key to the morality of difference.

I pass the el Muayyad mosque where the great ramparts and massive gate seem as familiar as the Palais des Papes in Avignon, and turn right towards el Azhar University, diffidently, an infidel entering its holiness, stepping into the lovely courtyard of the mosque. It is crossed by a wide, worn and beautiful carpet covering the golden marble and leading the students sitting on it to the beautiful cloisters below castellated arches with a plain, keep-like centrepiece and a low dome flanked by minarets behind. The shade keeps off the pitiless sun, but the cloister is breathlessly hot. Beyond it is another, dusty little garden with bleached grass and thirsty palms. This is the traditional organisation of space in Islam. Round the courtyard stands the severe, expressionless wall, pierced only by slits or ornately latticed, wooden fenestration. A small door opens. Shoeless and disarmed, you are admitted as a guest and friend to the shade and spaciousness within.

The tourist has walked and walked. Finally, he takes a taxi to the City of the Dead, where Sultan Barquq was buried out in the desert in 1399 and which is now a suburb of half a million live inhabitants and no one knows how many dead ones. Sultan Qaytbay's huge, filigreed dome of 1472 far outdoes the founder, and round him the city of tombs spreads just like any city, with quarters for rich and poor, little stone walls built in rectangles marking off the grand from the mere headstones or the low marble bars outside.

Twelve hundred years of Muslim dead lie here, and thousands of their descendants live around and on top of them, while thousands more turn up for the markets among the tombs and on the regular holy days of el-Hurayn (the prophet's grandson), of Imam el-Shafi'i, and two dozen or so others come for the *moulids*, which is to say to picnic lavishly and make a good night out.

These few excursions, some hot walks, a magnificent railroad ride, a trip on the Nile, frequent stops for tiny cups of bitter coffee behind the curtained slots in the bare walls of dark, narrow lanes, can they be said to be enough to provide an image with 'a structure and an identity', of this vast city sprawling endlessly across level sands shrouded by its own dust and smoke? I found edges, paths, landmarks, nodes, in other words, *form*, enough of it; I found variety, colour, strangeness, stereotypes of picturesquerie and of fearsome poverty. Alone in the dark of Sharia el-Muizz, the roofline of the mosques sharp against the rich starscape of Egypt, I was afraid, and with cause. In 1998 a busload of tourists was pointlessly butchered by trigger-happy Islamic terrorists as they visited Luxor, gunned, it seems, with relish, the throats of the wounded cut, all in the name of recalling a sane, pious, courteous nation to the impossible medievalism of Quranic law as the gunmen saw it.

Structure; identity; form; and the moral of it all is one package tourist with a livelier sense of the variousness of things; of the resplendence of this city and the thrill of cities in general, especially ones with lots of sun; of a few truths and falsehoods in 'orientalism'; of what great good Abdul Nasser did; of how one hopes that the rich countries of the Mediterranean are doing enough to help the poorer ones; of how the dust chokes and the desert is beautiful; of how dignified and austere are the cobalt blues and sand yellows of Islamic architecture.

V

Whatever else, Cairo is a city in which the past is coterminous with the present. (The terrible bullets confirm that.) The mighty cities of the European tourist freeway which Thomas Cook extended to Cairo have a certain difficulty at present with their past. Christine Boyer puts it unsympathetically like this:[18]

> The contemporary arts of city building are derived from the perspective of white, middle-class architectural and planning professionals who worry in a depoliticised fashion about a city's competitive location in the global restructuring of capital, and thus myopically focus on improving a city's marketability by enhancing its imageability, livability and cultural capital.

These men (and a few women) have experienced a loss of faith in pure modernism and the drives of uncriticised progress such as put the freeway through the Bronx. Well they might. They are left with the task of rehabilitation. A new precept dictates (though by no means everywhere) that rather than demolish, planners and developers should always seek to retain, restore, rehabilitate, even if they only keep the façade of the old building. Judgement by this token is a mere caprice of the taste of the day, so no one will risk anything irrevocable.

This may be good as far as it goes, but it goes towards a refrigeration of the city in which everything is frozen after the patina of restoration has been sprayed upon it. Then, by and large, all that planners can think to do with what they have preserved – the railway marshalling yards at Swindon, the massive warehouses of Albert Dock in Liverpool, the baroque cast-iron of Les Halles or the Quai D'Orsay railway station in Paris, the civil elegance of Faneuil Hall in Boston – is turn them into some sort of merchandising establishment, paying the rent and something back on the investment by selling fashion and the arts, along with their own pleasantly lit, airy and spacious sort of benignant boredom.

The more redolent the building, of course, the more the tourists are sure to turn up. It was a stroke of Parisian genius to put the splendours of nineteenth century French art from Courbet to Gauguin in the Quai D'Orsay. The tourist thrills to his and her very own music at the sight of those magic destinations carved along the friezes of the building – Orléans, Tours, Poitiers, Bordeaux – and thrills again at walking on the spot where the railroad ended, before taking the escalator up to call on Cézanne and Monet.

Paris, we shall say, has best met – on behalf of its millions of tourists as well as its own city-dwellers – what Christine Boyer calls 'our desire for authentic memories and city experiences [which] reveals an empathy for lost totalities'.[19] She admits to such an empathy herself;[20] who would not?

> The public realm of the City of Collective Memory should entail a continuous urban topography, a spatial structure that covers both rich and poor places, honorific and humble monuments, permanent and ephemeral forms, and should include places for public assemblage and public debate, as well as private memory walks and personal retreats.

We have touched such walks and retreats with André Aciman; I cannot doubt that one may find a little bit of Paris that is for ever Cairo.

Boyer is stern with the postmodern theory of the world which has shaped her. Modernism disgraced itself, with demolition, with a heedless dedication to the automobile, by its complicity with both Fascism and Stalinism, by its disrespect for the pleasures of city life inseparable from disorderliness. 'Leave a couple of black bags on the corner and in a few days you'll have a trash heap,' somebody said, and went on, 'culture is like that'. But this bits-and-pieces approach of the postmodern, its theories of fragmentation, do nothing for a vision of a city whose pathways, landmarks and nodal points effect a narrative of what the city means to those who take their vacations there because it is so famous.

A capital city is an emblem: of state, nation and country – none of which terms are synonymous, all of which grow more cloudy every day. Boyer invokes (in spite of herself) the grand vision of Paris's planners under Napoleon III who, emphasising history itself as the great unifier of a city's totality, sought to imagine

> [a] new representational order ... an expansive and majestic panorama that drew the totality together, outlining only its significant sites for public embellishment and inspiring its citizens, through the contemplation of its sublimity and grandeur, to be rational and orderly in their public affairs.[21]

This is a city whose narrative was addressed to its citizens. But it was also the city which became, in Benjamin's phrase, 'capital of the nineteenth century' and therefore one in which all the new tourist classes, high, middle and small bourgeoisie, who were within reach of the railway would take vacations in search of high fashion, low life and a lot to eat and drink. It had therefore to be a city eloquent, indeed, in structure and identity; the vacationers must be able to find their way round it easily enough but also interestedly enough, and it must speak to them condescendingly and familiarly of the glory of France.

From that day to this, from Napoleon III to Mitterand, such a politics has issued in the plainly visible and legible narrative of Paris. Baron Haussmann, at Napoleon's behest, started it all with his *grandes percées*[22] (which, it has to be admitted, fired emulation in Robert Moses) which were thrust through old, close, crabbed Paris as wide and splendid avenues flanked by *hôtels de villes*, solid Third Empire masonry with heavy quoins and plateglass windows up to seven storeys. The axis and focus of this quite unprecedented city lay along the seventeenth century line of the mighty Louvre, Madame de Maintenon's ladylike gardens in the Tuileries, up the new, swaggering *Champs d'Elysées* to the deliberately named *Arc de Triomphe*, finally to be extended to the huge, brutalist *La Défense* of Mitterand's 1980s Paris.

Such a conception erases, as most capitals do, any official reference to the violence, discord and oppressions of past and present. It remains a literal effrontery that the site of the revolutionary guillotine is now *Place de la Concorde* and an amazing erasure that the city brings off in so wiping all traces from Montmartre of the 1871 commune and its mass murders. The Paris the tourists are given to read now is nonetheless a coherent and compelling, a sufficiently truthful and a richly impregnated Official History. The city was principled enough, or lucky enough, to escape the collaborator government under the Nazis which went to Vichy, and so it may gracefully wear a few stone medallions commemorating the resistance of July 1944.

The right and the left banks of the Seine correlate with satisfying exactitude the classical dichotomy of modern politics.[23] On the right bank, the Bourbon palaces, the President, the *Bourse*, the police headquarters, the *Opéra*, the Louvre housing the grand Davidian paintings of the Republic; on the right bank also, the Rue de Rivoli and the most expensive clothes in the world. On the left bank, the sixth arrondissement and the Latin quarter (so-called because Latin was the local tongue for students

Figure 9.3 Paris
Source: Hilary Britland

from every corner of the then intellectual world until the seventeenth century), the great university and the *grandes écoles*, founded to train the administrators and intellectuals of what was to be the most rational and efficient state in modernity, now the nursery of what Pierre Bourdieu calls 'the state nobility',[24] a *noblesse des bureaux* become the securest élite in history.

Left bank and right bank, therefore, live in a mutually essential opposition and complementarity. Ministers once students at the *grandes écoles* entertain their *maîtres à penser* to lunch.[25] The tourist paces happily along the left bank towards the *Pont Neuf* and feels the daring of old revolutionary gestures stir the blood. Over the river is ranged in absolute and confident serenity the skyline of rule; behind, along the crowded sweep of the Boulevards Saint Germain des Prés and Saint Michel stand the courts of reason and criticism. Thickly intertwined in the narrow streets, following the lines of medieval settlement, in many cases made of the medieval stones, are the bookshops, publishers, cafés and restaurants in which the weapons of critique are sharpened and blunted and covered with the rich sauces of Escoffier's great tradition.

Everyone loves Paris. All the songs say so. What makes them do so, so ungovernably? It may be its clarity. Each district is so firmly edged, each so distinctive. It may be its homeliness. The scale of the centre is so walkable, its points of rest so frequent and so happily matched to the panorama. It is surely the grace of its counterpoint between openness and closure, narrow streets and large places. It is also the magnificence with which old and new assertions have been rhetorically combined, as I.M.

Pei's famous glass pyramids in the courtyard of the Louvre set off the massive stone façades and the celebratory statuary of French literature at their summits.

When Ernest Hemingway, heartiest of all literary tourists and holidaymakers, went to Paris in 1921, like every other aspiring writer and artist of his day, he joined Joyce, Ezra Pound, Gertrude Stein, Ford Madox Ford, Man Ray, Matisse, Picasso and Miro in the buzzing cafés, Closerie de Lilas, the Rotonde, the Coupole, the Procope. He lived in appropriate poverty, writing and effortfully rewriting *The Sun Also Rises*.

Forty years later he published posthumously a loving little memoir of the city,[26] and a caustic one of his associates. It combines, I would say, the happy tourist's best memories in a single structure. He recalls the cafés and their food in a wonderful elegy to cold draught beer, oysters *portugaises* and cold boiled potatoes in olive oil and pepper. He joins the Cézannes in the Luxembourg palace on a fine frosty day and, hungry himself, feels the hunger in the paintings. And he walks, pondering his Parisian novel, walks past the fishermen fishing for *goujons* beside the Seine, walks the two boulevards of the Latin Quarter, greets the statue of Marshal Ney and as it begins to rain thinly sets a cracking pace up to Montmartre, and the bare little apartment he rents with his wife Hadley, here remembered as beloved, his baby boy and their stout tom cat.

Hemingway, always on the move, always an exile in the city of strangers, has many friends, a loving wife, a terrific zest for Paris, a terrific zest for life. The first few chapters of his brief memoir are as good a self-portrait as I know of the happy holidaymaker, and a guide to how to love a strange city, enormously changed and much as it was.

VI

Paris is a shaped city: deliberately shaped by its rulers but, on the whole, shaped to the reasonable acquiescence of its citizens. When the tourist arrives in Paris, he or she must take the city on Parisian terms. Jonathan Raban, writing of London,[27] speaks of 'soft cities', which is to say cities softly responsive to the imprint of any and all personalities, cities whose identity is capacious enough to mirror all permissible desires. Paris is certainly flexible enough to take in many strangers and not just students and artists, but all the peoples of its sometime empire, Cambodians, Vietnamese, Egyptians, Algerians, Ethiopians, let alone the tides of refugees from central and eastern Europe, the ruling classes of Russia, the American robber barons.

In each case, however, Paris put an imprint on *them*. She is not so soft, after all. Part of what a city classically *is*, in the sense in which I have been discussing it in this chapter, is a living historical and aesthetic entity with its own features and characteristics. It has therefore a character of its own, and cannot be made into just anything. To this extent, any account of why one may love Paris or Venice or New York or Cairo must take account of what the city is truly like.

This is such an obvious thing to say it is almost an embarrassment. In any one of those cities, you are so obviously *there* and not elsewhere. Whatever culture is, it is most easily pointed at and differentiated when we point at and compare Cairo with Paris, or London with New York. All are human artefacts and therefore comparable; all are sublimely different. It is this the tourist goes to discover, and goes back to turn difference not into sameness but into something better known and, one hopes, well loved.

Compare what I have said about the experience of Paris with that of first, Venice, then New York. Venice is indeed a city whose every stone carries a value in the currency of cultural capital. It has only itself to sell: belvederes, architecture, art and the supporting industries of food and fashion. It ought to be no more than a museum. But there, museums today all laudably attempt to transform themselves from spectacles to experiences. Venice brought off this same transformation with extraordinary ease during the nineteenth century. As it lost political, strategic and financial significance, it became *a place to stay*, and having time to settle into this new sort of identity, devised ways of life and forms of exchange which would confirm it in that new kind of political economy.

Of course, it had in this devising its own extraordinary endowments by way of Tintoretto, Palladio and Sansovino. But its success fairly shines upon it now. Venice, *La Serenissima*, can afford to be serene so long as she can hold off the encroachments of the Lagoon, precisely because her 60,000 permanent inhabitants know how to handle such an economy, and have taught the rest of the tourist-visited world the rudiments.

Venice, therefore, is an enclave whose vivid life is confirmed by its meaning as a place to stay and be looked at. New York, like Paris and Cairo, is a frankly quotidian kind of city. Holidaymakers come, in their millions, but New York has infinite purposes to which they are not privy. They come to spend, to look and see, to wonder. They come back, like André Aciman, to find the corners they learn to love. But the city does not welcome them, as Venice does and does so for a living. New Yorkers are always courteous to strangers in my experience, but New York itself has other things on its mind. The tourist may certainly come to love it; but he or she will always, in virtue of being on holiday, be a stranger there.

Yet it is easy to know. The guidebooks should start in the right, the only place to start, by walking over Brooklyn Bridge to gaze entranced at the most entrancing, most famous, most spectacular cityscape in the world.

I have Geoffrey Moorhouse's in my hand, a history with a bounce to match the city itself.[28] He starts from spectacularity, and quite right too. But he quickly turns to history, dividing New York precisely into its clear districts and matching each to a social class or an ethnic group. It is a good way to grasp a lived-in city. Neighbourhood architecture, local mores, pride of address. Easy with Paris, hard with London. In New York, blacks in Harlem and Brooklyn, Jews in the Bronx and lower East Side, the rich in Morningside and on Long Island, the Italians and Chinese starting out from their eponymous ghettoes, the Bohemians in their Village. Paths, edges, districts, landmarks, New York is rich in all of them. The deep slotted canyons sweep you northwards up Manhattan until you are emptied out with a shock in the green lung of Central Park. You come hurtling back down beside the Hudson and pay your quarter to the Staten Island Ferry. As it draws you away across the water, the beautifully articulated twins of the World Trade Towers dance subtly about each other and a new version of the heartlifting skyline offers itself.

The tourist loves it, is overwhelmed by the international teemingness of it all, as though one tries to comprehend but is completely bedazzled by an immediate diorama of all America's demography, millions of people moving west and east from the rest of

Figure 9.4   Manhattan Island, looking at the World Trade towers
Source: Kathy Williams

the world, cramming the gateways of Ellis Island, the gangplanks of the tramps and liners, the long tubes of the 747s.

A holiday in New York is formally the same as anywhere else, especially in the simplified machinery of modern tourism: see the selected sights; walk the famous streets; eat the local food; revere the house art; purchase the local specialty. Keep moving, keep spending.

But the city will have its way with you, like all great cities; and you will find your own way through it, for as long as you can shake off your blessed guides and their schedules. That is why we all keep going back, why the cities hold up and out their ineffable promise. Modernity has not yet done for wonder.

VII

That is no sneer at guides and bus timetables. I love them, collect them, trust them. One lesson of this book is that the history of vacationing may be understood as the making of many guidebooks, several among them, whatever Ruskin said, sensitive, erudite, written in respectable prose. But the holidaygoers need to cherish old atavism like a talisman, never more so than when setting off for the eternal city.

Any one of them might accidentally pick up Italo Calvino's mischievous, dead serious masterpiece, *Invisible Cities*.[29] That sedulously enigmatic book is framed by two men, famous men, talking endlessly about cities. One is the omnipotent Kublai, great Khan of the Tartars; he listens to the other, the inveterate tourist-traveller from Venice, Marco Polo.

Marco tells him about the cities he has known, while the Khan seeks endlessly to match what the traveller tells him to all that he knows and does not know of his vast empire.

Cities and human beings alike have characters, dispositions, temperaments, births and deaths; they are fixed. Cities and human beings have moods, passions, caprices, changes of character and dissolutions of self, contradictions, nullity; they are mutable. This is not a pathetic fallacy. The character we give to the cities we visit must tally with what the cities are really like. Like André Aciman in Straus Park we can glimpse the other cities we want to remember in different aspects of our favourite corners, or find them suddenly at the bottom of an unknown street. Cities may lose themselves in modernity, so that the only way to restore them to comprehensibility is to place an imaginary frontier round their heart, generally of the old city (Florence), and reserve our affection for the compassable, the knowable, the walkable, the recognisable. Cities may break down, simply not function as cities – São Paulo, they say, Naples pretty nearly, Bangkok. Cities may renew themselves, recover from chaos (Barcelona), or from utter destruction (Warsaw, Lisbon).

In Calvino's classic he rehearses the many commonplaces of which we keep a stock in order to render cities intelligible:

> Arriving at each new city, the traveller finds again a past of his that he did not know he had; the foreignness of what you no longer are or no longer possess lies in wait for you in foreign unpossessed places.

One understands a new city as both a tight network of districts each announced by its landmark and as a glimpse of odd lives seen as one wandered past. One moves easily between the certainty that the old city as remembered in sepia postcards was more graceful, leisurely, courteous, ordered etc. etc. and the conviction that the new one is richer, more resplendent, prosperous, etc. etc.

Chirico the surrealist painted a picture of a quayside, a lighthouse, an empty piazza, an unknown figure. He calls it 'the nostalgia of the infinite'. Kublai Khan describes such a quayside where passengers are leaving families distraught with grief who watch in mute anguish as the ship carries away those they love; they wave their handkerchiefs desperately until it rounds the point. The Khan orders Marco to go there. Marco knows the place but knows also he cannot go there and return to tell the Khan about it. 'The city … knows only departures, not returns'.

This terrifies the visitor. Like everybody who has been happy on holiday in a new city, he or she dreads looking for the happiness again, and being unable to find it.

Every new city, if it comes up to scratch, is a new acquisition. What I have lost of cities which I no longer want to visit is replaced by the new one and its happiness. Prague has become too dark and mad and full of sorcerers. But Barcelona! Barcelona is high, wide and handsome.

There is a tourist's nightmare in which the new city pours out into networks of roads and tenement blocks without beginning or end; these are cities, Calvino says, 'in the shape of Los Angeles, in the shape of Kyoto-Osaka, without shape. If their day comes, there will be no cities.' Until then, full of hope and expectation, see, we depart, and the good old cities make themselves new for us.

10

FUTURES

Virtue on vacation

I

So far, this has been an unyieldingly sunny and optimistic account of the joys brought by holidays. It has offered no challenge to the policies of blind expansion pursued for obvious reasons both by those smaller, poorer countries for whom tourism is crucial to the economy and by the travel agencies who sell us their tickets for their own greater profit and not the greater good of humankind. Faced by the impending death of the Mediterranean, I have cited the success of collaboration between the Mediterranean nations in cleaning the sea by way of cheering us all up. The real foundations of this history are laid by 1950 or so, but in 1950 only two and a half million people travelled abroad worldwide.[1] (In 1939 the corresponding figure was only half that.)

Since the Second World War, the most compelling history is demographic. But sheer numbers have a way of stupefying, and the human consequence of stupefaction is stupidity. Nonetheless, it would be stupid not to quote some of the figures by way of gesturing at the colossal scale of the change in fifty years. You just can't think about the meaning of holidays or the political economy of tourism without these dark masses hovering above you as unignorable, as universal, as the weather.

We begin with tourism in one country. In 1965, only 159,000 Japanese travelled overseas. In 1986 the Japanese government, working closely, as is usual in its social policy, with Japanese corporations, began a programme of promoting overseas travel by way of dispersing its (then) enormous trade surplus and, it was hoped, not only diffusing the resentment of the other wealthy countries at how Japan kept its riches to itself, but also modifying that largely correct view of Japan as an inward-turning, private and exclusive nation as well as one of the great imperial powers of the century. The aim was to send ten million of its population abroad every year within five years. It worked.

There was a munificence intended here. The Japanese would spend some of the money earned by the extraordinary economic success they had shared with the German Federal Republic since Americans armed with dollars revived their battered industrial production system in 1945. This is, one supposes, a version of what has come to be called 'trickle-down economics': that if the rich make lots of money, they will spend it in such a way that the poor, making and providing what they can, will see some of the benefits.

It rarely works out. David Nicholson-Lord writes[2] that:

In some Caribbean countries, up to 80% of the nominal inflows of foreign countries flow straight out again, into the hands of airlines, tour operators and travel agents. Figures of 70% leakage [i.e. profits which leave the host country for outside corporations] have been estimated for a beach holiday in Kenya, 77% for charter operations in Gambia and 60% for Thailand. The World Bank has reported that in some countries as little as 10 cents in every dollar spent goes to local people. In Bali, where 200 people – an entire village – perform the Kechak dance for visitors, one study found that a group of tourists paid $250 in entrance fees to operators but the village received only $20 – 10 cents per performer.

Finally, Nicholson-Lord goes on to point out, government subsidies and tax breaks for hard-bargaining hotel chains and developers urging that they will bring construction work and service posts to the unemployed men and women of a poor country mean that, as he says, 'the poorest people often end up subsidising the holidays of the richest'.

This is globalisation and, as we have seen, it is a less straightforward business than many people suppose.[3] In some cases the small, the poor, the exploited countries might drive a harder bargain than they do. They own vital 'positional goods', which is to say that there are not so very many unspoiled silver beaches giving onto azure seas that the hotel chains and tour companies can simply take their business elsewhere, as it is said the multinationals can with their automobile assembly lines. In this connection it is a pleasure to report the formation in 1996 of the Ecumenical Coalition on Third World Tourism whose executive secretary said pungently that:

> tourism does not benefit the majority of people. Instead it exploits them, pollutes the environment, destroys the ecosystem, bastardises the culture, robs people of their traditional values and ways of life and subjugates women and children in the abject slavery of prostitution … It epitomises the present unjust world economic order where the few who control wealth and power dictate the terms.

No doubt, someone has to talk like that if poorer countries are to see anything like an equitable benefit from all they have to do to themselves in order to pull the tourists in (and even then, they are at the mercy of such structural constants as fashion and the collapse of consumer confidence). But straight cursing isn't going to stop the tourist traffic and a malediction spoken over the evils of oppression is as well levelled at local as at international élites. Indeed, even allowing for the more revolting aspects of the beer-swilling, loudmouthed, big-bellied Britisher abroad, I would risk saying that the more tourists there are from more nations, the more they observe the politics of politeness.

Putting things like that approaches the deep but personal question of virtue on vacation. How shall we do right and live well while visiting other countries? Everyone is now sufficiently a Marxist as well as a demographer to know that the frame of ethics is political economy and that the kindness of tourists must first be interpreted statistically. In either case, human intentions and willed preferences can only make a difference collectively. World studies of exploitation are prolific and much is made in them of the way rich countries keep poor countries poor, ensure their powerlessness, enforce their dependency. It won't quite do to say, 'not me or you', when you or I are complicit in the huge machinery of international travel merely by taking a vacation, whether at home or abroad.

The four leading industries of world capitalism are, as we saw: weapons; hard and soft communications technology; pharmaceuticals legal and illegal; and tourism. According to one United Nations report, tourism makes up an *eighth* of the world's gross product.[4] At the same time, there are degrees of implication. Complicity stands close whenever one goes on holiday, no doubt; nonetheless, whatever the exploitation, the money spent will certainly contribute to the subsistence wages of the room-cleaner, however much is stripped off by the tour operator, hence the tricky ethics of the tip.

Moreover, this moral argument is much modified by a return to the undressed figures of tourist mobility. Every summer, for example, the population of the Mediterranean littoral doubles to 260 million. The whole sea will, at this rate, soon be ringed by hotels. But the majority of this colossal number go to the northern coasts, where France, Spain and Italy at least are quite tough enough to force a square deal out of the industry. The same is even more bluntly true of visitors to the USA. Visitors of all kinds (whether for profit or pleasure or both) to New York City totalled 33 million in 1997, a rise of over 10 per cent on the previous year.[5] Wherever they came from – and only one in five came from outside the USA – we may be sure that New Yorkers themselves would hardly be the victims of the visitors.

Consider a handful of figures about tourists. In 1994 international receipts from tourism worldwide totalled $US337 billion (169 billion in Europe). The top tourist destination in Europe in 1994 was France with 61 million (19% of the total for the continent). In 1994 13.5 million Japanese went abroad (29% to the USA) while 16 million French people went elsewhere in Europe. In 1994 20 million tourists arrived in Britain, spending $14 million.[6]

These are part of the half billion people taking an international vacation each year, and for every one of them, four of five will go on holiday at home, meaning Parisians to Provence, New Jerseyites to Florida, Nova Scotians to Vancouver, Glaswegians to Cornwall, and Turinesi to Cefalu. For the first time, this vast movement of people, unlike all migratory or military movements of the past, is impelled neither by terror nor greed, not by starvation nor imperial longings. Whether they are in the home country or a foreign land, they are somewhere else, and they have come, casually and always temporarily, for fun, from curiosity, for a rest, for a touch of aesthetic improvement or of lubricity; but anyway, they have come peaceably and in search of that catchall, pleasure; even, it may be, fulfilment.

II

It is the argument of this book that all these millions have been, one way and another, shaped in the passions, desires, hopes and fears which they bring to each sojourn by the assorted voyages over the preceding two or more centuries of a very mixed crowd of fairly wealthy opportunists as they ranged the world.

Such influences do not, of course, move in a straight line. We have heard Francis Spufford tell us that our ideas, our forms of reasoning and, it is my concern to add to these, the frame of our feelings and the intensity of the values they express grow out of 'the imaginative compost' made by the past as it decays and decomposes.

The horticultural metaphor is not exact. My contention has been that the lives of the past both assumed and were given a narrative form. These narratives take shape and dislimn about us all the time. They are embodied in aspects of the lives we see and come to know well: our parents, brothers and sisters, neighbours, friends. They are made available in the social roles and forms of life which we join or into which we are inculcated: as students, clients, customers, citizens; as members of social classes to which we owe loyalty or which we resolve to defy; as representatives of generations, as each man and woman marks off the passages of the years, and moves from child to lover to parent to elder to memorial. In all these lived narratives as well as in the literal stories we tell ourselves about ourselves, in novels, memoirs, films and on television, the irreducible variety of biography pervades our being. We inherit its codes as we do our genes, commuting and redistributing them so that we look like and do not look like our parents.

Once again, the metaphor doesn't quite fit. In the case of our social narratives the play of voluntary choice flickers over the chords and strings of our inheritance. There are stories we *cannot* live in our society and be counted sane, but there is pretty well infinite possibility in the combination of narratives each individual may effect.

At the outer limits of the historical period of this book, more or less bracketed at its outset by the mid-eighteenth century and reaching forward, one guesses, at least until the middle of the first century of the third millennium, is the popular and universal story of the consumer. As I have often said in these pages, 'consumer' is yet another unsatisfactory metaphor, implying as it does the commodification of absolutely everything, the cancellation of memory, the eradication of love and trust from the facts of exchange, the reduction of happiness to expenditure. But the term has struck too deep roots in everyday language to be erased.

Instead, I have proposed that the many practices and meanings of consumerism have bound into themselves old and necessary values – values central to my exposition such as luxury, happiness, family love and indulgence, the solitary contemplation of natural beauty – which it found sedimented in the stuff of experience. These values are built, with different emphases, into the frameworks of being, feeling and interpretation which serve to make our life intelligible.

Such frameworks – as it were the little house in which we carry around our biography – ambivalently constituted by our character, our opportunity and our preference, contain, so far as they are able, the story of our lives. Their most typical operation is *to give form to* (i.e. comprehend) the events and situations we encounter. Thus, framework meets the facts of life and opens at its centre into feeling. The feeling we have – fear, joy, boredom, disgust, remorse – gives form to life. Then we know where we are.

Holidays on this side of the Atlantic, vacations on that, comprise one such framework, a room of one's own in the larger house of fictions which enjoin old life to shape up. Their beginnings were designed in the lives of grand tourists and partook evenhandedly of erudition and connoisseurship, debauchery and extravagance, companionship and meditation, interminable journeys stolidly endured and gleeful launchings-out to faraway places.

These broad attributes were matched to the available geography and then refined and extended by commercial processes. Starting at about the same time and continuing from our beginnings to the present day, however, a different make of voyager, fired by empire, its excitement and its profits, set off on even rougher journeys to even further away places, many of the most celebrated (James Cook, Robert Scott) never making it home. Their stories joined the cultural chorus antiphonally; they taught the awfulness of commercial tourists, the rightness of travellers.

Commerce won hands down, so much so that, as we have seen, present-day tourists pay a fortune to be turned into the traveller-explorers whose tales they have been told. The victory of commerce, however, went two ways. For then, even more drastically, capitalism slowly yielded to its intransigent progeny, the English industrial working class, two of the privileges of profit: more money and more leisure. A new kind of seaside was colonised out of the old, and Blackpool replaced Brighton as the eponym of the holiday.

With Whiggish inevitability, the great freedoms of the bicycle and the automobile brought mobility, clean air, open countryside, Bachelard's 'intimate immensity' to an enormous new class. Thereafter, once the Second World War had industrialised aircraft production, the rich world was ready to circle the globe and the two poorer worlds couldn't wait to join in. Culture and technology work together to make this vacationing playroom of the house rich in anticipation, refreshing in unaccustomed feelings, restorative of hope and happiness.

So procrustean a yarn is a bit simple, no doubt. But it encloses our history and allows for the rather more complicated account of the shaping of feelings into a sensibility – a sensibility which alters historically as well as personally – which is our subject. It can also be held up to the light of judgement and made to flash darkly or brightly.

The bright judgement is that the history of holidays is one of increasing happiness, fulfilment and opportunity. The evidence for this is there in the sheer numbers as well as in the steepling drop in airline prices since the first jet crossed the Atlantic in 1958. It is there in the millions of colour picture postcards sent back to the office and pinned on the board. It is there, where we began, in the bewitching imagery of TV holiday programmes broadcast in January nights.

But the darker judgement hangs unignorably on the holiday horizon. Its clouds shadow the grimmer tales in the folklore as well as the evidence of anybody's senses in the more crowded spots of vacationing delight.

No-one can deny, for a grim example, the ruin that has been made, mostly with sterling and by British visitors, of the east coast of Spain, the old way of life which was apotheosised at its last minute by Norman Lewis.[7] Lewis saw its gaunt beauty and its frugal, bitter culture. He learned to admire the male solidarity of the fishermen, the intimacy of their sea-knowledge, of fish and tides and boat; he felt their fierce localism and the hatreds it taught; he saw the almost-starvation of their skinny kids and silent wives; he revered their reverence for their working mixture of atheism and sparse catholicism; solitary himself, he loved the solitary place.

Over a mere three years in the 1950s, the way of life of the fishing village of Farol vanished. The money was put up to put up the monstrous blocks of holiday flats and hotels, three deep, overlooking the sea, nothing behind but the blank sierra. Lewis was not so much writing a threnody as trying to catch the dying moments of a life before it expired, unrecorded, for ever. But of course his *was* a lament. How could it not be?

What was lost to the tourists and their simple delight in – as they say – sun, sea, sand and sex, was a culture, which is to say a complete, self-sufficient and exclusive way of life. It was frugal and beautiful, stark and appealing, everything that consumerism is not. What has replaced it is much easier; even for the same fishermen's descendent families, better off, better-fed, illuminated by pop and telly and the cheap excitement of holiday streets.

Spain's own Nobel novelist Camilo Jose Cela told a similar, more quotidian tale when in 1946 he rambled unobtrusively from Madrid to Guadalajara to Pastrana and back.[8] Hardly a holiday route. One might even still find shrinking traces of the unassuming hospitality he found, the unlocked private houses, the easy-going familiarity of strangers, the dignified tramps, the rough food, the common courtesy. It is all there in Cela's little travel memoir, entirely persuasive, as far as we can tell, quite unidealised. This is Franco's Fascist Spain, nine years after the end of the Civil War.

What shall we regret today if we deplore the coming of tourism and holidaymaking to these places? The death of Franco? The passing of the military junta in Greece? After all, the colonels also wanted Greece to be exactly as it was in 1937: monks, milkmaids, proud bandits, goats, dour peasants. Jeremy Bentham famously taught the utilitarians of the 1820s that happiness can only be measured in quantities of material welfare and that progress simply equals more of the latter for more people. Even as one feels intuitively that this won't do at all, and that innumerable sources of happiness are not reducible to nor aggregable as quantities, it is difficult to see how otherwise to practise public policy. Faced by the wide streets, clean water and healthy inhabitants of Gandia, it takes an enormous effort to shake off modernity and turn back to Lewis's friends of the 1950s, Simon, Sebastian and Grandmother Elvira.

The whole speculation turns on our present understanding of the idea of 'well-being'.[9] In itself a sometime phrase in everyday use, it now has a slightly stilted air except when it is used in rather technical arguments deployed in debates intended to reconcile ethical theory and welfare economics.

Now that consumer capitalism has become our only intelligible name for an international system, economics, politics and ethics are, for the preoccupations of this book, mutually inextricable. Grasping the significance of this truth is part of what it is not just to be that public-private figure, the consumer-citizen, but rather more challengingly, what it is to be a decent person.

Moral questions are never very far away from our vacation plans exactly because those vacations are intended to prefigure some short-lived picture of the good life as each of us is able to live it for a fortnight or so every year. Each holidaymaking individual or group draws on the collective stock of stories about how holidays ought to be, and sets optimistically out.

The optimism, as we have also seen, is traditionally and highly coloured by the sense of comedy. The holiday snapshot albums of millions bear their witness to the power of the comic convention. Photographs depict everyone as smiling happily. Say 'cheese' your children call out eagerly, and we each do our best whatever our private thoughts. Comedy in this context is not just a matter of putting on a good face. It is an orientation towards the world as we want it to be.

Comedy has been, of course, the uncomic subject of much aesthetic reflection over the centuries, and faced by the horror of twentieth century politics and its warfare, one might well conclude that the only way to comprehend such ghastly and meaningless destruction is as tragic catastrophe arising from a too-bold hopefulness in the misapplication of theories of the good society. Yet with half the world in ruins half-a-century ago, by the chime of the millennium,we can surely see the outline of a future ruled for a couple of generations or so by the victorious comicality of a new world class, the international lower middle class visible in millions as they enter the airports of the world on the way to their next foreign trip.

It is a tricky thing to talk about at such a level of generality, and a couple of weeks' larking about and happy self-indulgence look absurdly thin ground upon which to stand a comic vision of the kindly world society. For a century and a half that particular fraction of the middle class has been, for all artists and intellectuals, a term of abuse, connoting all that is worst in British, French and North American respectability, combining that status-craving, narrowness of mind and grudgingness of feeling, privatisation of living and closing-down of the civic virtues which disfigures subtopia.

Amen to much of that. But as the industrial working class has dispersed as a historical force in the West, shattered by the elimination of the heavy male labour and systems of production which made it, and as its children have promoted themselves into the informal hierarchies of computer services, the settled victory of middle-class Allsorts has become clear wherever people have enough work to provide them with food, shelter, fondness and a bit of leisure.[10] It is a class whose members expect a home sufficiently of their own not to worry about it, a car to act as a private and mobile extension of that home and take them far enough for their wants, a family and friends whose ties, actual and necessary as the class wants them to be, are still loose enough to allow each individual liberty of movement and the space (as they say) to have things, on occasion, their own way.

The novelist V.S. Naipaul, better known perhaps for sternness than kindliness but rarely other than comic in his view of life, had the ambition to describe the achievement of this class as 'our universal civilisation'.[11] In a world threatened by natural disasters and human hate it is a bold thing to essay. He acknowledges this, with the sureness and fastidiousness of his kind of great writer. In the teeth of religious rage and global fears, he affirms what he takes to be the beauty and convincingness of this civilisation. It lies in two principles, he says: that each person seeks to become the best person it is in them to become; and that in this quest, each of us – as Charles Kingsley put it in that excellent socialist fable-for-children *The Water Babies* – will do as we would be done by. These are recastings of the canonical premises of liberalism, the demise of which has so often been announced but whose novel and ideal formation may be found, it is suggested by this book, in the principles and practice of a successful vacation.

Somewhere in the connection between the two principles is the most generally believed and believable picture we can presently contrive for well-being and living-a-good-enough-life. The comic side of things will always be pretty obvious wherever people strive to become their best selves, just as it will as they do to others as they would be done by, but like all good comedy, not only cheerfulness but also seriousness breaks in on the philosophising. When Richard Hoggart finds '"fair play" and its Siamese twin "trust" … still on the whole powerful tenets' in English life,[12] I not only want to cheer, I want to go on and make the insight something which, in a small way, Englishness can contribute to human welfare. Moreover, I want to find these values at work during playtime and in that corner of everyday life which is our subject and which, as has been so consistently asserted in these pages, is reserved for our best behaviour.

The holiday provides, after all, one of the few arenas left in which private lives are lived in public. In the resort, the camp, on the beach, in the theme park, we meet each other as strangers and test our politeness.

Manners make men and women. On vacation we look out (or so I say) for our best selves. At our best we treat others as we would like them to treat us. This is hardest to do but all the more pressing because of the difficulty when the others are foreign and do not speak English. At that point, homespun liberalism has to improve itself a little, and be to others what (one hopes) *they* would like one to be.

This sometimes stiff, sometimes ebullient comedy is played out wherever best behaviour meets up with other peoples. In a lovely poem, Philip Larkin – elsewhere in his poetry so often a touchstone for sardonic bitterness and the deliberate rejection of fellow-feeling and the 'civil affections' – catches exactly the way in which the seaside (here, Scarborough in 1969), then and now, keeps up with a grand continuity that putting-folk-on-their-mettle, that 'kindness and gentleness and capacity-for-being-pleased' which (so Dickens once said) are above all worth keeping of our childhood.

To step over the low wall that divides
Road from concrete walk above the shore
Brings sharply back something known long before –
The miniature gaiety of seasides.
Everything crowds under the low horizon:
Steep beach, blue water, towels, red bathing caps.
The small hushed waves' repeated fresh collapse
Up the warm yellow sand, and further off
A white steamer stuck in the afternoon –

Still going on, all of it, still going on!
To lie, eat, sleep in hearing of the surf
(Ears to transistors, that sound tame enough
Under the sky), or gently up and down
Lead the uncertain children, frilled in white
And grasping at enormous air, or wheel
The rigid old along for them to feel
A final summer, plainly still occurs
As half an annual pleasure, half a rite.

As when, happy at being on my own,
I searched the sand for Famous Cricketers,
Or, farther back, my parents, listeners
To the same seaside quack, first became known.
Strange to it now, I watch the cloudless scene:
The same clear water over smoothed pebbles,
The distant bathers' weak protesting trebles
Down at its edge, and then the cheap cigars,
The chocolate-papers, tea-leaves, and, between

The rocks, the rusting soup-tins, till the first
Few families start the trek back to the cars.
The white steamer has gone. Like breathed-on glass
The sunlight has turned milky. If the worst
Of flawless weather is our falling short,
It may be that through habit these do best,
Coming to water clumsily undressed
Yearly; teaching their children by a sort
Of clowning; helping the old, too, as they ought.[13]

At first sight this looks like an elegy for a lost seaside childhood, until one looks at the crowds still turning out onto English and Eastern seaboard beaches. No doubt, the concept, as the marketeers would be bound to say, of the holiday camp is due for revision and couldn't survive *Hi de Hi* and *Carry on Camping* unwounded. £180 million[14] are to provide new camps with 'skyline Pavilions', 'oases of calm' and sumptuous new cottages instead of chalets, all at £720 per week for four. It looks a long way from Larkin's 'miniature gaiety'.

And yet. And yet. The picnickers, bathers and donkeys are still there, on the beach at Scarborough, Blackpool, Weston-super-Mare. That lovely light still falls like breathed-on glass upon all Atlantic beaches to east or west of the ocean; the steamer sails away across every holiday horizon, for ever; and the parents still teach their children by a sort of clowning, helping, as they ought, the rigid old to soften stiff joints in the sun, watching in delight as their youngest child, staggering plumply on the sand, grasps for support from the enormous air.

Larkin does his recollection in tranquillity. His serious affection is alive to the comedy of his tableau and, just like Betjeman's beach twenty years before, he equably notes the occasional garbage drifting in the surf around the paddling feet. In another mood but the same frame of feeling, he would include details of the clowning and details also of how (comically) wrong holidays may go. Indeed, one favourite conceit in the folklore of vacationing is how badly things went: how dreadful the picturesque hotel was ... how deadly the food ... how terrifying the storms and squalid the tents, how extreme the dysentery ... how noisy the neighbours, repulsive the children ... finally, how appalling one was oneself ... There is no need to go on. Monty Python got everything in at Drury Lane twenty-odd years ago:

To all at number twenty two: weather wonderful, food very greasy but we have managed to find this tiny little place hidden away in the back streets where you can buy cheese and onion crisps and Watneys Red Barrel ... when you finally get to Malaga Airport everybody's swallowing Enterovioform tablets, and queuing for the bloody toilets and queuing for the bloody armed customs officers, and queuing for the bloody bus that isn't there waiting to take you to the hotel that hasn't yet been built. And when you get to half-built Algerian Ruin, called the Hotel del Sol, by paying half your holiday money to a licensed bandit in a taxi, there's no water in the pool, there's no water in the taps, there's no water in the bog and there's only a bleeding lizard in the bidet. And half the rooms are double booked and you can't sleep anyway because of the permanent 24-hour drilling of the foundations of the hotel next door, you're plagued by appalling apprentice chemists from Ealing pretending to be hippies, and middle-class stockbrokers' wives from Esher as they buy identical villas in suburban development plots just like Esher...[15]

The convention is clear. Dire hols are comic. The Monty Python voice masters the effect the others strain for. Its headlong garrulity is of a piece with the boringness of the people he has met. Once upon a time, as Paul Fussell has noticed,[16] the opening manner of the travel essay was 'I hate it here', here being specifically England. Thereafter the usual forces of old and new snobbery, bitter status competition, irreconcilable conflicts of taste and judgement, contradictions between wanting a gregarious and wanting a solitary time, all did their corrosive and bloodthirsty work, such that Torremolinos, Ibiza, Waikiki, Goa, all become places to detest because of their giddy popularity and Peru, Katmandu and the dustier corners of Turkey, Thailand and Sri Lanka[17] were listed as poisonous because they poison you, and are too much for everybody except the lunatic bounty-hunters, for whom abominable discomfort is a campaign ribbon to be worn proudly when you're back.

Kenneth Burke once remarked that 'the comic frame [of historical interpretation] should enable people to be observers of themselves, while acting'.[18] Comedy, for Burke and for the vacationer, 'is essentially *humane*, leading in periods of comparative stability to the comedy of manners, the dramatisation of quirks and foibles ...' Comedy by his token requires 'the maximum of forensic complexity'.[19]

One could hardly say that the present is a stable period, but with a bit of care vacations can be kept safe. There are hideous counter-examples, of course: the tourists shot and slashed to death in Luxor in 1998; the death of others in the lift of Bangkok's luxury hotel as its illegally-added top floors collapsed; the wretched child unconscious in the swimming pool of a Spanish hotel, the water of which was too filthy for him to be visible. These grisly little tales have, I suppose, their forensic complexity, and Burke would tell us to see them not as comic but as, perhaps, humanely ponderable.

They arise from commonplace human awfulness: bigotry, corruption, indolence. On the bad side, the moral vocabulary and experience of the virtuous tourist starts there, with the thick and juicy contents of words like those. On the good side, the special but, as I am arguing, 'utopia-representative' qualities of the holidaymaker equip him and her with a moral vocabulary which starts out from states of being such as cheerfulness, blitheness, active sympathy as well as a keen propensity to laughter. If these might be thought by more sardonic souls a bit much to meet up with in the echoing halls of the airport terminal and the easy-going egalitarianism of the departure lounge, let us say that an affable philanthropy is best disguised by a politic politeness.

III

The phrase has its relevance at the end of a book which speaks up for the duty due to cheerfulness. Our virtuous holidaymaker partakes of a general effort discernible in the victorious middle classes of the wealthy nations to conduct themselves better towards foreign peoples and parts.

It is, I claimed in the first chapter, reasonable to hope that holidays, meaning what they do, will do something to bring out the best in people. They are the occasion, as

Larkin told us, for teaching by clowning; for gathering all those towards whom one has immediate responsibility into the activity of the day; for pausing to see how beautiful this little intersection of nature and culture is (the crowd, the beach, the sea, the weather); for *keeping things going*: 'Still going on, all of it, still going on' – thank goodness, yes.

And goodness has a lot to do with it. If we close our ears to Monty Python's tirade and join the throng in the vast hangar-terminal at Gatwick we shall find, by and large, people on their best behaviour, happy enough to be going on with, excited, gentle-mannered, dressed in the instant garishness of vacation clothing, all of it somehow immediately dowdy and subdued in a reassuring kind of way. This on the whole English but still polyglot and multicultural crowd is a *civic* crowd, pleasantly anticipating the empty hour or so it has in which to patrol the silver shrine-like shops, buying nothing of the piled opulence of neckties, handbags, cameras, malt whiskies, shirts.

The Gatwick crowd takes in the cornucopia around it sedately. It is used to the effect. The grand terminal is enough of a symbol to stand for our consumerism and its leisurely dynamics in both its repellent aspects and its fine ones. It is extremely efficient: we are each of us divested of heavy luggage at the outset (except for those barbarians who carry corpse-sized shoulder bags onto the aircraft). The luggage is nonchalantly tagged and returned to us, with absolute reliability, thousands of miles away and after its long, blind, jerking transit through unpeopled catacombs. We wander off and gaze through the towering plate-glass walls at the lovely aircraft in their ordered dances on the tarmac. Occasionally a team of godlike aircrew pace by, the women trundling little wheeled suitcases behind them, their uniforms pleasantly implying the discipline of the armed forces amongst the immense casualness of the passengers.

James Ballard writes, 'Airports are time-free zones, an atlas of arrivals and destinations forever updating itself, where briefly we become true world-citizens.'[20] He loves the airport landscape, 'its instantly summoned village life', sees the concourses as 'the *ramblas* and *agoras* of the future city', each of us held in 'the unitary global culture of the departure lounge'.

Ballard overdoes it, no doubt. What on earth is a culture where all one can do is wait, eat or buy? But these are indeed actions we perform in markets, and airports sufficiently represent the ideal markets and meeting places somewhere near the heart of such good lives and good societies as may be confected out of the twenty-first century.

It is the point of intellectual life to show how the world is and to gesture towards how it ought to be. That might also pass, at a pretty low level, as the point of ordinary life. Nothing to jeer at in the two formulations, for if intellectual life does not address itself, out of its considerable privileges, its leisure, comfortable libraries and sufficient wages, to the conduct of everyday life, then it is worth nothing and merits the contempt sometimes voiced about it in the yellow press.

If one weighs up what is said in the academies about travelling leisure as, for this conclusion, I shall call all our vacationing lives, then, as is to be expected, the scales carry pretty equal loads of curses and blessings. In his intelligent brief essay on leisure theory,[21] Chris Rojek identifies four forces at work in the organisation of leisure under modern capitalism. Voting, more or less, with the Marxists for the view that all culture under capitalism is a fix intended to stupefy the people, alienate their allegiances and turn absolutely everything into a saleable commodity, Rojek names four grim gaolers of human spontaneity and creative expression. They are privatisation, individuation, commercialisation and pacification. The first keeps us at home in front of the television and the video, both gleaming with images of faraway. The second pretends that all our pleasures are peculiar to our very special selves (this is your niche); in so doing, it confirms the strong narcissism of leisure life, with its concentration on the brown and beautiful body, the distinctive attire, the holiday away from it all. The third makes profit into the one true value. The fourth keeps us quiet and obedient. The individual self is the site of all this exploitation.

You can't say he's wrong. You can only protest there is more to it than that. Indeed, he says so himself. He is pulled between two themes. In the first, 'leisure experience is not an essence of human societies, but an effect of systems of legitimation'. In the second, 'to live a life of leisure is to live a charmed existence'.[22] The grip of dominant forces – what Marxists call 'the hegemony' – is fierce. The power of human beings to make the world new – what Wordsworth referred to as 'certain inherent and indestructible elements of the human mind' – is a constant surprise.

Theorists of culture as a fix held the field for a long time. Their strength was that they taught the old-fashioned liberals that most of us are just how narrow are the margins of freedom and how invisibly heavy are the mind-forged manacles of social structure. Then theorists got fed up with this theory and provided another one, stressing the creativity and choiceful disposition of consumers. By this revised token,[23] the stylisations of consumer life are the autonomous products of everyday creativity and although these are still loaded down with the weight of masculine power and its ineffable self-regard, much can be and has been made of the unprecedented opportunities for personal self-definition.

We are forced back on the clichés of ambivalence – on the one hand this, on the other hand that. The present incantation by politicians and hucksters of the value of choice is filthy with dishonest use. All the same, we all want to be able to choose, if we have the chance and the money, to take a holiday and whereabouts it shall be. The common cry that pleasures are unequally allocated and access to them brutally restricted by the evil trinity of class, race and gender is at once true and crass. There are times when one keenly defends the barriers of class or generation and keeps them well repaired; on holiday, maybe. The bitter reproach from the intellectual spokesmen-and-women on behalf of tourist-dependent third world nations that tourists exploit or ignore the poverty and misery they see but will not look at on holiday hits home. It cannot be rebutted. While history remains the history of struggle, struggle for a better, juster, more trusting world, nonetheless neither the holidaymakers nor the consumer-citizen can live permanently posted on sentry duty, waiting for the opportunity to repair historical wrongs. The only answer is to act rightly and live well where you happen to be, and this returns us to the intense, commonplace satisfactions of human encounter, watchful alike for cheating or generosity. The cultural logic of capitalism, in Jameson's famous phrase,[24] is not so fixed in the new unfixities that all the conscientious intellectuals can do is keep on the watch for exploitation, make sure everyone is kept alertly miserable, and theorise desire as certain disappointment.

The furious buzz of conversation in academic circles which I have scanted here is only a more formalised version of the conversations of many societies in the wealthy half of the world as they work out how to conduct themselves towards the poorer half, and what sort of common good may be come at for the globe and its future. Some official at the United Nations found a very timely way of defining the moment of this new kind of modernism when writing:: 'Modern tourism was born out of the application of social policies which led to industrial workers obtaining annual paid holidays, and at the same time found its expression through the recognition of the basic human right to rest and leisure.'[25] This summarises one theme of this book admirably. If, of course, one has a right, someone else has a duty to provide for it. I don't think the case for our leisure lives need be put altogether in terms of rights, but it will do for now. What is more largely implied by the declaration is that tourism and its cognates – leisure, travel, vacationing and so forth – characterise a new sort of age. Daniel Miller says roundly that 'consumption has become the vanguard of history'[26] and that in a world in which, as William Morris foresaw, scarcity can be abolished and where the distribution of food dissolves seasonality. That invocation of history may be, as I said, rather too large a slogan for the understanding of vacations, but Miller braces us to see that something big is on the move, something which, in my account, began in the middle of the eighteenth century, but which only in the past quarter century has gathered the momentum to become the huge source of energy pouring through the millions wandering vaguely round the airport terminals.

IV

They are part, James Clifford[27] might put it, of the diaspora of 'discrepant cosmopolitanisms'. I would rather describe them, in a more homely idiom, as suburban gypsies. Both of us are trying to catch the contemporary traveller's best way of being-in-the-world. Clifford's phrase acknowledges that all contemporary travellers – our half-billion tourists per year – wear their own, varied and discrepant kinds of cosmopolitan knowingness. 'What is at stake,' he says, is 'a comparative cultural studies approach to specific histories, tactics, everyday practices of dwelling *and* travelling: travelling-in-dwelling, dwelling-in-travelling'. (This is André Aciman's purpose in Straus Square.) My suburban gypsy, wandering such safe vacation havens as Martha's Vineyard, Viareggio, the hill villages of old Tartary, the desert fortresses of the Yemen, brings with him or her the polite expectation of inviolability, a confidence that international credit cards will produce currency, food and shelter in most places, and the traveller's practical knowledge that you can make a little home out of anything, a hotel room, a clapboard chalet, a tent hooked to the back of the Range Rover.

What is coming into view is a new bundle of sentiments embodied in this timid wanderer. She starts, as I do, as does the UN Declaration on Tourism, from the supposition that there is a basic human need for rest and leisure. The Declaration says 'right' but let us stick to need, and say, moreover, that meeting such a need is one of life's primary goods.[28] This is not to say that desiring expensive vacations turns into a need which must be satisfied. It is to say that while each of us has a moral responsibility to mitigate expensive tastes in the name of fair shares, rest and leisure, and the search for active forms of movement which satisfy the desire for these constitute a primary good in life. It should therefore be part of efforts on behalf of a common good to provide both the leisure and the travel, each as part of the common and equal culture in the good society. Having the leisure during which one may compare other lives and histories becomes a condition of human emancipation.

It looks utopian to say so, until we think of our half-billion international air travellers per year, or our three billion (half the population of the globe) on the move in their own country. And as this book is earnest in emphasising, it is on holiday that one pictures little pieces of utopia. Paradise, it turns out, has the etymology from old Persian 'pairi' (around, about, as '*para*bola') and 'doeza' (wall);[29] hence Paradise, a secret garden. Every vacation makes an enchanted garden from which the holiday-maker ventures out to seek disenchantment. The delight with which we find out what the place and the people are really like frees us from the fantasy of exclusion so carefully built into the wall of the garden.

It is a moral rhythm. Tired out, we leave home to find the last homely house and its garden, where the spell holds, keeping out the bad world while rest restores us to health and vigour. Our children, happy and excited, leave home to find novelty and adventure, to make new friends and new stories about themselves, to gaze off the headland or at the ships on their urgent errands. We go out together to see what we can find.

We carry with us, just now, all the paraphernalia we need to understand this foreign, other place: videos, photographs, guidebooks, translations, etiquette manuals, credit cards. At times, what I have called the politics of politeness gives us a fit of moral hypochondria[30] in which we wealthy Americans or Europeans berate ourselves for bullying the others or old Nature herself by our patronage or extraction. But we get over it. If we are pioneers of a no-more-than thirty-year-old kind of late capitalism; if we stand at the van of the age of consumption; if a tenth of the world's people is travelling with us, generations of them pounding the earth dry; if nature, child of human culture is turning against us; we had better do things right. No wonder if some of the books express a little queasiness.

We set off, determined to see what is lovely and of good report, and, if possible, to agree with the reporters. If not, we shall be nice about it, keep our own counsel, make up our own minds. Our children hold onto either hand, full of beans and eager to look and see. We point out things to them, absurdly, teacherly. Respect, we say, rightly; respect the place, respect the people. It is a lovely day, sunny, a nice breeze, the gulls shrieking. Theodore Roethke once wrote a poem which began, 'The right thing happens to the happy man'. 'Damned if I'm just a consumer,' you think to yourself. 'I'm happy. So let the world be happy'. The holidays have started.

NOTES

1 THE PERFECT HOLIDAY

1 Fernand Braudel, *The Mediterranean and the Mediterranean World in the Age of Philip II*. Glasgow: Collins, 2nd revised edition, 1972, p.16.
2 John Berger, *About Looking*. London: Writers and Readers Co-operative, 1980, pp.197–8.
3 Walter Benjamin, *The Lyric Poet in the Era of High Capitalism*. London: New Left Books, 1974, p.134.
4 Theodor Adorno, *Minima Moralia: Reflections on a Damaged Life*. London: New Left Books, 1974, p.224.
5 Walter Benjamin, *The Lyric Poet*, p.134.
6 David Lodge, *Paradise News*. London: Secker and Warburg, 1991.
7 In a famous paper, Edward Thompson noted how the coming of capitalism brought with it the notion of '*spending* time', of time as money, in a way completely at odds with non-capitalist society. See his 'Time, work-discipline and industrial capitalism', reprinted in his *Customs in Common*. Harmondsworth: Penguin, 1991.
8 Wallace Stevens, 'Notes towards the supreme fiction' in *The Palm at the End of the Mind*. New York: Vintage Books, 1972, part ii, iv.

2 THE INVENTION OF TOURISM

1 John Fowles, *Daniel Martin*. London: Jonathan Cape, 1978.
2 Edmund Burke, *Philosophical Enquiry into the Origins of our Ideas of the Sublime and Beautiful*.
3 See J.H. Plumb, *The Growth of Political Stability in England 1675–1725*. Harmondsworth: Penguin, 1973.
4 Lawrence Stone traces this development in his now classic *The Family, Sex and Marriage in England 1500–1800*. London: Weidenfeld and Nicolson, 1977.
5 Figures in Jeremy Black, *The British and the Grand Tour*. London: Croom Helm, 1985, p.21.
6 Cesare de Seta, 'Grand Tour: the lure of Italy in the eighteenth century', in *Grand Tour*, Andrew Wilton and Ilaria Bignamini (eds). London: Tate Gallery, 1996, p.15.
7 Edward Wright, *Some Observations Made in Travelling Through France and Italy &c in the years 1720, 1721 and 1722*, London, 1730. It is hard to uncover publishing figures for the period for books of this kind. *The Gentleman's Magazine* had a subscription of 10,000. Wright's guide went through thirty-one editions. By the end of the first decade of the nine-teenth century, Dr Johnson's two travel books had sold 50,000 copies.
8 Paul Fussell, *Abroad: British Literary Travelling between the Wars*. Oxford: Oxford University Press, 1980.
9 Ibid., p.73.
10 Robert Halsband, *The Life of Mary Wortley Montagu*. Oxford: Clarendon Press, 1956, p.111.
11 List taken from Marcia Pointon, 'Killing pictures' in John Barrell (ed.), *Painting and the Politics of Culture*. Oxford: Oxford University Press, 1992, pp.39–73.

12 *The Complete Letters of Lady Mary Wortley Montagu*, ed. Robert Halsband, 3 vols. Oxford: Clarendon Press, 1966, pp.313–14.

13 *Complete Letters*, vol.II, p.79: 11 November 1740.

14 Lisa St Aubyn de Téran, *A Villa in Italy*. Harmondsworth: Penguin, 1994.

15 Lord Chesterfield, *Letters to His Son*. London: Dent, Everyman edition, 1951; see especially pp.168, 171, 193, 198.

16 *The Private Papers of James Boswell: Boswell on the Grand Tour – Italy, Corsica, France 1765–66*, ed. Frank Brady and Frederick Pottle. London: William Heinemann, 1955, p.109.

17 Ibid., p.15.

18 Ibid., pp.53, 62–3, 64–5, 66.

19 Alexander Pope, 'Moral Essays' in *Collected Poems*. London: Dent, Everyman edition, 1956, p.255. See also J.H. Plumb, *The Commercialisation of Leisure in 18th Century England*. Reading: University of Reading Press, 1973.

20 In 'The Golden Asses', 1761 (Lewis Walpole Library).

21 As witness *The Grand Tour*, Wilton and Bignamini (eds), 1996, as cited.

22 Johann Wolfgang von Goethe, *Italian Journeys*, (1789).

23 All these quotations found by Christopher Hibbert, *The Grand Tour*. London: Weidenfeld and Nicolson, 1969, pp.105–9. But see his whole chapter, 'Italy'.

24 These glimpses of Winckelmann are taken from *The Grand Tour*, Wilton and Bignamini (eds), 1996, especially the essay by Cesare de Seta, pp. 17–19. See also A. Potts, *Flesh and the Ideal: Winckelmann and the Origins of Art History*, New Haven, CT: Yale University Press, 1994.

25 The history of these dealings has been for half a century the remarkable life's work of the Italian scholar Carlo Pietrangeli. See his *The Vatican Museum: Five Centuries of History*. Rome: The Vatican, 1993. See also Francis Haskell and Nicholas Penny, *Taste and the Antique*. New Haven, CT: Yale University Press, 1981.

26 Mark Jones (ed.), *Fake? The Art of Deception*. London: British Museum, 1990.

27 Jack Lindsay, *Turner: His Life and Work*. St. Albans: Granada, 1966, p. 68.

28 See Francis Haskell, *Patrons and Painters*, Oxford: Oxford University Press, 1963; F. Davis, *Victorian Patronage of the Arts*, Oxford: Clarendon Press, 1963.

29 Kenneth Clark, *Landscape into Art*. London: John Murray, revised edition, 1976, pp.138–9.

30 Richard Wollheim, *Painting as an Art*. London: Thames and Hudson, 1987, pp. 81–4.

31 This is a compressed version of the argument in David Wiggins's famous paper, 'Truth, invention and the meaning of life'. See his *Needs, Values, Truth*. Oxford: Blackwell, 1987, p.106.

32 The disputed history of this nationalist transfiguration has been most recently rewritten by Linda Colley, *Britons: Forging the Nation 1707–1837*. London: Vintage Books, revised edition, 1987. See also Philip Corrigan and Derek Sayer, *The Great Arch: English State Formation as Cultural Revolution*. Oxford: Basil Blackwell, 1985.

33 Quoted by Malcolm Andrews, *The Search for the Picturesque*. Stanford, CA: Stanford University Press, 1989, p.153. I have counted much in what follows upon this admirable book.

34 Quoted by Andrews (1989), p.159.

35 See Hugh Trevor-Roper, 'The Highland tradition of Scotland', in Eric Hobsbawm and Terence Ranger (eds), *The Invention of Tradition*. Cambridge: Cambridge University Press, 1983. For Scott, see Donald Davie, *The Heyday of Sir Walter Scott*. London: Chatto and Windus, 1967.

36 Wordsworth's *Guide to the Lakes*, 5th edition 1838, facsimile reprint. Oxford: Oxford University Press, 1977, p. 47.

37 See *Turner in the North of England*, exhibition catalogue. London: Tate Gallery, 22 October 1996–9 February 1997.

38 S. Schama, *Landscape and Memory*. London: HarperCollins, 1995, p.555, my italics.

3 CONFECTING SEASIDE

1 The domestic details may be found in Peter Laslett, *The World we have Lost*. London: Methuen, 1965; and added to by Stone (1977) as cited; Plumb (as cited). Pat Rogers, *Literature and Popular Culture in 18th Century England*. Brighton: Harvester, 1995; and John Brewer, N. McKendrick and J. Plumb, *The Birth of a Consumer Society*. Bloomington: University of Indiana Press, 1982.

2 Jean-Didier Urbain, *Sur La Plage: mœurs et coutumes balnéaires (XIX–XX siècles)*. Paris: Editions Payot, 1996.

3 Stephen Greenblatt reviews his predecessors in his marvellous *Marvellous Possessions: The Wonder of the New World*. Chicago: University of Chicago Press, 1991.

4 Ian Watt, *The Rise of the Novel*. London: Chatto and Windus, 1957.

5 Their history is classically expounded by Elaine Denby in *Grand Hotels: Reality and Illusion*. London: Reaktion Books, 1999. See also Chapter 4 below.

6 This is the title (in translation) of Alain Corbin's classic study, here recapitulated: Alain Corbin, *The Lure of the Sea: The Discovery of the Seaside in the Western World 1750–1840*. Cambridge: Polity Press, 1994.

7 See Edgar Wind, 'Botticelli's birth of Venus' in his *Pagan Mysteries of the Renaissance*. Harmondsworth: Penguin, 1967.

8 Corbin (1994), p.283.

9 See R.R. Bolgar, *The Classical Heritage and its Beneficiaries*. Cambridge: Cambridge University Press, 1954. For the relation between city and country, see Keith Thomas, *Man and the Natural World*. Harmondsworth: Penguin, 1983; and Raymond Williams, *The Country and the City*. London: Chatto and Windus, 1973.

10 Corbin comes up with a rich haul of books of the time extolling the curative properties of the sea, e.g. Dr Robert White, *The Use and Abuse of Sea Water* (1775); A.P. Buchan, *Practical Observations Concerning Seabathing with Remarks on the Use of the Warm Bath* (1804); Dr John Awsiter, *Thoughts on Brighthelmstone, Concerning Sea-Bathing and Drinking Sea-water* (1768).

11 *A Dissertation on the Use of Seawater in the Diseases of the Glands, particularly the Scurvy, Jaundice etc.* (1769, but Latin edition 1752).

12 J.R. Pimlott, *The Englishman's Holiday: A Social History*. London: Faber and Faber, 1947, Chapters VI and VII. See also Mark Girouard's classic, *Sweetness and Light: The Queen Anne Movement, 1860–1900*. Oxford: Clarendon Press, 1977.

13 Edmund Gilbert, *Brighton: Old Ocean's Bauble*. London: Methuen, 1954. See also, of course, Nikolaus Pevsner, *Sussex: The Buildings of England*. Harmondsworth: Penguin, 1965 (with Ian Nairn).

14 Nikolaus Pevsner, *The Buildings of England: Devon*. Harmondsworth: Penguin, 1957.

15 Schama (1995), p.559.

16 Mrs. Gaskell, *The Life of Charlotte Brontë*. London: Dent Everyman edition 1966, p.117.

17 Quoted by Jonathan Raban in an excellent essay, 'On the waterfront', *New York Review of Books*, 14 July 1994. It is taken from James's *A Little Tour of France*. Harmondsworth: Penguin, 1983.

18 Schama (1995), pp.541–3; Andrews (1989), p.183.

19 Figures from E.J. Hobsbawm, *Industry and Empire: An Economic History of Britain since 1750*. London: Weidenfeld and Nicolson, 1968.

20 Ibid., p.97.

21 Ibid., p.92.

22 Edmund Swinglehurst, *The Romantic Journey: The Story of Thomas Cook and Victorian Travel*. London: Pica Editions, 1974; and Piers Brendon, *Thomas Cook: 150 years of popular tourism*. London: Elek Press, 1991.

23 See Denby (1999), Chapter 5.

24 Quoted by Swinglehurst (1974), p.58.

25 Brendon (1991), p.161.

26 The title of J.A.R. Pimlott's book (1947) as already cited; H. Butterfield, *The Whig Interpretation of History*. Harmondsworth: Penguin, 1973

27 John Walton, *The Blackpool Landlady*. Manchester: University of Manchester Press 1978, p.15. My brief history of the town relies on this book and on Pevsner's *Lancashire*.
28 Walton (1978), p.21. The town doubled in size between 1871 and 1891 and doubled again in the 1890s (Pimlott [1947] pp.177–8).
29 Walton (1978), p.26.
30 Quoted by Anthony Hern, *The Seaside Holiday*. London: Cresset Press, 1967, p.98.
31 *The Miners Gala: An Illustrated History*. Durham: The National Union of Miners, 1992.
32 Marriot Edgar, 'The Lion and Albert', in *Albert, 'Arold and others*. London: Francis, Day and Hunter, n.d.; Stanley Holloway, of course, performed the poems for posterity on 78 rpm records.
33 Transcript from files of Mass Observation, inquiry into Blackpool holidays 1935, verbatim report by Tom Harrisson (University of Sussex archive). I have made no attempt to orthographise the Lancastrian accent.
34 A telling phrase rescued by Clifford Geertz from Jeremy Bentham, of all people. See Geertz's *The Interpretation of Cultures*. New York: Basic Books, 1973.

4 THE MEANING OF LUXURY

1   This crucial factor in the economics of the cultural industries is given extended theoretic discussion in my *Media Theory*. Oxford: Blackwell, 1990.
2   Henry James, *Italian Hours*. New Jersey: Ecco Press, 1990, p.229.
3   John Ruskin, *Mornings in Florence*. Harmondsworth: Penguin, 1987, p.93.
4   Michael Frayn, *Sweet Dreams*. London: Secker and Warburg, 1973, pp.11, 23.
5   Given how powerful a political symbol 'home' universally is, it's a mystery so few of the professional political scientists write about it. But see W. Rybczynski, *Home: A Short History of an Idea*. London: Heinemann, 1988.
6   See Judith Herrin, *The Formation of Christendom*. Oxford: Basil Blackwell 1987, pp.59–83.
7   For the history of this process in the Netherlands, see Simon Schama, *The Embarrassment of Riches*. Berkeley, CA: University of California Press, 1988.
8   Christopher J. Berry, *The Idea of Luxury: A Conceptual and Historical Investigation*. Cambridge: Cambridge University Press, 1994.
9   Fred Hirsch, *Social Limits to Growth*. London: Routledge and Kegan Paul for the Twentieth Century Fund, 1977. See particularly Chapters 1 and 5.
10 Ibid., p.96. My italics.
11 See Edward Luttwak on 'Central-Bankism' in Peter Gowan and Perry Anderson (eds), *The Question of Europe*. London: Verso, 1997.
12 J.S. Mill, *The Six Great Humanistic Essays*, ed. Albert Levi, New York: Washington Square Press, 1963, p.188.
13 This brief passage of moralising is much at odds with what Jacques Derrida has to say on the subject, in his *The Gift of Death*. Chicago: University of Chicago Press, 1995.
14 Berry (1994), pp.11–12.
15 Compare Donald Olsen, *The City as a Work of Art*, New Haven, CT: Yale University Press, 1986, pp.190–1, 211–13, 235–6; and Denby (1999) in her admirable book, though grand hotels are hardly as done for as she suggests.
16 Vicki Baum, *Menschen in Hotel* (widely translated as *Grand Hotel*), 1932, later filmed with Heinz Rühmann and Sonia Ziemann. Here quoted in Ullstein Bücher edition, Berlin, 1991, p.118.
17 As it is the theme of Raymond Williams's famous study to point out. See his *The Country and the City*. London: Chatto and Windus, 1973.
18 *Selections from Ralph Waldo Emerson*, ed. Stephen Whicher. Boston: Houghton Mifflin 1957, p.329.
19 Henry Thoreau, *Walden*. Princeton, NJ: Princeton University Press, 1973, p.112.
20 Preface to the Puffin edition of *Swallowdale*, 1973.
21 Quoted from Escoffier by James Johnston, *A Hundred Years of Eating*. Dublin: Gill and Macmillan, 1977, p.7.

22 Theodore Zeldin, *France 1848–1945* (1977). Oxford History of Modern Europe: Clarendon Press, pp.725–62.
23 As Stephen Mennell points out in *All Manners of Food: Eating and Taste in England and France from the Middle Ages to the Present*. Urbana: University of Illinois Press, 1996, Chapter 6, 'Chefs and their publics'.
24 Ibid., Chapter 8, 'The Trade Press'.
25 Ibid., p.160.
26 Kenneth Grahame, *The Wind in the Willows* (1908), London: Methuen Children's Books, 1977, p.14.
27 Mary Douglas, 'Deciphering a meal', *Implicit Meanings: Essays in Anthropology*. London: Routledge and Kegan Paul, 1975.
28 Ibid., p.255.
29 A visit with a long provenance, provided by A. Corbin, *The Lure of the Sea*. Cambridge: Polity Press, 1994, pp.187–97.
30 A plenty now notoriously under threat. See *Cod: A Biography of the Fish that Changed the World* by Mark Kurlansky. London: Jonathan Cape, 1998, pp.261–73.
31 The details which follow are taken from Elizabeth David, *Italian Food*. London: Michael Joseph, revised edition, 1992. For the history of ice, see Mennell (1994).
32 The phrase is Jack Goody's, in his *Cooking, Cuisine and Class*. Cambridge: Cambridge University Press, 1982, chapter 5.
33 See James P. Johnston, *A Hundred Years Eating: Food, Drink and Daily Diet in Britain since the Late 19th Century*. Dublin and Montreal: Gill and Macmillan, 1977, pp.62–3.
34 Richard Hoggart, *The Uses of Literacy*. Harmondsworth: Pelican, 1958, p.53.

5 MAGNETIC DANGERS

1 Of which Theodore Zeldin and Peter Gay are the best-known practitioners. See Zeldin (1977), as already cited, and Peter Gay, *The Bourgeois Experience: Victoria to Freud*. London: HarperCollins, 1994.
2 This paragraph serves to summarise a scheme of Raymond Williams's in which he offered to distinguish between *values* as 'dominant, residual and emergent'. I use 'values' here as inseparable from feeling. See Williams's *Culture*. Glasgow: Collins, 1981.
3 In his classic essay, 'Notes on the Balinese cockfight', *The Interpretation of Cultures*. London: Hutchinson, 1975, pp.446, 450–1.
4 Particularly Anthony Giddens, in his *Modernity and Self-Identity*. Cambridge: Polity Press, 1991.
5 Francis Spufford, *I May Be Some Time: Ice and the English Imagination*. London: Faber and Faber, paperback, 1997, p.8.
6 As has been well known for a long time, full literacy was widely assumed in much more than half the population of Britain long before the Education Act of 1870 which established compulsory schooling. See R.K. Webb, *The British Working Class Reader 1790–1848*. London: Allen and Unwin, 1955.
7 Spufford (1997), p.1.
8 S. Junger, *The Perfect Storm*. London: Fourth Estate, 1998.
9 Charles Taylor, 'History, comparison, truth', *Philosophical Arguments*. Cambridge, MA: Harvard University Press, 1995, pp.150, 156.
10 Paul Fussell, *Abroad*. Oxford: Oxford University Press, 1980.
11 Wilfred Thesiger, *Arabian Sands*. Harmondsworth: Penguin, 1964, p.276.
12 Ibid., p.258.
13 Ibid., p.278.
14 Ibid., p.279.
15 Peter Fleming, *News from Tartary* (Jonathan Cape 1936). London: Abacus, 1994.
16 Ibid., p.58.
17 Ibid., p.325.
18 A heroic tale re-enacted in the movie, *Ill Met by Moonlight*, made by Michael Powell and Emeric Pressberger, in which Dirk Bogarde plays Leigh Fermor (1956).

19 Patrick Leigh Fermor, *Roumeli: Travels in Northern Greece* (John Murray 1966). Harmondsworth: Penguin, 1983. Robert Byron, *The Road to Oxiana* (Macmillan 1937). Harmondsworth: Penguin, 1992.

20 T.S. Eliot, 'Little Gidding', *Four Quartets*. New York: Harcourt Brace, 1943, p.50.

21 Jon Kracauer tells the story of the most notorious such debacle, in *Into Thin Air: A Personal Account of the Mt. Everest Disaster*. New York: Random House, 1997.

22 The best-known of the debunkers being Roland Huntford, *Scott and Amundsen*. London: Hodder and Stoughton, 1979.

23 Most recently, Jenni Diski, in her self-confirming and impressive memoir (a pretty queasy self, as it happens), *Skating to Antarctica*. Hopewell, NJ: Ecco Press, 1997.

24 Arthur Ransome, *Winter Holiday*. London: Jonathan Cape, 1953.

25 Joseph Conrad, *The Shadow Line*. London: Dent, 1917.

26 Jonathan Raban, *Old Glory*. Glasgow: Collins, 1981.

27 Fussell (1980), p.45, and his last chapter, 'The End'.

28 Redmond O'Hanlon, *Into the Heart of Borneo*. Edinburgh: Salamander Press, 1984; *In Trouble Again*. New York: Atlantic Monthly Press, 1988; *Congo Journey*. Harmondsworth: Penguin, 1997; Joe Simpson, *Touching the Void*. London: Vintage, 1997.

29 Mallory to his wife Ruth (24 April 1924) quoted by John Holzell and Audrey Salkeld, *The Mystery of Mallory and Irvine*. London: Jonathan Cape, 1986, p.190.

30 Holzell and Salkeld (1986), p.153.

31 Simpson (1997), p.21.

32 John Muir, *The Mountains of California* (1894). New York: Doubleday, 1961.

33 Muir (1961), pp.228–9.

34 Paul Theroux, *The Great Railway Bazaar: By Train through Asia*. Harmondsworth: Penguin, 1975.

35 Redmond O'Hanlon (1988), p.88.

36 O'Hanlon (1984), original italics.

37 O'Hanlon (1988), pp.169–70.

6 THE INDUSTRIALISATION OF MOBILITY

1 See Nigel Thrift, *Spatial Formations*. London: Sage, 1998.

2 The phrase is Edward Luttwak's, although he is by no means an uncritical apologist for the thing. See his *The Endangered American Dream*. New York: 1993; as well as *Turbo-Capitalism*. London: Orion Books, 1998.

3 In particular, Paul Hirst and Grahame Thompson, *Globalisation in Question*. Cambridge: Polity Press, 1996.

4 Ibid., Chapter 1. See also David Harvey, *The Condition of Postmodernity*. Oxford: Basil Blackwell, 1989.

5 Evelyn Waugh's first travel book was called *Labels* (London: Duckworth, 1930) and described an extended Mediterranean cruise in 1929.

6 See David Evans, *The Ingenious Mr. Pedersen*. Dursley:Allan Sutton, 1954.

7 J.A.R. Pimlott (1947), p.167.

8 James M. Laux in *First Gear: The French Automobile Industry to 1914*. Liverpool: Liverpool University Press, 1976, p.130.

9 Pimlott (1947), p.212.

10 Sidney and Beatrice Webb, *The Story of the King's Highway*. London: Longman, 1913.

11 By Raymond Williams in 'An epoch's end', *New Left Review*, 140, July–August 1983.

12 Laux (1976), pp.21–2.

13 James Ensor, *The Motor Industry*. London: *Financial Times* and Longmans, 1971, p.11.

14 See James Stilgoe, *The Metropolitan Corridor: Railroads and the American Scene*. New Haven, CT: Yale University Press, 1983.

15 See Joseph J. Thorndike, *The Coast: A Journey Down the Atlantic Shore*. New York: St. Martin's Press, 1993, pp.117–18.

16 Alexander Wilson, *The Culture of Nature: North American Landscape from Disney to the Exxon Valdez*. Oxford: Blackwell, 1992, p.28.

17 Ibid., p.29.
18 A.J.P. Taylor, *English History 1914–1945*, vol.15, Oxford History of England. Oxford: Clarendon Press, 1965, p.303. See also Philip Bagwell, *The Transport Revolution*. London: Routledge, 1974, p.219. It is worth adding that more people were killed by cars in 1934 than in 1994.
19 Eric Hobsbawm, *Age of Extremes: The Short Twentieth Century 1914–1991*. London: Michael Joseph, 1994, p.101.
20 H.J. Dyos and D.H. Aldcroft, *British Transport: An Economic Survey*. Leicester: Leicester University Press, 1969, pp.374–5.
21 John B. Rae, *Climb to Greatness: The American Aircraft Industry 1920–1960*. Cambridge, MA: MIT Press, 1968, p.1.
22 Graham Greene, *England Made Me*. Oxford: Bodley Head, 1935.
23 Constance Babington Smith, *Amy Johnson*. London: Collins, 1967. See also Mary Russell, *The Blessings of a Good Thick Skirt*. London: Flamingo, 1994.
24 Rae (1968), pp.10–11.
25 Philip Bagwell (1974), p.274ff.
26 Dyos and Aldcroft (1969), p.384. See also Robin Higham, *Britain's Imperial Air Routes 1918–1939*. London: Foulis & Co., 1960.
27 Ibid., pp.100, 348.
28 R.H. Tawney, *The Acquisitive Society* (1921). London: Collins, 1961, p.26.
29 Pimlott (1947), pp.214–15.
30 Quoted by Stephen G. Jones, *Workers at Play: a social and economic history of leisure 1918–1939*. London: Routledge and Kegan Paul, 1986, p.19.
31 Jones (1986), p.20; Pimlott (1947), p.219.
32 Jones (1986), p.31.
33 See *All our Working Lives*, ed. Peter Pagnamenta. London: BBC Publications, 1984.
34 Jones (1986), p.199.
35 Sidney Pollard, *The Development of the British Economy 1914–1980*. London: Edward Arnold, 1983, p.322.
36 Jones (1986), p.200.
37 My evocation gestures towards John Arlott's incomparable cricketing history of that year, *Vintage Summer 1947*. London: Eyre and Spottiswoode, 1967.
38 Figures taken from John Urry, *The Tourist Gaze: Leisure and Travel in Contemporary Societies*. London: Sage, 1990. See also J. Jakle, *The Tourist*. Lincoln: University of Nebraska Press, 1985.
39 Edward Thompson, review-articles of Raymond Williams's *The Long Revolution*, *New Left Review*, nos. 9,10,11, 1961.
40 Their tale is marvellously reassembled by Patrick Wright in his *The Village that Died for England*. London: Jonathan Cape, 1995.
41 John Lowerson, 'Battles for the countryside' in Frank Gloversmith (ed.) *Class, Culture and Social Change: A New View of the 1930s*. Brighton: Harvester, 1980.
42 Ibid., pp.268–77.
43 Ibid., p.273.

7 THE MEDITERRANEAN

1 The word is chosen by Pierre de la Ruffinière du Prey in his *The Villas of Pliny from Antiquity to Posterity*. Chicago: University of Chicago Press, 1995, from which I take all the following account. De la Ruffinière is, like me, at pains to show just how much of our present imaginings of the Mediterranean and the good life lived beside it we owe to the Latin classics.
2 Nikolaus Pevsner, *The Buildings of England: Northumberland*. Penguin: Harmondsworth, 1957, p.286.
3 Letter to Voconius Romanus in *Pliny: Letters and Panegyrics*, Loeb Classical Library, translated by Betty Radice, vol.II, pp.23–5. London: William Heinemann, 1969.

4 One charming example of the transcontinental tendency is worth a bit of research for the tourist in Wales. From about 1925 the extraordinary Anglo-Welsh architect, engineer, designer and building speculator, Clough Williams-Ellis, devoted himself to developing an explicitly Italianate and Mediterranean village on the sheltered side of Tremadoc Bay where the Gulf Stream swirls busily in to keep the coastline warm. Portmeirion was this amazing project, equipped with harbour, pilot house, campanile, traditional inns, all to Williams-Ellis's own designs, all quoting the piled, stacked, amicably crowded and always shapely effect of the prettiest fishing towns of Italy: Portafino, Sorrento, Amalfi. When the whole place is also decked out in Caprese pastels the result bears witness to the spell cast on northern imaginations by the Mediterranean (see *Portmeirion Further Explained*, ed. Noel Carrington, 3rd edition. Birmingham: Kynoch Press, 1935).

5 The figures are brutally incomprehensible; but for what it's worth, we know that 52 million tourists arrived in Italy in 1994, 60 million in France and 43 million in Spain; source: *Tourism Market Trends Europe, 1985–1994*. Madrid: World Tourism Organisation, 1995.

6 Nearly 70 years ago, in Adrian Stokes, *Stones of Rimini* (1934). New York: Schocken Books, 1969, especially chapter III. The idea is powerfully reworked by David Attenborough in his BBC TV series, published in book form as *First Eden*. London: Collins/BBC, 1987.

7 Braudel, as cited, second revised edition, 1972, pp.232ff.

8 Ibid., pp.241, 243.

9 Stokes (1969), p.61.

10 Ibid. (1969), pp.70–2. He is building here on ideas first voiced in Jules Michelet's classic of 1861, *La Mer*. For Michelet, the sea became finally tamed only by the laying of the first telegraph cables.

11 For his key discussion, see David Ekserdijian, *Correggio*. New Haven, CT: Yale University Press, 1997.

12 A contention fully developed by Wollheim (1987), as cited.

13 Stokes is writing about Agostino di Duccio's marble relief carvings in the Tempio Malatestiano (1447–1461) in Rimini, but the same points can be readily made about Correggio or Giorgione.

14 Foucault is the first thinker (though anticipated by Henry James) to identify the mixture of possession, appropriation and insolence in the bourgeois gaze. John Urry then ingeniously captures the term to classify the two orders of tourist gaze – the 'solitary' (or Romantic) and the 'collective'. See Urry, as cited (1992).

15 F. Scott Fitzgerald, *The Great Gatsby*. New York: Scribners, 1925, pp.49–50.

16 E.M. Forster, *A Room with a View*. Harmondsworth: Penguin, 1990, p.194.

17 See Zeldin (1977), p.793ff, 'Individuation and the Emotions', and more specifically T.J. Clark, *The Absolute Bourgeois: Art and Politics in Nineteenth Century France*. London: Thames and Hudson, 1973.

18 Vincent Van Gogh, *The Letters*, selected and edited by Mark Roskill. London: Collins, 1983, p.268.

19 The phrase is John Pemble's, in his *The Mediterranean Passion: Victorians and Edwardians in the South*. Oxford: Clarendon Press, 1987; but I wonder if he is quite attentive enough to the colour of the money.

20 Mary Blume, *Côte d'Azur: Inventing the French Riviera*. New York: Thames and Hudson, 1992, p.30.

21 Blume (1992), p.117.

22 Patrick Heron, 'Solid space in Cézanne', pp.16–17, *Modern Painters*, 1996, vol.9, no.1.

23 John Pemble, *Venice Rediscovered*. Oxford: Clarendon Press, 1995.

24 The term has been made a formal one by Edward Said in his *Orientalism*, (Harmondsworth: Penguin, 1985) but the thing, as it is his point to make, long precedes this classic work.

25 In his travel book *Vathek*, quoted by Pemble (1995), p.118.

26 John Ruskin, *The Stones of Venice: a selection*, edited by Jan Morris with the original illustrations. London: Faber and Faber, 1981, p.171.

27 John Ruskin, *The Seven Lamps of Architecture*. London: George Allen, revised with a new preface, 1890, pp.357–8 (Ruskin's italics).

28 John Ruskin, *Mornings in Florence*. Harmondsworth: Penguin, 1987, pp.7–8. See also the admirable discussion of Ruskin versus Forster in James Buzard, *The Beaten Track: European Tourism, Literature and the Ways to Culture*. Oxford: Clarendon Press, 1993, pp.288–91.

29 Norman Lewis, *Naples '44: An Intelligence Officer in the Italian Labyrinth*. London: Collins (Eland Book), 1983, p.203.

30 Ibid., p.53.

31 Peter Ritchie-Calder, *The Pollution of the Mediterranean*. Berne: Herbert Land, 1973, p.43.

32 Quoted by Peter Haas, *Saving the Mediterranean: The Politics of International Environmental Co-operation*. New York: Columbia University Press, 1990, p.xx.

33 Jürgen Habermas, *Towards a Rational Society*. Boston: Beacon Press, 1970, Chapter 2.

34 Haas (1990), p.182.

8 FOREIGN BODIES

1 Blume (1992), p.75.

2 Michel Foucault, *The History of Sexuality*. Harmondsworth: Penguin, vol. I, 1985.

3 E.M. Forster, 'What I believe' in *Two Cheers for Democracy*. Harmondsworth: Penguin, 1968.

4 Edward Luttwak's phrase (1998), as cited.

5 D.H. Lawrence, *Collected Short Stories*. New York: Viking Press, 3 vols, 1961, vol.III, pp.528–45.

6 Norman Douglas, *Siren Land: Anecdote, Philosophy and Myth: A Celebration of Life in Southern Italy*. Harmondsworth: Penguin, 1983, p.75.

7 See *The Worktowners*, as cited, chap.5.

8 *Rain*, later filmed sensationally as *Miss Sadie Thompson* in 1953 with Rita Hayworth is probably the best-known and most suggestive.

9 The history of the Singapore prostitutes over this period is remarkably retrieved by James Francis Warren in *Ah Ku and Karayuki-san: Prostitution in Singapore 1870–1940*. Oxford: Oxford University Press, 1993.

10 e.g. Sir Roland Braddell; Warren (1993), p.176.

11 Conan Doyle wrote a well-known and impressive Sherlock Holmes story called 'The Opium Den' a little time before.

12 In 1916 no European woman could be found working in any Singapore brothel.

13 Very much so according to Rita Nakashima Brock and Susan Brooks Thistlethwaite in *Casting Stones: Prostitution and Liberation in Asia and the United States*. Minneapolis: Fortress Press, 1996. Similarly, Cynthia Enloe, *Bananas, Beaches and Bases: Making Feminist Sense of International Politics*. Berkeley, CA: University of California Press, 1990.

14 Brock and Thistlethwaite (1996), p.59. They took the 60 per cent figure from a doubtful source in Pico Iyer, *Video Night in Katmandu and Other Reports from the Not-so-Far East*. New York: Vintage, 1988.

15 Cleo Odzer, *Patpong Sisters: An American Woman's View of the Bangkok Sex World*. New York: Blue Moon Books, 1994, chapter 2.

16 Jeremy Seabrook, *Travels in the Skin Trade: Tourism and the Sex Industry*. London: Pluto Press, 1996.

17 Seabrook (1996), p.19.

18 Odzer (1994), p.47.

19 Some of their life-histories are told by Pasuk Phongpaichit in *From Peasant Girls to Bangkok Masseuses*. Geneva: ILO, 1982.

20 Seabrook (1996) chapter 2; Benedict Anderson, 'From miracle to crash in the Far East', *London Review of Books*, 16 April 1998; Ryan Bishop and Lillian S. Robinson, *Night Market: Sexual Cultures and the Thai Economic Miracle*. New York: Routledge, 1998, especially chapter 4.

21 Bishop and Robinson (1998), p.154.

22 Steven Marcus, *The Other Victorians*. London: Pan, 1969.

23 J.G. Ballard, *The Kindness of Women*. London: HarperCollins, 1994.

24 Ibid., p.242.
25 Roland Barthes, *Camera Lucida*. London: Flamingo Books, 1988.
26 Ballard (1994), pp.249–50.
27 Charles Nicholl, *The Fruit Palace*. New York: Vintage, 1988, p.58.
28 Alec Garland's novel *The Beach* (1997), already cited and to be released as a film in 2000, melodramatises the way these trips might go horribly wrong, when eager Edenists bump into the hard drugs trade.
29 *The Rough Guide to Thailand* (London: Rough Guides, 1995 edition) is caustic about all but a handful of them.
30 Nicholl (1988), though an Englishman, speaks up eloquently for this discovery.
31 First turned into fiction, I think, by Angus Wilson in his novel *As If by Magic*, London: Secker and Warburg, 1981.
32 Their astonishing handbook is *Fielding's The World's Most Dangerous Places*, compiled by Robert Young Pelton, Coskim Aral and Wink Dulles. California: Fielding Worldwide Inc., 3rd edition, 1998.
33 Ibid,. p.174.

9 CITY STATES

1 Raymond Williams, *The Country and the City*. London: Chatto and Windus, 1973, pp.5–6.
2 Gaston Bachelard, *The Poetics of Place*, Boston: Beacon Press, 1969.
3 Bachelard (1969), pp.xxxi–xxxii.
4 Kevin Lynch, *The Image of the City*. Cambridge, MA: MIT Press, 1960.
5 Ibid., p.25.
6 Mike Davis, *City of Quartz: Excavating the Future of Los Angeles*. London: Verso, 1990.
7 John Urry (1990) suggests, it will be remembered, the 'romantic' and the 'collective', as the two such types.
8 André Aciman, 'Shadow cities', *New York Review of Books*, 18 December 1997.
9 Christopher Alexander, 'A city is not a tree', in Gwen Bell and Jacqueline Tyrwhitt (eds), *Human Identity in the Urban Environment*. Harmondsworth: Penguin, 1972, pp.401–32.
10 Ibid., p.405.
11 Marshall Berman, *All that is Solid Melts into Air: The Experience of Modernity*. London: Verso, 1983, p.165.
12 Jane Jacobs, *The Death and Life of Great American Cities*. New York: Vintage, 1961, pp.148 and 51. But see Lewis Mumford's biting review, 'Mother Jacobs' home remedies for urban cancer', *New Yorker*, 1 December 1962.
13 Berman (1983), p.293.
14 Lynch (1960), p.82.
15 For Reyner Banham, it is the one right view. See his *The Architecture of the Well-Tempered Environment*. Chicago: University of Chicago Press, 1984.
16 Lewis Mumford, *The City in History*. Harmondsworth: Penguin, 1965, Chapter 17, 'The myth of Megalopolis'.
17 As Lynch (1960) says strongly, so much so that he recommends to planners that they aim to incorporate such prospects in their plans; pp.108ff.
18 M. Christine Boyer, *The City of Collective Memory: Its Historical Imagery and Architectural Entertainments*. Cambridge MA: MIT Press, 1994, p.4.
19 Ibid., p.4.
20 Ibid., p.9.
21 Ibid., p.14.
22 I take much in what follows from Godfrey Hodgson's learned, relaxed and admirable *A New Grand Tour: How Europe's Great Cities Made our World*. Harmondsworth: Penguin, 1995, Chapter 2.
23 Hodgson (1995) p.31ff is very stylish on this subject.
24 Pierre Bourdieu, *The State Nobility: Élite Schools in the Field of Power*. Cambridge: Polity Press, 1996.
25 James Hillis Miller, *Topographies*. Stanford: Stanford University Press, 1995, p.330.

26 Ernest Hemingway, *A Moveable Feast*. New York: Scribners, 1964.
27 Jonathan Raban, *Soft City*. Glasgow: Collins, 1974.
28 Geoffrey Moorhouse, *Imperial City: The Rise and Rise of New York*. London: Hodder and Stoughton, Sceptre editions, 1989.
29 Italo Calvino, *Invisible Cities*. New York: Harcourt Brace, translated by William Weaver, 1974.

10 FUTURES: VIRTUE ON VACATION

1 UNESCO report: *Tourism and Economic Development Outside Europe*. Paris: UNESCO, 1965, fig.2. See also N. Singh, *The Impact of Tourism on the Balance of Payments*. Athens: CPER, 1984.
2 David Nicholson-Lord, 'The politics of travel: is tourism just colonialism in another guise?', *Nation* (NY), 6 October 1997. See also Singh (1984), p.191.
3 See Hirst and Thompson (1995), as cited.
4 UN Conference Report: *World Conference on Sustainable Tourism*. New York: UN, 1995.
5 *New York Times*, 26 August 1998.
6 All figures from *Tourism Market Trends*. Madrid: WTO, 1995.
7 Norman Lewis, *Voices of the Old Sea*. London: Picador, 1996.
8 Camilo Jose Cela, *Journey to the Alcarria* (1948). New York: Atlantic Monthly Press, 1990.
9 The now classic work on the topic is by James Griffin, *Well-Being*. Oxford: Clarendon Press, 1986.
10 In his Leslie Stephen lecture, *Pessimism and Morality* (Cambridge: Cambridge University Press, 1972), Stuart Hampshire lists the distribution of food, shelter, obstacles to the taking of life, the regulation of sex and rights and duties in respect of money and property, as the four essentials which shape a universal morality. I also take a good deal of support from Ralf Dahrendorf's *Reflections on the Revolution in Europe*. London: Chatto and Windus, 1990.
11 In *The New York Review of Books*, 19 January 1991.
12 Richard Hoggart, *Townscape with Figures: Farnham – portrait of an English town*. London: Chatto and Windus, 1994, p.200.
13 Philip Larkin, 'To the Sea', *Collected Poems*. London: Faber, 1989.
14 *Independent*, 4 September 1997.
15 I owe this transcript to the Python scholar, Hilary Britland.
16 Fussell (1982).
17 See Malcolm Crick, *Resplendent Sites, Discordant Voices: Sri Lanka and International Tourism* (Chur: Harwood Academic Publishers, 1994) for a sharp jolt to the benign view expressed here that tourism will work out all right for everybody in the end. The novel *The Beach* by Alec Garland (New York: Viking, 1997) is an extreme fiction about how paradisal holidays are sure to go murderously wrong.
18 Kenneth Burke, *Attitudes towards History*. Los Altos: Hermes Press, 1959, p.171.
19 Burke (1959), p.42.
20 J.G. Ballard, 'Going somewhere', *Observer*, 14 September 1997.
21 Chris Rojek, *Capitalism and Leisure Theory*. London: Tavistock Publications, 1985, pp.18–23 and chapter 8, 'The sociology of pleasure'.
22 Ibid., p.178.
23 Their position is usefully summarised in textbook form by Celia Lury, *Consumer Culture*. Oxford: Blackwell, 1996.
24 Fredric Jameson, in his collection *Postmodernism, or the Cultural Logic of Late Capitalism*. London: Verso, 1991.
25 United Nations Declaration on Tourism, 1980.
26 Daniel Miller, in his own introduction to the collection he edited, *Acknowledging Consumption: A Review of New Studies*. London: Routledge, 1996, p.xiv.
27 James Clifford, *Routes: Travel and Translation in the Late 20th Century*. Cambridge, MA: Harvard University Press, 1997, p.36.

28 I take much in the following paragraphs from *The Quality of Life*, a study prepared for the World Institute for Development Economics Research, edited by Martha Nussbaum and Amartya Sen. Oxford: Clarendon Press, 1993. See particularly Sen's own contribution, and those by G.A. Cohen, Charles Taylor and Thomas Scanlon.
29 James Clifford (1997), p.154. Also *OED*.
30 The phrase is Clifford Geertz's, considering the condition in younger anthropologists of his acquaintance. See his *Works and Lives: The Anthropologist as Author*. Princeton, NJ: Princeton University Press, 1988.

BIBLIOGRAPHY

Aciman, A. (1997) 'Shadow cities'. *New York Review of Books*, 18 December.

Adorno, T. (1974) *Minima Moralia: Reflections on a Damaged Life*. London: New Left Books.

Alexander, C. (1972) 'A city is not a tree'. In G. Bell and J. Tyrwhitt (eds), *Human Identity in the Urban Environment*. Harmondsworth: Penguin.

Anderson, B. (1998) 'From miracle to crash in South East Asia'. *London Review of Books*, 16 April.

Andrews, M. (1989) *The Search for the Picturesque*. Stanford: Stanford University Press.

Arlott, J. (1967) *Vintage Summer 1947*. London: Eyre and Spottiswoode.

Attenborough, D. (1987) *First Eden*. London: Collins / BBC.

Awsiter, J. (1768) *Thoughts on Brighthelmstone, Concerning Sea-Bathing and Drinking Sea-water*.

Babington Smith, C. (1967) *Amy Johnson*. London: Collins.

Bachelard, G. (1969) *The Poetics of Place*. Boston: Beacon Press.

Bagwell, P. (1974) *The Transport Revolution*. London: Routledge.

Ballard, J.G. (1994) *The Kindness of Women*. London: HarperCollins.

—— (1997) 'Going somewhere'. *Observer*, 14 September.

Banham, R. (1984) *The Architecture of the Well-Tempered Environment*. Chicago: University of Chicago Press.

Barrell, J. (1986) *The Political Theory of Painting from Reynolds to Hazlitt*. New Haven, CT: Yale University Press.

Barthes, R. (1988) *Camera Lucida*. London: Flamingo Books.

Baum, V. (1991) *Menschen in Hotel*. Berlin: Ullstein Books edition.

Benjamin, W. (1974) *The Lyric Poet in the Era of High Capitalism*. London: New Left Books.

Berger, J. (1980) *About Looking*. London: Writers and Readers Co-operative.

Berman, M. (1983) *All that is Solid Melts into Air: The Experience of Modernity*. London: Verso.

Berry, C.J. (1994) *The Idea of Luxury: A Conceptual and Historical Investigation*. Cambridge: Cambridge University Press.

Bishop, R. and Robinson, L.S. (1998) *Night Market: Sexual Cultures and the Thai Economic Miracle*. New York: Routledge.

Black, J. (1985) *The British and the Grand Tour*. London: Croom Helm.

Blume, M. (1992) *Côte d'Azur: Inventing the French Riviera*. New York: Thames and Hudson.

Bolgar, R.R. (1954) *The Classical Heritage and its Beneficiaries*. Cambridge: Cambridge University Press.

Bourdieu, P. (1996) *The State Nobility: Élite Schools in the Field of Power*. Cambridge: Polity Press.

Boyer, M.C. (1994) *The City of Collective Memory: Its Historical Imagery and Architectural Entertainments*. Cambridge, MA: MIT Press.

Brady, F. and Pottle, F. (eds) (1955) *The Private Papers of James Boswell: Boswell on the Grand Tour – Italy, Corsica, France 1765–66*. London: William Heinemann.

Braudel, F. (1972) *The Mediterranean and the Mediterranean World in the Age of Philip II*, 2nd edition. Glasgow: Collins.

Brendon, P. (1991) *Thomas Cook: 150 Years of Popular Tourism*. London: Elek Press.

Brewer, J., McKendrick, N. and Plumb, J. (1982) *The Birth of a Consumer Society*. Bloomington: University of Indiana Press.

Brock, R.N. and Thistlethwaite, S.B. (1996) *Casting Stones: Prostitution and Liberation in Asia and the United States*. Minneapolis: Fortress Press.

Buchan, A.P. (1804) *Practical Observations Concerning Seabathing with Remarks on the Use of the Warm Bath*.

Burke, E. (1756) *Philosophical Enquiry into the Origins of our Ideas of the Sublime and Beautiful*.

Burke, K. (1959) *Attitudes towards History*. Los Altos: Hermes Press.

Butterfield, H. (1973) *The Whig Interpretation of History*. Harmondsworth: Penguin.

Buzard, J. (1993) *The Beaten Track: European Tourism, Literature and the Ways to Culture*. Oxford: Clarendon Press.

Byron, R. (1992) *The Road to Oxiana* (Macmillan, 1937). Harmondsworth: Penguin.

Caillois, R. (1960) *Man, Play and Games*. Paris; (1962) London: Thames and Hudson.

Calvino, I. (1974) *Invisible Cities*. New York: Harcourt Brace, trans. by William Weaver.

Carrington, N. (ed) (1935) *Portmeirion Further Explained*, 3rd edition. Birmingham: Kynoch Press.

Cela, C.J. (1990) *Journey to the Alcarria* (1948). New York: Atlantic Monthly Press.

Chesterfield, Lord (1951) *Letters to His Son*. London: Dent, Everyman edition.

Clark, K. (1976) *Landscape into Art*. London: John Murray.

Clark, T.J. (1973) *The Absolute Bourgeois: Art and Politics in Nineteenth Century France*. London: Thames and Hudson.

Clifford, J. (1997) *Routes: Travel and Translation in the Late 20th Century*. Cambridge, MA: Harvard University Press.

Colley, L. (1987) *Britons: Forging the Nation 1707–1837*. London: Vintage Books.

Conrad, J. (1917) *The Shadow Line*. London: Dent.

Corbin, A. (1994) *The Lure of the Sea: The Discovery of the Seaside in the Western World 1750–1840*. Cambridge: Polity Press.

Corrigan, P. and Sayer, D. (1985) *The Great Arch: English State Formation as Cultural Revolution*. Oxford: Basil Blackwell.

Crick, M. (1989) 'Representations of tourism'. *Annual Review of Anthropology*, 18, pp.301–44.

—— (1994) *Resplendent Sites, Discordant Voices: Sri Lanka and International Tourism*. Chur: Harwood Academic Press.

Dahrendorf, R. (1990) *Reflections on the Revolution in Europe*. London: Chatto and Windus.

David, E. (1992) *Italian Food*. London: Michael Joseph.

Davie, D. (1967) *The Heyday of Sir Walter Scott*. London: Chatto and Windus.

Davis, F. (1963) *Victorian Patronage of the Arts*. Oxford: Clarendon Press.

Davis, M. (1990) *City of Quartz: Excavating the Future of Los Angeles*. London: Verso.

Denby, E. (1999) *Grand Hotels: Reality and Illusion*. London: Reaktion Books.

Derrida, J. (1995) *The Gift of Death*. Chicago: University of Chicago Press.

Diski, J. (1997) *Skating to Antarctica*. Hopewell, NJ: Ecco Press.

Douglas, M. (1975) 'Deciphering a meal'. *Implicit Meanings: Essays in Anthropology*. London: Routledge and Kegan Paul.

Douglas, N. (1983) *Siren Land: Anecdote, Philosophy and Myth: A Celebration of Life in Southern Italy*. Harmondsworth: Penguin.

Dyos, H.J. and Aldcroft, D.H. (1969) *British Transport: An Economic Survey*. Leicester: Leicester University Press.

Edgar, M. (n.d.) *Albert, 'Arold and Others*. London: Francis, Day and Hunter.

Ekserdijian, D. (1997) *Correggio*. New Haven, CT: Yale University Press.

Eliot, T.S. (1943) *Four Quartets*. New York: Harcourt Brace.

Elwell, R.W. (ed.) (1977) Brochure written for the West Jersey Railroad Company for the season of 1877.

Enloe, C. (1990) *Bananas, Beaches and Bases: Making Feminist Sense of International Politics*. Berkeley CA: University of California Press.

Ensor, J. (1971) *The Motor Industry*. London: *Financial Times* and Longmans.

Evans, D. (1954) *The Ingenious Mr. Pedersen*. Dursley: Allan Sutton.

Fitzgerald, F.S. (1925) *The Great Gatsby*. New York: Scribner's.

Fleming, P. (1994) *News from Tartary* (Jonathan Cape, 1936). London: Abacus.

Forster, E.M. (1968) *Two Cheers for Democracy*. Harmondsworth: Penguin.

—— (1990) *A Room with a View*. Harmondsworth: Penguin.

Foucault, M. (1985) *The History of Sexuality*, vol. 1. Harmondsworth: Penguin.

Fowles, J. (1978) *Daniel Martin*. London: Jonathan Cape.

Frayn, M. (1973) *Sweet Dreams*. London: Secker and Warburg.

Fussell, P. (1980) *Abroad: British Literary Travelling between the Wars*. Oxford: Oxford University Press.

Garland, A. (1997) *The Beach*. New York: Viking.

Gaskell, Mrs (1966) *The Life of Charlotte Brontë*. London: Dent, Everyman edition.

Gay, P. (1994) *The Bourgeois Experience: Victoria to Freud*. London: HarperCollins.

Geertz, C. (1973) *The Interpretation of Cultures*. New York: Basic Books.

—— (1988) *Works and Lives: The Anthropologist as Author*. Princeton, NJ: Princeton University Press.

—— (1997) 'Cultural tourism'. In W. Nuryanti *Tourism and Heritage Management*. Jakarta: Gadjah Mada University Press.

Giddens, A. (1991) *Modernity and Self-Identity*. Cambridge: Polity Press.

Gilbert, E. (1954) *Brighton: Old Ocean's Bauble*. London: Methuen.

Girouard, M. (1977) *Sweetness and light: The Queen Anne Movement, 1860–1900*. Oxford: Clarendon Press.

Goody, J. (1982) *Cooking, Cuisine and Class*. Cambridge: Cambridge University Press.

Grahame, K. (1977) *The Wind in the Willows* (1908). London: Methuen Children's Books.

Greenblatt, S. (1991) *Marvellous Possessions: The Wonder of the New World*. Chicago: University of Chicago Press.

Greene, G. (1935) *England Made Me*. Oxford: Bodley Head.

Griffin, J. (1986) *Well-Being*. Oxford: Clarendon Press.

Haas, P. (1990) *Saving the Mediterranean: The Politics of International Environmental Co-operation*. New York: Columbia University Press.

Habermas, J. (1970) *Towards a Rational Society*. Boston: Beacon Press.

Halsband, R. (1956) *The Life of Mary Wortley Montagu*. Oxford: Clarendon Press.

—— (ed) (1966) *The Complete Letters of Lady Mary Wortley Montagu*, 3 vols. Oxford: Clarendon Press.

Hampshire, S. (1972) *Pessimism and Morality*. Cambridge: Cambridge University Press.

Harvey, D. (1989) *The Condition of Postmodernity*. Oxford: Basil Blackwell.

Haskell, F. (1963) *Patrons and Painters*. Oxford: Oxford University Press.

Haskell, F. and Penny, N. (1981) *Taste and the Antique*. New Haven, CT: Yale University Press.

Hemingway, E. (1963) *Islands in the Stream*. New York: Scribner's.

——. (1964) *A Moveable Feast*. New York: Scribner's.

Herbert, R.L. (1994) *Monet on the Normandy Coast: Tourism and Painting, 1867–1886*. New Haven, CT: Yale University Press.

Hern, A. (1967) *The Seaside Holiday*. London: Cresset Press.

Heron, P. (1996) *Modern Painters*, vol. 9, no. 1.

Herrin, J. (1987) *The Formation of Christendom*. Oxford: Basil Blackwell.

Hibbert, C. (1969) *The Grand Tour*. London: Weidenfeld and Nicolson.

Higham, R. (1960) *Britain's Imperial Air Routes 1918–1939*. London: Foulis & Co.

Hirsch, F. (1977) *Social Limits to Growth*. London: Routledge and Kegan Paul for the Twentieth Century Fund.

Hirst, P. and Thompson, G. (1996) *Globalisation in Question*. Cambridge: Polity Press.

Hobsbawm, E.J. (1968) *Industry and Empire: An Economic History of Britain since 1750*. London: Weidenfeld and Nicolson.

—— (1994) *Age of Extremes: The Short Twentieth Century 1914–1991*. London: Michael Joseph.

Hodgson, G. (1995) *A New Grand Tour: How Europe's Great Cities Made Our World*. Harmondsworth: Penguin.

Hoggart, R. (1958) *The Uses of Literacy*. Harmondsworth: Pelican.

—— (1994) *Townscape with Figures: Farnham – Portrait of an English Town*. London: Chatto and Windus.

Hollis, M. (1988) *Rational Economic Man*. Cambridge: Cambridge University Press.

Holzell, J. and Salkeld, A. (1986) *The Mystery of Mallory and Irvine*. London: Jonathan Cape.

Huntford, R. (1983) *Scott and Amundsen*. London: Hodder and Stoughton.

Inglis, F. (1990) *Media Theory*. Oxford: Blackwell.

Iyer, P. (1988) *Video Night in Katmandu and Other Reports from the Not-So-Far East*. New York: Vintage.

Jacobs, J. (1961) *The Death and Life of Great American Cities*. New York: Vintage.

Jakle, J. (1985) *The Tourist*. Lincoln: University of Nebraska Press.

James, H. (1983) *A Little Tour of France*. Harmondsworth: Penguin.

—— (1990) *Italian Hours*. Hopewell. NJ: Ecco Press.

Jameson, F. (1991) *Postmodernism, or the Cultural Logic of Late Capitalism*. London: Verso.

Johnston, J.P. (1977) *A Hundred Years of Eating: Food, Drink and Daily Diet in Britain since the Late 19th Century*. Dublin and Montreal: Gill and Macmillan.

Jones, M. (ed.) (1990) *Fake? The Art of Deception*. London: British Museum.

Jones, S.G. (1986) *Workers at Play: A Social and Economic History of Leisure 1918–1939*. London: Routledge and Kegan Paul.

Junger, S. (1998) *The Perfect Storm*.London: Fourth Estate.

Kracauer, J. (1997) *Into Thin Air: A Personal Account of the Mt. Everest Disaster*. New York: Random House.

Kurlansky, M. (1998) *Cod: A Biography of the Fish that Changed the World*. London: Jonathan Cape.

Larkin, P. (1989) *Collected Poems*. London: Faber.

Laslett, P. (1965) *The World We Have Lost*. London: Methuen.

Laux, J.M. (1976) *First Gear: The French Automobile Industry to 1914*. Liverpool: Liverpool University Press.

Lawrence, D.H. (1961) *Collected Short Stories*. New York: Viking Press.

Leigh Fermor, P. (1983) *Roumeli: Travels in Northern Greece*. Harmondsworth: Penguin.

Lewis, N. (1983) *Naples '44: An Intelligence Officer in the Italian Labyrinth*. London: Collins (Eland Book).

—— (1996) *Voices of the Old Sea*. London: Picador.

Lindsay, J. (1966) *Turner: His Life and Work*. St Albans: Granada.

Lodge, D. (1991) *Paradise News*. London: Secker and Warburg.

Lowerson, J. (1980) 'Battles for the countryside'. In F. Gloversmith (ed.) *Class, Culture and Social Change: A New View of the 1930s*. Brighton: Harvester.

Lury, C. (1996) *Consumer Culture*. Oxford: Blackwell.

Luttwak, E. (1997) 'Central-Bankism'. In P. Gowan and P. Anderson (eds) *The Question of Europe*. London: Verso.

—— (1998) *Turbo-Capitalism*. London: Orion Books.

Lynch, K. (1960) *The Image of the City*. Cambridge, MA: MIT Press.

Marcus, S. (1969) *The Other Victorians*. London: Pan.

Mennell, S. (1996) *All Manners of Food: Eating and Taste in England and France from the Middle Ages to the Present*. Urbana, ILL: University of Illinois Press.

Michelet, J. (1861) *La Mer*. Paris: Plon.

Mill, J.S. (1963) *The Six Great Humanistic Essays*, ed. Albert Levi. New York: Washington Square Press.

Miller, D. (ed.) (1996) *Acknowledging Consumption: A Review of New Studies*. London: Routledge.

Miller, J.H. (1995) *Topographies*. Stanford: Stanford University Press.

Moorhouse, G. (1989) *Imperial City: The Rise and Rise of New York*. London: Hodder and Stoughton.

Muir, J. (1961) *The Mountains of California* (1894). New York: Doubleday.

Mumford, L. (1962) 'Mother Jacobs' home remedies for urban cancer'. *New Yorker*, 1 December.

—— (1965) *The City in History*. Harmondsworth: Penguin.

National Union of Miners (1992) *The Miners' Gala*. Durham: NUM.

Nicholl, C. (1988) *The Fruit Palace*. New York: Vintage.

Nicholson-Lord, D. (1997) 'The politics of travel: is tourism just colonialism in another guise?'. *Nation*, NY, 6 October.

Nussbaum, M. and Sen, A. (eds) (1993) *The Quality of Life*. Oxford: Clarendon Press.

Odzer, C. (1994) *Patpong Sisters: An American Woman's View of the Bangkok Sex World*. New York: Blue Moon Books.

O'Hanlon, R. (1984) *Into the Heart of Borneo*. Edinburgh: Salamander Press.

—— (1988) *In Trouble Again*. New York: Atlantic Monthly Press.

—— (1997) *Congo Journey*. Harmondsworth: Penguin.

Olsen, D. (1986) *The City as a Work of Art*. New Haven, CT: Yale University Press.

Pagnamenta, P. (ed) (1984) *All our Working Lives*. London: BBC Publications.

Panofsky, E. (1993) *Meaning in the Visual Arts*. Harmondsworth: Penguin.

Pemble, J. (1987) *The Mediterranean Passion: Victorians and Edwardians in the South*. Oxford: Clarendon Press.

—— (1995) *Venice Rediscovered*. Oxford: Clarendon Press.

Pevsner, N. (1957a) *The Buildings of England: Northumberland*. Harmondsworth: Penguin.

—— (1957b) *The Buildings of England: Devon*. Harmondsworth: Penguin.

—— with Nairn, I. (1965) *The Buildings of England: Sussex*. Harmondsworth: Penguin.

Phongpaichit, P. (1982) *From Peasant Girls to Bangkok Masseuses*. Geneva: ILO.

Pietrangeli, C. (1993) *The Vatican Museum: Five Centuries of History*. Rome: The Vatican.

Pimlott, J.R. (1947) *The Englishman's Holiday: A Social History*. London: Faber and Faber.

Plumb, J.H. (1973a) *The Growth of Political Stability in England 1675–1725*. Harmondsworth: Penguin.

—— (1973b) *The Commercialisation of Leisure in 18th Century England*. Reading: University of Reading Press.

Pointon, M. (1992) 'Killing pictures'. In J. Barrell *Painting and the Politics of Culture*. Oxford: Oxford University Press.

Pollard, S. (1983) *The Development of the British Economy 1914–1980*. London: Edward Arnold.

Pope, A. (1956) 'Moral essays', *Collected Poems*. London: Dent, Everyman edition.

Potts, A. (1994) *Flesh and the Ideal: Winckelmann and the Origins of Art History*. New Haven, CT: Yale University Press.

Raban, J. (1974) *Soft City*. Glasgow: Collins.

—— (1981) *Old Glory*. Glasgow: Collins.

—— (1994) 'On the waterfront'. *New York Review of Books*. 14 July.

Radice, B. (trans.) (1969) *Pliny: Letters and Panegyrics*, vol. II. Loeb Classical Library, Cambridge, MA: Harvard University Press.

Rae, J.B. (1968) *Climb to Greatness: The American Aircraft Industry 1920–1960*. Cambridge, MA: MIT Press.

Ransome, A. (1953) *Winter Holiday*. London: Jonathan Cape.

—— (1973) *Swallowdale*. Harmondsworth: Puffin.

Ritchie-Calder, P. (1973) *The Pollution of the Mediterranean*. Berne: Herbert Land.

Rogers, P. (1995) *Literature and Popular Culture in 18th century England*. Brighton: Harvester.

Rojek, C. (1985) *Capitalism and Leisure Theory*. London: Tavistock Publications.

Rough Guides (1995) *The Rough Guide to Thailand*. London: Rough Guides.

Ruffinière du Prey de la, P. (1995) *The Villas of Pliny from Antiquity to Posterity*. Chicago: University of Chicago Press.

Ruskin, J. (1908) *The Seven Lamps of Architecture*. London: George Allen.

—— (1981) *The Stones of Venice: A Selection*, ed. J. Morris. London: Faber and Faber.

Ruskin, R. (1987) *Mornings in Florence*. Harmondsworth: Penguin.

Russell, M. (1994) *The Blessings of a Good Thick Skirt*. London: Flamingo.

Russell, R. (1769, but Latin edition 1752) *A Dissertation on the Use of Seawater in the Diseases of the Glands, particularly the Scurvy, Jaundice etc.*

Rybczynski, W. (1988) *Home: A Short History of an Idea*. London: Heinemann.

Said, E. (1985) *Orientalism*. Harmondsworth: Penguin.

St Aubyn de Téran, L. (1994) *A Villa in Italy*. Harmondsworth: Penguin.

Schama, S. (1988) *The Embarrassment of Riches*. Berkeley, CA: University of California Press.

——. (1995) *Landscape and Memory*. London: HarperCollins.

Seabrook, J. (1996) *Travels in the Skin Trade: Tourism and the Sex Industry*. London: Pluto Press.

Seta de, C. (1996) 'Grand Tour: the lure of Italy in the eighteenth century'. In A. Wilton and I. Bignamini (eds) *Grand Tour*. London: Tate Gallery.

Simpson, J. (1997) *Touching the Void*. London: Vintage.

Singh, N. (1984) *The Impact of Tourism on the Balance of Payments*. Athens: CPER.

Spufford, F. (1997) *I May Be Some Time: Ice and the English Imagination*. London: Faber and Faber.

Stevens, W. (1962) *The Palm at the End of the Mind*. New York: Vintage Books.

Stevenson, R.L. (1984) *Travels with a Donkey in the Cevennes*. Oxford: Oxford University Press.

Stilgoe, J. (1983) *The Metropolitan Corridor: Railroads and the American Scene*. New Haven, CT: Yale University Press.

Stokes, A. (1969) *Stones of Rimini*. New York: Schocken Books.

Stone, L. (1977) *The Family, Sex and Marriage in England 1500–1800*. London: Weidenfeld and Nicolson.

Swinglehurst, E. (1974) *The Romantic Journey: the story of Thomas Cook and Victorian travel*. London: Pica Editions.

Tawney, R.H. (1961) *The Acquisitive Society* (1921). London: Collins.

Taylor, A.J.P. (1965) *English History 1914–1945*. Oxford: Clarendon Press.

Taylor, C. (1995) *Philosophical Arguments*. Cambridge, MA: Harvard University Press.

Theroux, P. (1975) *The Great Railway Bazaar: By Train through Asia*. Harmondsworth: Penguin.

Thesiger, W. (1964) *Arabian Sands*. Harmondsworth: Penguin.

Thomas, K. (1983) *Man and the Natural World*. Harmondsworth: Penguin.

Thompson, E. P. (1961) Review articles of Raymond Williams's *The Long Revolution*. *New Left Review*, nos. 9,10,11.

—— (1968) 'Time, work-discipline and industrial capitalism'. Revised and reprinted in his *Customs in Common*. Harmondsworth: Penguin 1991.

Thoreau, H. (1973) *Walden*. Princeton, NJ: Princeton University Press.

Thorndike, J.J. (1993) *The Coast: A Journey down the Atlantic Shore*. New York: St Martin's Press.

Thrift, N. (1998) *Spatial Formations*. London: Sage.

Tourism Market Trends Europe 1985–1994 (1995). Madrid: World Tourism Organisation.

Trevor-Roper, H. (1983) 'The Highland tradition of Scotland'. In E. Hobsbawm and T. Ranger (eds) *The Invention of Tradition*. Cambridge: Cambridge University Press.

Turner in the North of England, exhibition catalogue. London: Tate Gallery, 22 October 1996–9 February 1997.

UN (1995) Conference Report *World Conference on Sustainable Tourism*. New York: UN.

UNESCO (1965) *Tourism and Economic Development outside Europe*. Paris: UNESCO.

Urbain, J. (1996) *Sur La Plage: mœurs et coutumes balnéaires (XIX–XX siècles)*. Paris: Editions Payot.

Urry, J. (1990) *The Tourist Gaze: Leisure and Travel in Contemporary Societies*. London: Sage.

Van Gogh, V. (1983) *The Letters*. London: Collins.

Walton, J. (1978) *The Blackpool Landlady*. Manchester: University of Manchester Press.

Warren, J.F. (1993) *Ah Ku and Karayuki-san: Prostitution in Singapore 1870–1940*. Oxford: Oxford University Press.

Watt, I. (1957) *The Rise of the Novel*. London: Chatto and Windus.

Waugh, E. (1930) *Labels*. London: Duckworth.

—— (1993) *Brideshead Revisited* (1945). London: Dent, Everyman Library edition.

Waymark, P. (1983) *The Car Industry*. Bath: Sewells.

Webb, R.K. (1955) *The British Working Class Reader 1790–1848*. London: Allen and Unwin.

Webb, S. and Webb, B. (1913) *The Story of the King's Highway*. London: Longman.

Whicher, S. (ed.) (1957) *Selections from Ralph Waldo Emerson*. Boston: Houghton Mifflin.

White, R. (1775) *The Use and Abuse of Sea Water*.

Wiggins, D. (1987) 'Truth, invention and the meaning of life'. In *Needs, Values, Truth*. Oxford: Blackwell.

Williams, R. (1973) *The Country and the City*. London: Chatto and Windus.

—— (1981) *Culture*. Glasgow: Collins.

—— (1983) 'An epoch's end'. *New Left Review*, 140, July–August.

Wilson, Angus (1981) *As If by Magic*. London: Secker and Warburg.

Wilson, Alexander (1992) *The Culture of Nature: North American Landscape from Disney to the Exxon Valdez*. Oxford: Blackwell.

Wilton, A. and Bignamini, I. (eds) (1996) *The Grand Tour*. London: Tate Gallery.

Wind, E. (1967) 'Botticelli's birth of Venus'. *Pagan Mysteries of the Renaissance*. Harmondsworth: Penguin.

Wollheim, R. (1987) *Painting as an Art*. London: Thames and Hudson.

Wordsworth, W. (1977) *Guide to the Lakes*, 5th edition (1838), facsimile reprint. Oxford: Oxford University Press.

Wright, E. (1730) *Some Observations Made in Travelling Through France and Italy &c in the Years 1720, 1721 and 1722*. London.

Wright, P. (1995) *The Village that Died for England*. London: Jonathan Cape.

Young Pelton, R., Aral, C. and Dulles, W. (eds) (1998) *Fielding's The World's Most Dangerous Places*, 3rd edition. California: Fielding Worldwide Inc.

Zeldin, T. (1977) *France 1848–1945*. Oxford History of Modern Europe: Clarendon Press.

INDEX